Donated in Loving Memory of
Janice Kathryn Miller
by
Russell Miller

1.05

How The World Began

The world is the everlasting caricature of what it should be.
—Marcel Achard

It is God's nature to make something out of nothing. This is why God cannot make anything out of him who is not yet nothing.
—Martin Luther

The past in its pastness is not what concerns me, but the past as something present. . . . I am delving into Adam in order to unriddle him and myself.
—Gerhard Nebel

How The World Began

Man in the First Chapters of the Bible

By Helmut Thielicke

Translated with an Introduction
by John W. Doberstein

JAMES CLARKE & CO. LTD.
CAMBRIDGE & LONDON

First published in Great Britain 1964
Second Impression 1970

Translated from *Wie die Welt begann. Der Mensch in der Urgeschichte der Bibel* by Helmut Thielicke
Quell-Verlag (1960), Stuttgart, Germany

Printed in Great Britain by
Lewis Reprints Limited, Port Talbot, Glamorgan

Contents

THE BEGINNING

1. In the Beginning 3
2. The Primeval Witnesses 12
3. The Light of the World 26
4. God's Autograph 41

THE CREATION OF MAN

5. Man—the Risk of God 59
6. Creation and Evolution, Faith and Science 72
7. The Meaning and Order of the Sexes 87
8. The Great Sabbath 103

THE STORY OF THE FALL

9. How Evil Came into the World 121
10. The Bridgehead of the Tempter 136
11. Guilt and Destiny 152
12. The Mystery of Death 170

THE STORY OF CAIN AND ABEL

13. The Cain Within Us 187
14. Where Is Abel Your Brother? 202
15. Insecure Man 218

The Story of the Flood

16. Floods and Fires 235
17. Noah—The Adventure of Faith 252

The Building of the Tower of Babel

18. The Fear of Our Fellows 273
19. Outlines of a New World Order 289

Postscript for Theological Readers

20. Postscript for Theological Readers 303

Translator's Introduction

This is the fourth of Helmut Thielicke's books which I have had the privilege of translating—with two more already completed and on their way to publication. When the first, the sermons on the parables of Jesus, was sent on its way in English, I had no idea that the pressure of demand would lead me, not only to continued labors on succeeding volumes, but to a warm and stimulating friendship with the author of these books. Both the work of translating and the friendship have entered into my life and strengthened my apprehension of the gospel for which we stand.

These sermons on the first eleven chapters of Genesis are great preaching on texts that often daunt the preacher today. The editor of the *Expository Times* wrote of one of Thielicke's volumes of sermons: "A valuable tool is placed in the hands of preachers and teachers when a book is published by a scholar who is also a successful preacher. Such a gift is Professor Helmut Thielicke's sermons." As a teacher of preachers I can say to preachers what I say to my students: If you want to know how to preach to the man of today on the Old Testament and particularly these first chapters of the Bible, read these sermons!

In the first sermon and the "Postscript for Theological Readers" the author has stated the purpose of these lecture-sermons and the problems connected with their preparation but an excerpt from a personal communication to the translator is worth passing on to the reader. He states that his first aim was to hew out the *message* of the text as in any proper sermon. His second purpose was to enter into the current discussion of the relationship between the Old and the New Testament by this means of preaching as a Christian on Old Testament texts. The third intention was to help people to grapple with the intellectual difficulties they face in this world today in which the antitheses of faith and thought, kerygma and cosmogony, religion and science create barriers for doubters and misgivings for believers.

"Every sermon," the author says, "must run the gamut of this *whole* complex of questions. This made the labor I expended on these sermons the most difficult and trying task I have ever tackled. There were shoals of problems, both of theory and method, that needed to be dealt with in connection with each sermon.

"The recompense for all this was the unusual intensity with which the hearers listened and also their quantity. The services had to be repeated in each case because of the tremendous overflow attendance. Theological courses of study for laymen, which were conducted by my co-workers, endeavored to deepen the impact of the sermons. And these in turn had to be scheduled in duplicate in order to accommodate the numbers who came. As in the case of previous series, the audiences were made up of all kinds of people—university professors and students, dock workers and executives, Christians and pagans."

Mount Airy, Philadelphia. J.W.D.

THE BEGINNING

1

In the Beginning

We have a long and adventurous road ahead of us. Therefore it may be well to have a brief talk with the reader to let him know what awaits him and what the author has tried to do. Those who do not need these preliminary instructions may begin their reading at once, starting with page twelve.

The question of where we come from and where we are going is one of the elementary challenges of life. Perhaps it is *the* question of life. Only when we get an answer to it do we learn who we are.

Often we meet a person we cannot quite make out. Then we are likely to inquire about the family he comes from and his social milieu. Medical men inquire into a criminal's hereditary background; psychologists probe into the traumata of youth, the first impressions of life and even prenatal influences; astrologists determine the configuration of the planets at the time of birth; and the contemporaries of Jesus said: "He comes from Nazareth, a hick town. Can anything good come out of Nazareth? Such a commonplace origin disproves his claim to be someone extraordinary."

And always these inquiries, the serious ones and the superstitious ones, proceed on the same assumption: If I know the origin of a man (or of "man" himself), if I know where he comes from, then I also know what he amounts to, then I know his secret.

It is certainly worth asking whether the great interest that our generation has shown in prehistory and primitive history may not likewise be explained from this point of view. Books with titles like *Gods, Graves, and Scholars; I Searched for Adam*, and many others, are best sellers today. Why is it that people, who live so much in the present as we do and who watch the future of atomic development with such fascination and anxiety, should be seeking in such great numbers to penetrate the veil that covers the past and wanting to trace back as far as possible the trail of mankind? This is surely remarkable and it should make us stop and think.

I do not believe that this is primarily scientific curiosity, that it is merely a prehistorical hobby, so to speak, or even a flight from the problems of the day into what is remote. I rather think that here again is the upthrust of the same disturbing question: Where do we human beings come from? Quite simply, we are seeking the secret of our life. We no longer know what we are. What a strange and enigmatic breed we are! Presently we shall be flying in space, but at the same time we are threatening to blow up the base of this voyage into space, namely, our own planet. We conquer space and time with our machines, but these machines also appear to be conquering us. We change the face of the earth, but on our own faces are the same old runes of guilt, suffering, and death. Despite everything we have created, we are still the same as the men of old: Cain and Abel, Achilles and Thersites, Siegfried and Hagen. Who are we, really; where do we come from?

This question of origin is thus a good one, but it is not being put in the right way.

In any case, we ask quite different questions about *nature*. For example, if we want to know what a rose is, we do not inquire about its origin, we do not look at its seed or its bud, but rather examine the full-blown blossom. Only when it has reached its utmost maturity, its final form, do we learn what colors, forms, and odors the rose holds within itself, and therefore what its nature is. Anselm of Canterbury, the great theologian, once said:

If you want to know what quartz is, you do not investigate the rock from which it comes, but rather the crystal into which it is developing. Only then will you know what quartz is, and get at its nature.

Now this way of putting the question sounds quite plausible. If I want to know what technology is, I do not go to the German Museum in Munich and look at the first miserable steam locomotive. Rather I look for the latest and most highly developed product of technology; I look at an electronic brain or an atomic pile.

But, applied to us men, this would mean that, if we want to know what man is, we must examine him at the height of his development. And perhaps today this would be to examine him at the point where he is about to conquer social misery and is moving toward the welfare state, where his medical science is adding decades to human life, where his chemistry is extracting food for millions from the earth, and automation is about to provide us with two sabbath days in a week and thus surpass the paltry beginning of creation in which God could spare us only *one* day off.

But the remarkable and highly disconcerting fact is that we do *not* proceed in this way. The fact is that when we want to know who we men are, we do not investigate, as we do with a rose, the final stage of maturity. We do not ask how far progress can bring man today or by 1984 and what kind of a being he may reveal himself to be. No, the fact is that we inquire about the *bud*, we examine his prehistoric origins; in the last analysis we inquire about Adam and Eve. Even Marxism has done the same thing; it sees the nature of man realized in his first germinal beginnings, namely, when primitive communism still prevailed. Subsequent history is then not simply a maturing and advance, but more a fall from this prototype and goal; it is a process of degeneration, namely, a history of class struggles.

Why is it that when we are dealing with man we go backwards to search out his origin?

The answer is that we human beings know very well, or at least dimly suspect, that when we grow older and when the whole human race grows older something is going on that is totally different from the blooming, ripening, and self-unfolding which we observe in nature and in a rose. For what is growing in human life is not only the gifts and blessings God put into our life. The seeds the dark Adversary planted in our hearts by night are also springing up.

True, as we grow older, our mind and understanding grows too, and this is a gift of God. But think of all the crooked pursuits and evil thoughts with which this mind occupies itself! After all, every crook, every tyrant has at his disposal a considerable quota of this gift of God. But what does he, what do we, do with it? Sometimes it might be well if we were a little more stupid.

Then there is another thing that is true. When mankind matures it is true that it flowers and produces many advances; but in the midst of all that is positive and good the same old poisonous weed springs up alongside it. We utilize the forces of nature, we subdue the earth, we accept all the potentialities which God has placed in his creation; but at the same time we use them to destroy, to kill, to poison, and to hate.

So, obviously, we can no longer recognize *what* God meant us to be when he created us, *what* he had in mind when he planned the image of man, by looking at what we really are and what we are today. And, because we know this, we go back to the bud, we go looking for the original design. We go hunting for the origin of man in order to find out what man really was before the catastrophe that disfigured and defaced him.

Now it would certainly be naïve to think that the primitive age of mankind could furnish us with any information that would help us at this point. Nevertheless, it may be some kind of correct instinct that leads us in this direction. Might not the first pages of the Bible, which tell us about the beginning of the world, be of some help to us? Might not these pages be able to give us an answer to our feckless question of what God really and originally intended man to be?

For it is these first pages of the Bible that deal with the problem. There we are shown *why* men do not simply develop as flowers do and why they do *not* reveal what they are in the process of flowering and maturing. For, according to these first pages, we are told that we are no longer what we were when we left the hands of God, but instead that something happened in between—that man seized the forbidden fruit, that he desired to be more than a child and creature, and that now a disastrous rift has been driven through history by Cain and Esau and Nebuchadnezzar and Judas—in short, that we have become something different from the image we were intended to be.

So if I want to know who I really am and what God intended me to be, I must go back behind the lost paradise, I must look to the morning of creation and try to hear the first words that God spoke to me and my father Adam.

So let us enter upon a journey back to that first day of the world. We are setting out for a great and very exciting goal. It will be, so to speak, a voyage of study and discovery which we begin with the exposition of these ancient texts; and therefore we shall conduct ourselves as explorers do when they are on an expedition. No matter who they were, Sven Heden or Amundsen, they all had one decisive question in their minds, one question they were seeking to solve and which determined the whole route of their journey. We too have a question which we propose to explore. It is the question of who we are, whence we came, and what God intended when he gave us life. We are not going to study prehistory and archeology; rather we hope to learn something about the meaning of our life.

The chapters of this book contain addresses which the author delivered over a period of two years to an audience made up of all professions and ages in the large Church of St. Michael in Hamburg. In this difficult task—how could it be otherwise with these texts that tower above us like mountain peaks—he was encouraged above all by the sight of large numbers of young people and their attentive faces. In numerous discussions and letters they besieged him with their questions and difficulties, and the inevitable result was that these discussions somehow got themselves written into and between the lines of this book and thus acquired a presence which helped to overcome the danger of their becoming a mere monologue.

I think back with gratitude upon these hours of thinking together, of teaching and learning, of preaching and listening.

Each time I began by saying, "Today we hear what is written in Genesis, chapter so and so, verse so and so," it had only been a short time since this member of the audience was still at work in the harbor, another in his office, and a third somewhere on an assembly line or a building construction. And so it may have been that at first these stories appeared not only strange and unfamiliar but also a bit remote from the reality of the world. The Garden of Eden looked so completely different from our garden plot at home or the neighborhood park. And never before had we met a serpent like this, which was able to carry on a religious discussion, not even in a circus or a zoo. The Flood was quite unlike any rainstorm we had ever experienced. The tower of Babel too had something strange and archaic about it, standing there like a bizarre prehistoric monster beside the Eiffel Tower and the Empire State Building and all the other skyscrapers of our time. We citizens who live our lives between asphalt and concrete were somewhat at a loss as we contemplated the primitive rock of these strange, primeval, lunar peaks.

But once we entered this massif, once we took hold of the words of these ancient texts and turned them over in our minds, these messages suddenly became relentless in the way they struck straight home to us. Sometimes they were comforting and sometimes they were also threatening; but always we felt that they were surrounding us. The serpent suddenly became more aggressively present than the dog that barks at me in my neighborhood. Noah's ark was closer than the subway from which I had just alighted. And God's great "Let there be!" suddenly became so tremendously real that compared with it the screaming advertisements on the billboards, the hundred-fold ballyhooing of toothpastes, margarines, and tourist attractions became as unreal as soap bubbles. Here it suddenly became relentlessly clear that the God who caught up with Adam and said, "Where are you?" is also my God. The guilt of Cain toward his brother is exactly the same as that which stands between me and my neighbor. The altar of Noah on the first bit of dry land is also a summons to me: "How oft the Lord of grace did spread his wings above thee!" And the rainbow that shone like an arc of divine promise above the receding Flood is also a sign for me from another world when I walk through the valley of the shadow and cry out from the depths.

There is still another respect in which we are all related to these people of the primeval age, even though they still used bow and arrow and walked the fields and deserts on foot whereas we launch atomic rockets and rush from pole to pole in stratospheric clippers: for them and for us today God was far away and invisible. None of them ever saw him face to face. They saw him only in a mirror dimly and heard him only through his dark Word (I Cor. 13:12). Eve saw only the shining apple, swinging in the breeze of paradise. She heard only the words of the serpent. God seemed to be playing no part in this scene. He was remote and seemed unreal compared with the fascination of the moment. Only in the cool of the evening were his footsteps heard in the distance. Nor did Cain see God. He saw only his hated brother whom he would kill; and then he saw "red." But God was not in this red. Nor did Noah see God. He saw only the endless, hopeless flood and his lonely ship in the midst of the void. And all the signs were against the coming of a rescuer, of a hand that could cope with these turbulent elements.

And, finally, the people who built the tower of Babel did not see God either. They were bewitched by what they were able to accomplish. They were the ancestors of the atomic strategists of today and the space-travelers of tomorrow. They felt confirmed and vindicated when they succeeded in building up into the boundless blue and nobody seemed to stop them. To them Sputnik was more real than the "good Lord."

None of them saw God. They all saw something totally different. They *saw* what they loved and hated; they *felt* what made them freeze and sweat; and they *wanted* what each day required of them, work in the fields and their daily wages. They wanted their food and their physical pleasure; they wanted sleep and their possessions and their prestige. They saw and they felt and they wanted a thousand things—everything except God. For them he was very far away, he was hardly even true.

But a few of them were very near to him, though in a mysterious way: Abel perhaps and Noah and later Abraham. They were so close to him that the fear in their hearts, the flood, and the strange country hardly mattered to them, so close that God became the most real thing in their lives and they lived in his peace as in arks, fortresses, and homesteads. *But*—they had him only in the sense that they had to *believe* in him.

What is this then, this faith that caused them to endure life, that put solid ground under their feet, and above their heads the shining rainbow of God?

So, actually, this book is concerned with only one question: What does it mean to believe?

Believing is by no means merely a question of *what* I believe in, but always also the question of *against what* I believe. For faith must always struggle against appearances. We do not see what we believe, at any rate not until the moment comes when faith is permitted to see what it has believed, and unbelief is *compelled* to see what it has *not* believed.

Among the many things that distort our view of God, and "against" which we must therefore believe, are our misunderstandings. Often misunderstandings are based upon the fact that we confuse the figurative, mythical, ancient-cosmological forms of expression in these texts of the first chapters of Genesis with the thing itself, instead of seeing in them the code language of a time long past which we must translate into the clear words of our own language. In this way the biblical form of expression, which ought to be transparent for some very elementary news which is of immense importance to us, becomes for many of us an iron curtain that hides them from our view and cuts them off from our ears like a soundproof wall.

I am not concerned with cheap apologetics when I seek to remove misunderstandings. For I have no desire to tone down these texts and prepare them appetizingly so that respectable citizens of the twentieth century can swallow them with pleasure and digest them without getting a stomach-ache. It is only when we are led through all these misleading misconceptions—which provoke a *wrong* offense—to the thing *itself*, that the real excitement begins. For only then do the real, decisive questions arise. And then there will also be provocations and offenses, but in any case decisions, made necessary by the claim of these texts.

It is obvious that it takes some labor of thought to arrive at this point. The message of these texts is not to be had cheaply. Not infrequently was the preacher himself driven to the edge of despair when after an effort of thought he failed to express the ultimate result in the simplicity and naturalness which befits the fateful questions of existence.

So I leave this book to its reader not without misgivings and yet in the hope that Another will know how to make something out of the fragments of an imperfect person. For in the hands of the Master even faulty instruments can be made to sing and to perform a work that is significant.

2

The Primeval Witnesses

> In the beginning God created the heavens and the earth. The earth was without form and void, and darkness was upon the face of the deep; and the Spirit of God was moving over the face of the waters.
> —*Genesis 1:1–2*

When it became known that I proposed to deal with the biblical story of creation in a series of sermons, I received a letter in which the sender, with fine frankness, said, "What do you think you know about creation anyhow? Who was there when it happened? After all, there were no reporters there to hear those words, 'Let there be!' Yet the Bible acts if it were presenting an eyewitness account."

I consider this question to be serious and also reasonable. If we stop to think about it, we shall actually be pursuing a clue that will help us to understand the creation story better.

One thing is right, naturally: there were no reporters and eyewitnesses. So the first pages of the Bible could not have come from them. But perhaps, we may conjecture, it was the ancient "scientists" who set down here their ideas about the origin of the world in the same way that present-day geologists or astronomers do (even though the latter may proceed in a far more modern and critical way and with incomparably more precise methods of research!).

But this assumption would surely put us on the wrong track, for the Bible is not at all concerned merely with the beginning of things or with times past. If it were, the way it proceeds and poses its questions would be altogether different. This can be observed in many of the myths concerning the origin of the world which are in fact (even though not exclusively) concerned with the beginning.

In these myths it is said, for example, that the world was made or generated by the gods. But the question of what came *first* of all goes still further back and finally forces one to ask, "Then who made the *gods?*" Thus one arrives at longer and longer genealogical lists, dimmer and dimmer primeval ages dissolving in the distance, and dotted lines growing thinner and thinner. The gaze of man is taxed, so to speak, to despair in the effort to penetrate the veil of the primeval age. But finally one must stop at the uttermost limit of time, just as the astronomer's telescope finally arrives at the ultimate nebula beyond which it cannot penetrate. Time and space make us aware of the limits of our field of observation. And even the speculations of our reason are not unlimited in their radius of action.

Now it is remarkable that the author of the first pages of the Bible betrays no sign of this strained gazing into the mighty past. Not even between the lines do we perceive even the slightest suggestion of the question of what God may have been doing *before* the creation and perhaps even where he himself originated. Someone once asked Luther what God occupied himself with before he made the world and he was given this drastic answer: "He was cutting switches with which to flog inquisitive questioners."

So this possibility of explaining the creation story falls to the ground too. It could not have been a scientific interest; otherwise we would surely see in it the attempt to drive the drill still deeper into the bedrock of the world and to go back behind the world of creation.

These first pages of the Bible have a totally different interest. Their purpose is to show what it means for me and my life that God is there at the beginning and at the end, and that everything that happens in the world—my little life with its cares and its joys, and also the history of the world at large extending from stone-age man to the atomic era—that all this is, so to speak, a discourse enclosed, upheld, and guarded by the breath of God.

So once more the question hits us, even more sharply than before: "If there were no reporters and if there were no scientists at work here—who then is speaking? What right does a man have simply to assert: 'In the beginning God created . . .' and 'God said, "Let there be . . ."'?"

We might even carry this question further. People who would like to believe have difficulty with many other things in the Bible. Perhaps they are in despair about it and finally brush it aside in resignation. What right, for example, does anybody have to talk about the end and the world beyond? Who has ever been *there*—at the Last Judgment, the resurrection of the dead, in heaven, in hell, in the region of the departed? Isn't all this nothing but visionary dreaming? Isn't this the work of men who lack the necessary knowledge and sense of moderation, men who allow their thoughts to go wandering about, men who obviously have high-pressure imaginations? Ought they not rather to concentrate on what needs to be done *today*? Wouldn't it be better if they confined themselves to this world and their everyday life, examining "the finite on every side" and at best honoring the unsearchable in silence?

We have an excellent illustration of this question in the parable of the rich man and Lazarus.[1] You remember the main features of the story. The hardhearted rich man dies and sinks into the torment of everlasting separation from God. Poor Lazarus, however, enters into Abraham's bosom where he can see the glory of God. And then as the rich man suffers the torment of his banishment —alone and hopeless, having played out all his cards—for the first time he feels something like love stirring in his heart. He thinks of his five brothers and the fact that in their unsuspecting carelessness the same fate that causes him to languish in hell may

---

[1] Cf. Thielicke, *The Waiting Father; Sermons on the Parables of Jesus* (New York: Harper, 1959), pp. 41-51.

come upon them. And here the parable presents an incident that accounts for our reference to it here.

There follows a passionate dialogue between the rich man and Father Abraham, as it were, a dialogue between hell and heaven. And in this dialogue we suddenly hear what I might call the cry of the rich man for a reporter. He says, "Please, Father Abraham, send a messenger to my five brothers to warn them not to miss the decision of their lives." But Abraham answers, "No, that is impossible! They have the men of God, Moses and the prophets. They can learn everything they need from them." But the rich man replies (I am changing the words a bit, but not the meaning), "No, Father Abraham, if you were to send a reporter from the realm of the dead to give them a firsthand report of how our earthly decisions work out in the world beyond, then they will listen." But Abraham refuses, "If they do not hear the prophets and close their minds to the Word of God, neither will they listen to any such reporter."

That's the end of it. The dialogue is over. The silence settles down again upon the man in his banishment and he sinks back into his everlasting brooding.

So, as far as the beginning and the end and the "beyond" are concerned, there are no reporters. Enlightened people of today have always known this. But that the Bible too knows it is at least interesting.

I find that now our question really becomes exciting, almost sensational. *If* all this is so, how did the Bible arrive at its statements about the beginning and the end and the "beyond"? Is it really enough that Moses and the prophets and the men of God have spoken about it?

Basically, the answer is very simple. The men of the Bible know something about who God is. They know it because God was good enough to seek out men to whom he revealed himself and whom he made his friends. Jesus was pointing to these men when he spoke of Moses and the prophets. But if this ever happened, if there really were men who lived and breathed close to God (to this day when we read these stories we sense something of the excitement and also the unspeakable peace of these encounters with God), then there is really nothing else to do except to see everything that happens to us in the light of what has dawned upon us when we were close to God.

This is how the psalms of creation and nature came into being, and also the hymns in our hymnals in which we praise God because he rules the moon and the stars, because he makes the springtime return, because we are surrounded by such a beautiful world.

But even when Job, the servant of God, loses house and home by one disaster after another, when his children die and illness and despair flood down upon him, he can no longer simply suffer it all in dull passivity, like a sick horse that suffers as a dumb creature. No, immediately he must bring even *this* into relation with God. Then he begins to argue with God and take issue with him, flinging his question into his face: "Why do you permit all this to happen? I have always served you faithfully. Don't you have any sense of justice at all? Why do you play these dirty tricks on me?"

But the very fact that Job must relate to God everything he experiences and suffers only makes his suffering greater and more ghastly. For the worst thing for Job was not at all his itching sores, his business losses, and his family tragedy. After all, these might have been met with some kind of stoic indifference. What really shook and tormented him was that he could not understand God, that this put him on the outs with Him, and thereby pitched him into nothingness and meaninglessness.

And so it is with us too: We can somehow endure everything, even the worst things in our life, with a certain courage, if we can "accept" it and discover a way to put up with it. But it becomes intolerable and can drive us to the brink of madness when we can no longer find *any* meaning in what we have to suffer, when we quarrel with it and are overwhelmed by the question: "Why should this happen to *me*, why should *I* be pursued by bad luck, while others who are not one whit better always land on their feet and have everything arranged just right for them?" Cancer is bad enough in itself. But the person who has to struggle with the question of why God permits it besides, has something even harder to bear.

In such life situations, which we all know, we are basically having it out with God. Anybody who once meets God can never again do anything else but constantly come to grips with God in every situation of his life: on the one hand thanking him for the many fulfilments in his life, but on the other hand also protesting when God appears to be refusing him, praying to him when we have wishes, but also warning him in case he should not grant them.

The Bible, this so thoroughly human book, is literally filled with a buzzing confusion of voices, of sounds of joy and quarreling, of gratitude and protest, of despair and praise. And the reason is that the men of the Bible—Adam and Abraham, Job and Isaiah, Peter and Judas, and all the rest of them—could never do anything else but accept from God everything they experienced and endured, or refuse to accept it and thus go on strike. They cannot simply accept things as they are and simply go jogging on, presenting a thick and callous skin to the accidents and inevitabilities of life. No, everything that happens to them gets caught up in the magnetic field of their encounter with God. And that makes it easier for them, but sometimes harder too.

Once God has become the theme of a man's life it becomes tremendously exciting, even adventurous. For one never knows how God will lead him and what he has in mind. And it can be very exciting, even dramatic, to reflect that on the one hand God wants to be my Father and be faithful to me, and that on the other hand much that I go through seems to prove just the opposite and looks more like fate and accident than purposeful guidance. When God becomes the theme of a man's life everything that happens to him becomes both a question and a call to trust. That's why the Christian's life is so exciting and that's why he is a stranger to the nihilist's boredom.

All this must be clearly understood if we are to understand the *message* of the creation story. For now these men, whom God meets and for whom he has become destiny, quite understandably proceed to pose this *other* question: If God is the God we know (from his Word and everything we experience with him), then what does this mean for the beginning and the end of the world; what does it mean here and beyond, for the dead and the living?

If we see the question in this way, there are two things we will understand.

First, we will understand that the men of the Bible were not trying to pierce the primeval fog because of biological and geological curiosity, but rather that they were quite simply spelling out, in a kind of prophecy turned backwards, the meaning of the phrase, "As it was in the beginning, is now, and ever shall be from everlasting to everlasting," and that they expressed this praise of God (for this is precisely what it is) in the sublime pictures of the beginning and the end which we find in the first pages of the Bible and the Revelation of John.

The second thing that becomes clear when we put the question this way is: All that interests these men in the beginning of the world is not the condition of the world before history began, but rather the certainty that here, before the foundation of the world, there begins the history of a great love and a great search. Here there begin to take shape those higher thoughts that God is thinking even about my life. Long before I can think of God and love him he has already thought of me and anticipated me.

Yes, I realize something further, that even though man soon laid waste the paradise of creation and made it a theater of war and a vale of sorrow, those same hands are still at work as they were in the first hour of the world, punishing and blessing and guiding to goals that are contrived by a wise and very loving counsel. And *my* life too is fashioned and guided by the same hands that beckoned the stars and the flowers at the world's dawning and made the day and the night. And if he commanded the sun to shine, he will also master that cosmic sun of Satan caused by the unchained atom. If he knows that the earth with its plants and animals needs rain, and therefore separates the waters under the firmament from those above the firmament, he will also know all the needs of the Queen of England, the orphan child in a children's home, and the aged pensioner. If a thousand years in his sight are but as yesterday, then in his eyes even my little cares will weigh no less than the immensities of Sirius; then for him the tiny stretches of my daily journey, for which I ask his blessing, are just as important as the light years that measure the reaches of cosmic space.

So I cannot read the story of creation without seeing that I am in it too. In every verse I hear that God is thinking of *me* and that he stopped at no expense to draw me to himself.

> Who points the clouds their course,
> Whom winds and seas obey,
> He shall direct thy wandering feet,
> He shall prepare thy way.

Because the men of the Bible knew this God, they were certain (and this they tried to express in pictures and parables) that he had created the world and also would be there at the end, when the graves open and the sun is darkened, and when God for the last time will cry, "Adam, where are you?"

This is the source of the statement—or better, the profession of faith—concerning what happened at the beginning of the world.

But we must seek to uncover another feature of the creation story in which this strange relationship between the vast scale of the world's origin and the small dimension of my little life becomes clear. And it is to be found in an almost hidden passage which often escapes the attention even of careful readers of the Bible.

In the second verse it is said that the "earth was without form and void" before God spoke his first word. The church has always understood these words, "without form and void" to mean "nothingness" and therefore it has always interpreted this verse as saying that God created the world from nothing. The original text employs for the word "create" a term which is never used to denote any human activity and which is reserved only to the prerogative of God.

This means that the biblical writer is obviously attempting to express something quite specific. He is saying that what God is creating and making here possesses a quality fundamentally different from anything created and made by a human artist, or architect. How, actually, does an artist work when he fashions a work of art? After all, what he does is to give form to material which is already at hand, perhaps wood or stone. In the molding of his figure he is therefore bound to what the material itself presents. He must, as it were, wrest the image from the material; and the material, from which he wrings the image, speaks, as it were, along with the image. In other words, the material does not allow *everything* to be done with it; it sets limits to the freedom of the artist.

Now, we are told in our text that God did *not* make the world of material that was already there, to which he was bound, and whose qualities he had to take into account. On the contrary, he created from nothing; and consequently that which is created bears only the marks of God himself, it is the drossless, undistorted reflection of his thoughts. So God's creation proceeds in a sovereign freedom that suffers no other influence or limitation.

A sermon is not an academic lecture, but I must endeavor to give my listeners some idea of how unprecedented and extraordinary this statement of the Bible is in the whole history of religion.

That is to say that when one looks at the nonbiblical myths of creation from this angle the result makes us sit up and take notice: this statement that God created the world "from nothing" appears nowhere else. The world arises either out of a process of generation or it is fashioned from pre-existing matter. And as a rule this matter is tainted and accursed. It is not, as it were, innocent matter, like a piece of linden wood, but generally has behind it a dark and guilty history.

We may refer only to one of the Germanic creation stories and mention the outstanding features in this account. Here the world is made of the corpse of the giant Ymir, the sea of his blood, the heaven of his skull, and the clouds from his brains. But this Ymir, from whose body the world was made, was murdered by Odin and his brothers, even though they were related to Ymir through their mother and thus committed the heinous crime of killing a relative. Thus the world has a gruesome origin and at its beginning there was an unutterable outrage.

Why do I mention this bloodstained story? It would be unfair if I were merely to say: "Look at how much more clean and happy and festive the biblical account of creation is!" We are not at all concerned here to establish moral superiorities. I mention it rather because this Germanic story says that the world was made of curse-ridden matter. The world which is described thus does not bear only divine features; instead the dubious matter of which it is made is constantly breaking through. So whenever guilt and horror appear in the world, when treachery occurs as in the *Nibelungenlied*, when tragedies of infidelity happen, when hatred between men breaks out, when wars explode, when the heady cup of the will to power makes men drunk, it is this prenatal dowry of the world that is erupting. Then suddenly the poisonous genes of the world are manifesting themselves and the fatal curse that was invested in it at the beginning is growing virulent. Then it is the giant Ymir who is rising up.

The people who contrived these myths were therefore in their own way doing something that was similar to what the prophetic poets of the biblical creation story did: they were trying to understand the world by harking back to its beginning, its origin. They knew (just as we all do, even if we are not Christians) that we men are always incurring guilt and exposed to fear, that this is a cruel world, full of murder and the victims of murder. But, this being so, they did not say, "Yes, this is the way 'I' am; hidden within 'me' there is a murderer, an adulterer, a thief; there is nothing that is terrible in this world which is not lurking within me too." No, what they say is: "That's the way the 'world' is; it is made of accursed matter. Therefore it is our fate (note this: our 'fate') to be imperfect, deluded, cruel. This is simply the innate disposition of the world. These are the genetic laws of the cosmos. So in the last analysis we are exculpated. After all, what can a man do about his chromosomes? How can we be blamed for having been made of the corpse of the giant Ymir?"

I should think that it has become clear that it was not my intention to deliver a lecture on the history of religion when I undertook this little excursion into Germanic mythology. What I mean is far more than that. It is only when one sees these first words of the Bible that say that God made the world from nothing against the lurid background of such a *tragic* notion of the world's beginning that one really sees what the Bible was trying to say here. For then we learn to understand two messages in this text.

The first is very hard and so trenchantly earnest that it makes us flinch. For *if* God made the world from nothing, then this means that I came forth from his hands. And therefore some day he will demand me back again just as I was when I left his hands. He has lent me to myself, as it were, entrusted gifts and talents to me, and one day he will require them back. He will say to me: "Now I shall see what you have done with yourself." Then I shall have to give myself back, just as I must return a car I have borrowed. And the owner will then see whether I have treated it and cared for it properly. If a piston grinds or there is a dent in the body, he will count me responsible for it.

What am I going to say when God looks at me and says: "What have you done with your body, which I lent to you, with your gifts, which I gave to you, with your wife, your children, your associates, your friends, whom I gave you along the way?" What will I say when I stand there as one who has misused his body, squandered his gifts, filled them with scratches and dents?

What will I say? Will I timidly remark: "That's the way the world is; one never gets through it unshorn. What I did wasn't 'me' at all; it was heredity. In the last analysis it was the world-matter of the giant Ymir, from which you, God, made the world"?

The fact is that we men do answer in this way. We say: When this or that happens (note that we do not say we have "done" this or that, but rather that this or that "happened" to me), this is because of lack of talent, or our social environment, or a movie that stirred up our blood, or an incident in the service. It is everything, except *me*.

The following conversation took place not long ago between a journalist and a young prisoner he was visiting in jail.

"Why are you really here?"

He hesitated a bit. "I entered a store."

"Get much?"

"Forty-five dollars," he answered.

"How long did you get for it?"

"Nine months."

After a brief pause the journalist asked, "Is it worth it?"

"What's the use of this bosh about whether it's worth it; I can't help it."

"Aha," said the journalist, "so you're innocent?"

"No, not innocent, but neurotic."

The young fellow gave basically the same answer we all are inclined to give. No, we are not innocent. We wouldn't be quite so crazy as that. But it is fate. It is some higher force that made me do this or that. I have a neurosis, I had an unfortunate childhood. I got involved with slot machines. The corpse of the giant Ymir is making itself perceptible in the world and there is a sickly sweet and soporific smell in the air.

But this is precisely what we can no longer say, once we

have rightly heard the first sentences of the Bible. Then I cannot point to the curse with which the world is endowed. Then all I can say is what the prodigal son said when he came back home: "Father, I have sinned against heaven and before you; I am no longer worthy to be called your son. I cannot give myself back to you as I was when I received myself from you. I cannot go on playing the game of passing the buck; I cannot go on putting all the blame on other things, on all the people and situations that misled me in the far country. I can no longer shrug off my sin and simply call it fate. No, I stand here all by myself and for the life of me I haven't a single thing to say."

So this is the *first* thing to be learned here: Under the spell of the giant Ymir there are nothing but concatenations of fates and tragedies. But before the living God there is no such thing as talking oneself out of it with tragic stories. Here I must accept responsibility for myself.

But this is not the only thing that is said here. For the God who confronts us here in this hard, unbending rigor is at the same time the Father of Jesus Christ. He is the Father whose picture the Man of Nazareth painted when he said in his parable that the father embraced the lost son, kissed him, and pressed him to his heart. Everything Jesus said and did and suffered is nothing else but a chain of pointers that keep saying this one thing over and over again: "The Father is seeking you. He never gives you up, and even when he is obliged to refine you in the fires of tribulation, the greatest pains are still his visitations, his efforts to bring you back home."

So let this be the last thing we hear today: God is faithful, he never lets us down. He is not, like the gods, "entangled" in the universal cosmic process. He himself is not a mere part of the world. He is the Lord and Creator of the world and he dwells in majestic remoteness from all things made, from all creatures. But even though he is the Lord of the world who stretches his commanding hand above the universe, he comes to meet me, he knows me, and he clasps me to his heart. He will never give me up. I shall always be his child, even when I depart from him—or when death comes—or when the world ends. His faithfulness will never cease.

But what else can there be in this world (this world of which he is the Lord) that could separate us from him: tribulation, or distress, or persecution, or famine, or nakedness, or peril, or sword? Do I see that this hand that is reaching out for me and will not let me go is a severe hand, but also a very loving hand? Do I see that I must let go of myself and surrender, if this hand is to catch and hold me?

Luther said, "God created the world out of nothing. As long as you are not yet nothing God cannot make something out of you."

3

The Light of the World

And God said, "Let there be light"; and there was light. And God saw that the light was good; and God separated the light from the darkness. God called the light Day, and the darkness he called Night. And there was evening and there was morning, one day.

And God said, "Let there be lights in the firmament of the heavens to separate the day from the night; and let them be for signs and for seasons and for days and years, and let them be lights in the firmament of the heavens to give light upon the earth." And it was so. And God made the two great lights, the greater light to rule the day, and the lesser light to rule the night; he made the stars also. And God set them in the firmament of the heavens to give light upon the earth.

—*Genesis 1:3–5, 14–17*

Many of us, surely, remember that passage in Joseph Haydn's oratorio, "The Creation," where the words occur: "And there was light." The first three words are sung moderately, but at the word "light" the orchestra and choir bursts forth in extreme fortissimo, in a wild transport of ecstasy. It is as if all the suns and lights in the cosmos blazed up at one stroke, like a fountain of light ascending to the heavens. "The world is here, the world is here, for light has come."

So the first "Let there be" rolled through the primeval darkness and out of the formless darkness there rose the contours of structured spaces. And the great light came from God.

A few verses later the biblical text says, "And God saw that the light was 'beautiful' " (for this is the literal translation). So the first response the young, dew-fresh creation evoked from the heart of God was joy in its beauty, the rapture of the creator.

So the Bible begins with a word about beauty. And even before the heavens began to praise the Eternal Majesty, God's own heart was filled with joyful song that there should be something so beautiful arising here in the shimmer of the first light. Above the nascent world lay the serenity of God.

I think this is the very first thing we should hear in this text, because we have lost this higher happiness of the morning of creation. And perhaps it is least of all from the Bible that we expect this proclamation of an unspeakably beautiful world and we are a bit surprised that this call to rejoice in life should come to us particularly from *this* quarter.

Some time ago a mother whose son wants to study theology told me her friends and neighbors were much surprised by his decision and said to her, "What! Your Johnny wants to be a minister? But he's such a jolly fellow and religion is so awfully sad. Is he, perhaps, having love trouble?" These good people probably reflect quite correctly the general feeling that the Bible is rather a sad and melancholy book. Isn't it significant in itself that it is bound in somber black and often, when it is stamped with gold besides, reminds us of a first-class funeral? This book talks about sin and hell and the Last Judgment. If you let yourself in for that kind of thing, you might as well say goodbye to laughter, and rock 'n' roll doesn't go with it either.

But here it is said that God—the very God this black book tells about!—found the world beautiful and saw it spread out before him in the hilarious brightness of the morning. How does this tally?

Perhaps we Christians with our woebegone faces have contributed something toward fostering the prejudice that faith is a very sad and melancholy thing and that one must wait until the next world comes before one may expect a few compensations. What Nietzsche once said is probably quite true, that we Christians will have to look more redeemed if people are to believe in our Redeemer. And the fact is that there must be something festive and resilient in our life if people are to be convinced of the gaiety of the first light of creation.

I believe, therefore, that it is tremendously important that we should quite simply take note of this message of delight in the world and learn to understand it. For we have lost this joy. Gottfried Benn once fashioned this loss of the joy of creation and this dread of the world into a macabre vision:

"Can you imagine yourself," he asks, "as you look out your window on the earth, entering into the thoughts of a God who created anything so soft and gentle as the plants and the trees? Rats, plague, noise, despair—yes—but flowers? There is a fourteenth-century picture called the 'Creation of the Plants.' In it there is a small, crook-backed, black-bearded god, lifting up an outsize right hand, as if he were lifting out of the earth the two trees that stand beside him. Otherwise the picture is quite empty. Can you imagine this kindly Creator today? Vice, worms, maggots, sloths, skunks—yes, that, in masses, continuations, installments, 100 per cent, in ever new editions—but a little tender God lifting up two trees? No trees, no flowers—but robot brains . . . artificial duplication of chromosomes to produce bastard giants—subrefrigeration, superheating . . ." this is what *we* see the world becoming and what we have to fear.

And isn't Gottfried Benn pretty largely right? Just think of the accidents and catastrophes in our created world reported by our big dailies day after day. How far removed is this pain over the lost creation from the joy God found in the good and beautiful light, the joy that can still be found in Matthias Claudius' verses:

> I thank thee, God, and like a child
> Rejoice as for a Christmas gift,
> That I am living—just alive—
> Just for this human face I wear,
> That I can see the sun, the sea,
> The hills and grass and leafy trees,
> And walk beneath the host of stars
> And watch the lovely moon above.

I am not saying this in order to point out in a derogatory way how *miserable* we men have become with our anxiety, our worry about the atom, and our preoccupation with decadence, and how far we are from being able to see the exultant joy of life expressed in this account of the creation. It is rather a certain sadness that prompts me to refer to it, a heaviness of heart over the fact that God intended the world to be so completely different from what we see it to be today, that *he* brought it forth in a festival of light, whereas *we* have banished its festive light and, despite all our technical and social advances, often feel that our life is nothing but misery and drudgery.

This drastic contradiction calls one as a Christian, as a messenger of the gospel, to come to the fore. Here God has created a rich and abundant world, but we—we suffer from meaninglessness, anxiety, and boredom. Here Jesus Christ walked the earth and spoke his word of judgment upon guilt, suffering, and death; but we men go on living as if all this had never happened, tormenting ourselves with our wounded conscience, with unabsolved guilt and worry about the unknown future—when in reality all of this has been taken care of by God. It is as if a man were starving beside a stack of loaves of bread and perishing of thirst beside a rippling stream.

We really ought to learn to see our inner condition in this light. For we not only squander and throw away what Jesus did and suffered for us when we do not claim his gifts and go on living as if he were nothing at all. We also lose the Creator, and finally we lose our delight in the world, in nature, in the trees and the animals.

And hasn't it actually come to this pass? Is it really joy in the beauty of the world that drives us through the country at sixty to seventy miles an hour, that disgorges troops of tourists from their buses in the great and famous spots only to be sucked up again—after sending off a few hundred postcards—as with a vacuum sweeper? And a hundred yards away from these fat pastures of the travel industry, a hundred yards from the scenic competition of popular resorts, there where the crickets sing, nobody is to be found. Are the mountains we visit on our vacations ever a liturgy of creation for us? Are they ever pointers to the peace of worship? Or is not all this just wasted "sightseeing," because in the depth of our inner emptiness we hunger ever more insatiably for sensations and diversions and thus we swallow down the mountains, the sea, and the lakes in a merely optical sense?

When I say this I do not mean it to be a merely statistical statement. On the contrary, it has something to do with the disease that has infected our faith. Let me explain briefly what I mean by this.

A person who separates himself from the Lord of creation in time also loses creation itself. He loses its secret and also its charm. Then the world changes—as a sunlit landscape changes when a dark storm cloud passes over it. Then suddenly the world becomes a frightening zone of tension between East and West, a battleground of the will to power, a murky scene of atomic visions.

It is not only the newspapers we need to read to find this out. We can also let the specters of existentialism, that muffled shriek of desolation and hopelessness, have its effect upon us, or we can look at a few of Picasso's pictures, in order to recognize over and over again that not only have we renounced our Redeemer and thus lost our peace, but that, at the same time and directly related to this, we have also lost the world which God intended and created for us.

This loss can be ascertained by a very simple test question, which is this: Can we still honestly recite what Matthias Claudius was capable of saying about the beauty of the world and what he so unforgettably expressed in that most beautiful of all evening songs, "The moon has risen"? Do we have an idea at all of that quiet chamber of night where we can forget the day's cares and relax without a care? For which of us is the moon, only one side of which we see, really a parable of the many things in life "which we confidently laugh at, because our eyes do not see them"?

I should like to permit myself to give this bit of counsel. Just sit down some quiet hour and read the evening hymns in the hymnbook and see how the mystery of creation reveals itself here. See how the expanse of night and the security of its chamber looms before your eyes, and discover that many things are actually "seen" there which we do *not* see in the neon lights, the asphalt, the metropolitan smog, the constant rush and inner confusion of our waking hours.

Then all this will be perceived not merely with eyes that are hungry for beauty, and thus merely with an esthetic interest, but will at the same time become a transparency for him who is the "Eye and Watcher over Israel," who watches over us and surrounds our troubled dreams with his peace. Or may it not be the other way round? May it not be that we begin learning to see the flowers, the stars, the crickets, the mountain meadows, and all the other things in our world only if we have first discovered the Heart of all things? In other words, only if we have first come to know the One who moves and sustains all these things and who therefore—*therefore!*—also finds ways to "direct my wandering feet" and transforms the "clouds, the air, and winds" into signals of his kindliness.

In an allusive and, so to speak, discreet way this first chapter of the Bible expresses the fact that what it is thinking of is really this Heart of all things, and that only as we start with him can we understand the fulness of creation.

So not for a moment when we are dealing with this text—this is now clear—can we be content with the merely esthetic impression of Light. Here something far more, something completely different is said and suggested. This is brought out by a peculiar sequence in the narrative, which some of you may perhaps have already noticed when we read the text.

We scientifically schooled people would naturally assume that the sun would first have to be created in order for there to be light. But here it is the other way around. First God made the light and only then, it is said, did he set two lights in the firmament, the sun and the moon. To these two stars he assigned the task of determining the rhythm of day and night. Literally, the original even says, with an undertone of very mild depreciation, that God hung two "lamps" in the firmament.

Here the Bible actually reverses the processes of nature and detaches the essence of light from the object, that is, from the material vehicles of light which we see, a detachment which we may perhaps describe in modern terms as "surrealistic."

Now even an ancient writer, like the man who wrote these verses of the Bible, could hardly have been so blind and innocent in a scientific respect that he failed to see that light comes from the sun. If this were so, modern, informed men could only smile a sophisticated smile. But, of course, the biblical author was not that stupid. So when he placed the creation of light *before* the creation of the sun and moon, he must have intended to say something quite specific, which he could not say in any other way.

And this is the case. I shall briefly try to make this clear. The fact is that this account of the creation was addressed to a world that believed in astrology and put its trust in horoscopes. It was a world not too far removed from our own in which the newspapers give space to astrological counselors, horoscopes, and the slogan "the stars cannot lie." How many people today read their daily prophecies as people used to read their daily Bible passages in more pious times!

This belief in astrology asserts that the course of the planets determines life on this earth down to the smallest detail and even our life is under the sway of the stars. Hence we are living under the dictatorship of cosmic necessities, and we have only a very limited scope for our action. So the people of old, like some today, scanned their horoscopes to discover what was in store for them and what they might do to take better advantage of the chances provided by more favorable constellations or at least escape a threatening planet. In many respects the situation is worse today than it was then, for now a host of shrewd, glib writers (with their tongues in their cheeks) are at work instilling a bit of mendacious optimism into poor, misguided people and giving them a few miserable crumbs of consolation for their anxieties.

Against this anxiety of fate in the face of the planets, against this dictatorship of a deified cosmos the creation story of the Bible protests when it says: "The stars have no power. They have definite functions to perform, they are 'to separate the day from the night'—and that's all there is to it!" And this probably explains the depreciatory undertone in which the Bible speaks of the sun and moon as mere "lamps." "The stars in no way create light, but are merely intermediary bearers of a light which existed without them and before them" (Gerhard von Rad). Their function is therefore merely to transmit something they themselves have not produced at all. They are mere trustees of the light, cosmic stewards who have been employed and have no will of their own.

The light itself, however, comes from God. It is he whose hand is directly at work, and he is not dependent upon any planet or any other force of nature.

I wonder whether we really understand how comforting is this message. Let me try to explain it in a few sentences.

What the Soviet Union may be up to or what America may do, what will happen to our fragmented country, the fate of my children, my professional career, the course of my illness—none of this depends upon the orbit of the stars or any other anonymous intermediary powers, black cats, lucky numbers, charms, or nocturnal dreams. On the contrary, everything comes—as does the light of the world—from the Lord who utters his majestic "Let there be." "Nothing can happen to me, except what he has foreseen and what will prove best for me."

So no matter what may happen to me, there is always One who has a hand in it. And this One is not an unfeeling globe of fire like the sun. No, he has a heart that seeks me and knows my most secret thoughts and sighs, my yearnings and my fears.

It was, of all people, Theodor Däubler, the great spokesman

of nonobjective art, who once uttered, in connection with Goethe's "Theory of Colors," a profound and thoroughly Christian word about light which challenges our thinking. "Painting," he said, "is suffering and structured light ... It bears witness to the suffering and the action of light. But the word is the man." Theodor Däubler is really pointing to the background of creation: the artist, he is saying, celebrates the creation by exhibiting the light that comes from God in its variations and vicissitudes. He does this either by allowing it to shine in its splendor upon things and objects (and thus actually brings it into view), or he does so (as in many areas of modern art) by celebrating the action of light *without* recourse to the objects of nature, that is, "nonobjectively." There is only one being who does not fit into this light-flooded world of creation and whose secret is somewhere else: this being is man. For man is determined by the Word and only through the Word can this mystery be solved.

What Däubler is saying is that men, you and I, are not merely "shone upon" by God's light, as are the other creatures, like trees, animals, and houses; rather we men are "addressed" by the Word of God. When the Word of God is beamed upon us, do we then light up? No, it is terrible to say, man can remain in the dark nevertheless. We can withhold ourselves from this Word. But there is one thing we cannot do. We cannot evade the decision whether we shall stand beneath this Word or whether we shall desire to be our own masters. Once this Word has struck us we are involved in an encounter with God which we cannot escape. We must say either Yes or No to him.

Only as we understand that we thus are involved in a struggle with God that will make or break us will we also understand that we are not simply a species "which is striving out of the dark into the light," as Goethe once said, but that we actually shun the light of God. After all, it should give us pause that the Bible is constantly obliged to record men's *flight* from the light of God.

This account of our flight begins already in the Psalms. There it is said: "Thou hast set even my secret, my unacknowledged sins in the light of thy countenance" (Ps. 90:8); and this can only result in our having to shun this light. And another psalm (139) tells of a man, shaken by qualms of conscience, who simply flees from God because he cannot endure feeling that these consuming eyes of the Omniscient are searching him through and through. He flings himself into one diversion after another, he travels to the ends of the earth, in order to escape himself and the pursuit of these eyes. And finally he tries to switch on something like Morgenstern's "dark lamp" and says: "Let the darkness cover me that I may escape in the night from the eyes of this pursuing God." But the Psalm goes on: "Even the night is light. Though I disguise myself in a thousand ways before men and am able to present a serious figure, God's searchlight finds me out." And to stand in this light—this can be a frightening, a devastating thing.

Even the night of Bethlehem was no simple, harmless festival of light, in which the shepherds danced their folk dances in the fields beneath the ringing skies as the brightness of the star shone upon them. Oh, no; the shepherds "were sore afraid"— just as Peter was when suddenly the luminous grandeur of Jesus dawned upon him and he flung himself flat upon the ground, unable to endure it: "Depart from me, for I am a sinful man, O Lord" (Luke 5:8).

The fact is that we men are *not* the species which is striving toward the light, at least not the light of God. On the contrary, we shrink from it. This is the only way we can explain that dark and distressing saying in the Gospel of John: "The light shineth in darkness; and the darkness comprehended it not." We shall never understand the story of Jesus' passion, the story of Gethsemane and Golgotha, if we overlook this deep truth that man is afraid of the light of God and that he employs every trick and dodge he knows to escape it.

This does not become clear to us in the creation story itself, for here the mood of Joseph Haydn tends to come upon us when suddenly the world is bathed in the radiant freshness of the first morning of creation.

But as soon as God appears, not only in light, but in word, as soon as Adam and Eve are confronted with decision, and as soon as God's question, whether we propose to live under him, is addressed to you and me, then we begin to draw back.

In closing, let me try to make this withdrawal from the light of God a bit clearer.

How many have asked me: "How does one really go about becoming a Christian?" And in order to answer this question, the first thing one must know is what is involved in this drawing back from the light.

In order to get this clear, let us think back once more to the parable of the Good Samaritan.[1] The priest and the Levite passed by the poor fellow who had fallen among thieves. In other words, for these two ecclesiastical gentlemen this meeting with an unfortunate victim of highway robbers contained an unpleasant truth. And the truth it contained was this: "Here you've got to help, even if the situation is somewhat dangerous and the partisans break out of the woods again and perhaps beat you up the way they did the other fellow." On the other hand it would have been just too painful for these two gentlemen to have had to say to themselves, "Actually, I ought to pitch in and help here, but I'm not going to expose myself, because I'm simply afraid; and besides, this delay with all its to-do will not fit into my schedule." So both of them, as the original says, made a wide detour around the man who had fallen among thieves. Thus they suggested to themselves: "Shucks, he was so far away you could hardly see him." So both of them played dead when they were faced by a truth. They repressed the truth. They fled from the searchlight of God.

During the Third Reich I knew a splendid student who was

---

[1] Cf. Thielicke, *The Waiting Father*, pp. 158–69.

studying theology because of honest conviction and was quite carried away with the mission of bringing the saving good news to men. Then suddenly, almost overnight, as it were, he began coming repeatedly to my consultation period to tell me about every imaginable doubt that occurred to him. It began with doubt whether Jesus Christ was the Son of God and finally ended with his doubting the existence of God himself. It struck me that he was actually holding on to his doubt with ferocity, almost as if he took pleasure in it, and that he hardly listened to what I said. At times it seemed to me that he was afraid of losing his doubt, as if he had fallen in love with it and were clutching it with both fists. Some time later he gave up the study of theology and shortly afterward he left the church altogether. Only later did I learn what was in the background: the Black Shirts had taken a fancy to his tall Nordic figure and were courting him with stipends and promises of a great career, and they finally won him over.

Naturally, he was far too decent (I mean this seriously!) to admit to himself that these people were offering him more than this poor, moribund show called the church and therefore he should be opportunistic and desert. He was far too smitten by his conscience to be able to slip out that cheaply and transform his faith into a purely business calculation. So he had to produce a moral alibi to satisfy his conscience. "If I can succeed," he argued, "in atomizing my former faith by means of genuine doubt, then nobody, neither God, nor this gullible professor, not even my own conscience can call me a deserter. For how can one desert someone who doesn't even exist and about whom one was wrong anyhow?" So he availed himself of doubt in order to play dead to the truth which is Christ. He denied the light in order to be able to carry on his dark doings in the dark. (Just recently I heard to my joy that he has returned from this far country and found his way home.)

Why do I tell this story? I tell it because it shows at least one thing very clearly and that is, that Jesus Christ, who is the light of the world, can be a terrifying and at the same time burdensome thing to us. Once we join him we shall have to see men differently from the way we did before. Then we shall have to see them the way Jesus saw them, not from the point of view that says, "This my neighbor will have to look out for himself; nobody ever helped me." Or the point of view that says, "If this my neighbor cannot cope with himself or his marriage or his finances, then let him go to the welfare agency or the minister or his congressman or the question-and-answer column in the local newspaper."

No, then everything is changed. When one stands beneath the eyes of Jesus, then suddenly people count for something. Then one can no longer pass by the man who has fallen among thieves, but must bind up his wounds. Then suddenly the other fellow is much more than a mere "associate"; then he is someone for whom Jesus Christ suffered.

This is what happened to me one time in connection with a student who took his own life. He had always sat in our group. It was true that I noticed that he often sat there in brooding, melancholy silence. But I thought he was probably worrying about his examinations or that he simply had a moody temperament. "In any case," I thought, "if he has something on his mind, he can come to me." But he did not come; he simply took his quiet way out. And we, we who had let him go, had denied our Lord. Again we had played dead. But Jesus Christ cannot find us when we play dead. And this is often the reason why we do not gain peace and never find the key to being a Christian.

We are surrounded by all these questions every day of our lives. Just read the many letters that people send in to the newspapers and the questions they ask. You find nothing but disappointments in love, boredom, burdensome marriages, and business troubles. And yet these are always people who live around us somewhere. Who else would send such letters?

But normally we never even see these people, though they

live all around us. We stick our heads in the sand and therefore they too take flight into the anonymity of these letters to the columnists. But the love we receive from Jesus and then learn for ourselves not only makes us inventive but also causes us to find the people in need. It gives the kind of sight that seeks and knows.

This is certainly a hardship from one point of view. For one who loves is always in a state of mobilization; he is always on the alert. And this very moment, despite my weariness and despite my full schedule, I may be detailed to follow the track of my neighbor who is in trouble. Now, may it not be fear of being involved in this constant alert that keeps us from joining Jesus Christ? May it not be this fear that causes us to go on living in the state where we can't be bothered?

We ought to examine ourselves about this sometime. For, as a rule, it is not some doctrine that is preventing us from becoming a Christian, but something quite different: the fear of stepping out into this light, the fear of being seen through, even to the hidden lumber rooms of our soul, the fear of having to be always ready to act and ready to follow this Lord wherever he goes.

And yet, once we take our chances with him, we shall find that this is the real happiness and the real fulfilment of our life. If we begin today to give a cup of water to one of our neighbors in His name, we shall hear the beating heart of our Savior and be blessed by his nearness. We shall begin to learn how dark and cold life is without him and then in our own lives we shall feel the freshness of that morning of creation when the Word sounded forth: "Let there be light."

The great light is already here. The festival of light has already been inaugurated by God for you and for me. We need only to throw open the shutters of our dark house and let in its flooding fulness.

Otherwise, if we always keep the shutters closed, how should we ever know what God wants to do for us? But he who plants himself in this light, he who dares to make the leap from his own dark life into this light will begin to shine himself. He will experience a new form of joy, a joy that will fill his eyes with tears.

4

God's Autograph

And God said, "Let there be a firmament in the midst of the waters, and let it separate the waters from the waters." And God made the firmament and separated the waters which were under the firmament from the waters which were above the firmament. And it was so. And God called the firmament Heaven. And there was evening and there was morning, a second day.

And God said, "Let the waters under the heavens be gathered together into one place, and let the dry land appear." And it was so. God called the dry land Earth, and the waters that were gathered together he called Seas. And God saw that it was good. And God said, "Let the earth put forth vegetation, plants ,yielding seed, and fruit trees bearing fruit in which is their seed, each according to its kind, upon the earth." And it was so. The earth brought forth vegetation, plants yielding seed according to their own kinds, and trees bearing fruit in which is their seed, each according to its kind. And God saw that it was good. And there was evening and there was morning, a third day.

And God said, "Let there be lights in the firmament of the heavens to separate the day from the night; and let them be for signs and for seasons and for days and years, and let them be lights in the firmament of the heavens to give light upon the earth." And it was so. And God made the two great lights, the greater light to rule the day, and the lesser light to rule the night; he made the stars also. And God set them in the firmament of the heavens to give light upon the earth, to rule over the day and over the night, and to separate the light from the darkness. And God saw that it was good. And there was evening and there was morning, a fourth day.

And God said, "Let the waters bring forth swarms of living creatures, and let birds fly above the earth across the firmament of the heavens." So God created the great sea monsters and every living creature that moves, with which the waters swarm, according to their kinds, and every winged bird according to its kind. And God saw that it was good. And God blessed them, saying, "Be fruitful and multiply and fill the waters in the seas, and let birds multiply on the earth." And there was evening and there was morning, a fifth day.

And God said, "Let the earth bring forth living creatures according to their kinds: cattle and creeping things and beasts of the earth according to their kinds." And it was so. And God made the beasts of the earth according to their kinds and the cattle according to their kinds, and everything that creeps upon the ground according to its kind. And God saw that it was good.

—*Genesis 1:6–25*

A person must surely be a snob or be utterly "hard-boiled" if he is not moved by these primeval words, if his heart does not leap up in the early light of this morning of creation. If we ask ourselves what the cause of this enchantment may be, there is only one answer that comes to me: here we stand before the vision of the "world intact." Here there is no room for tensions and the anxiety of life. Here there are no natural catastrophes, but rather there still reigned the ancient refrain according to which the sun "sings in confraternal contest with the spheres," and "the incomprehensibly lofty works are glorious as on the first day." Nobody has ever so movingly expressed the shimmering innocence and charm of this infant day of the world as has Joseph Haydn in his oratorio "The Creation" (whose description of light we have already referred to): even the thunder and lightning and snowstorms, being given, as it were, their first paradisean performance, are delightfully harmless, playing together like young animals.

But why is it really that this encounter with what is perfect and whole always makes us a bit sad? What is the source of that faint touch of melancholy on the faces of Greek statues in their perfection? Why do beauty and sadness dwell so close together? Why is it that the clear, bell-like tones of a boy soprano not only delight but also fill us with aching pain? Why is the utmost of beauty so heartbreaking?

That all this is so is doubtless to be attributed to the fact that the intact world has slipped away from us and that this innocence lies behind us. The Bible itself tells us that this is so.

According to this primeval story, God created the beasts and the plants each according to its kind. The infinite variety of forms, structures, and characteristics is an expression of the overflowing abundance of creation, and everything that creeps and flies, everything that lives in the water, on the earth, or in the air, the prickly cactus and the sweet violets, the living, blooming things of nature and inorganic nature—all this chimes together like a symphony and combines in a soaring song of praise that rises to the dazzlingly new firmament.

But one needs only to turn over a page or two and there you will read how man broke away from this concert of creation and this exultant song of praise, how he set himself up as the soloist, indeed, the star of creation, and how he finally entrenched himself in this his present world by building a tremendous bunker in Babylon.

And here the theme of infinite variety emerges again; but this time as the sign not of the abundance of creation, but of judgment. The languages are diverse because they are confused; the peoples live "each according to its kind," but because of their diversity they have become enemies; what before was wealth and abundance is now a curse.

Truly, our world has changed. It is as if human hands had messed with everything God's creator-hands summoned into the light, and changed them all. That which God poured forth in living abundance—"each according to its kind"—now becomes a sign of separation, enmity, and lack of understanding.

And even the lights which God fixed in the firmament, the moon and the stars, no longer revolve as they did on that first day of the world; for now Sputnik has joined them, and soon there will be systems of cosmic highways and red and green lights will blink in a universe which has retained for the longest time the untouched state of the first day of creation.

And the remarkable thing is that we do not find it easy to incorporate Sputnik into the Creator's composition. It is hard for us to say that here in this conquest of space God's creation reaches its finale (after all, he promised that we should have dominion over the earth and therefore, no doubt, over the universe!). Sputnik's "beep-beep" doesn't quite fit in with the music of the spheres. The voice of man and the sound of his gadgets clash with this harmony, for man is no longer on God's side. Therefore we know that Sputnik and its progeny are not simply enrichments of the fulness of the universe, but that at the same time they will infiltrate the universe like partisans, like man's fifth column, that they will become spying eyes, emissaries of destruction, and messengers of mischief.

But here we must guard against simply falling into the romanticism of horror. What is *really* different after the Flood and the tower of Babel, what is really different in the atomic age and on this Sputnik-encircled earth from what it was on that morning of creation, can be expressed in a brief formula:

Everything that was here summoned to life by the divine "Let there be"—the trees and the whales, the birds and the stars—all these still bear the traces of the Creator, all of them are similes and signs that point to him. One can still read the autograph of the Creator on every stone and flowering twig. And this is precisely what we can no longer do. The autograph of God has disappeared from a great many things in our experience and the traces of the words "Let there be" have been erased.

Otherwise, why should we be doubting and despairing over many things that torment us and asking the protesting, anxious question: "How can God permit this?" How could he allow the blood-bath in Hungary to happen? How could he permit the "Pamir" to sink? How could he countenance the mass graves of the air-raid victims in the Ohlsdorfer cemetery in Hamburg? Charon, the boatman of Hades with the Sphinx-like smile on his face who is to be seen in the little temple there, would appear after all to be the appropriate autograph for all the insanity of blind fate and human cruelty, or is it . . . ?

Surely, the signature written in the horrors of refugee camps, mental hospitals, and the tears of those who grieve in loneliness, and also the vaunting pride of Western prosperity swaggering in the night clubs, surely this is not the signature of God's creator-hands, or is it . . . ? Surely, this must be somebody else's hand?

Or is it conceivable that, along with the words "Let there be light" and "Let there be waters," still other words were spoken, like: Let there be cancer, let there be the infirmity of old age, let there be radioactive pollution, let there be anxiety, let there be war? Is it possible to think of these two things together: Let there be spring *and* let there be frost in the springtime? Let there be an infant child in a mother's arms *and* let there be infantile paralysis?

Obviously, none of this is compatible. The handwriting of God seems to have become illegible. The idea that everything temporal is a parable of the Eternal has been shaken, for the likeness has been terribly distorted. May not this be the cause of that little pang at the bottom of our hearts which we feel when we read the account of the morning of creation? God can no longer be had directly. God has become indiscernible. Isn't that our trouble?

It really is the only trouble that exists. For the really tormenting thing in our life is not at all that we must go through illness, that our dearest must die, that we suffer business reverses, that we fail examinations. All of this is hard enough in all conscience. But it would be child's play if we were able to accept it from God's hand, if we could see God's autograph at the bottom of the cup of suffering. Then we would know why and for what purpose all this was happening to us. Then we should find peace.

If we could find even *one* hint that there is a fatherly heart in all that happens to me, a heart that means well toward me, then at least the anxiety and the self-tormenting argument with God would be over. Then my heart would have peace even though pain continued to shake my body and mind. Just one little trace of God, one tiny trace! What a comfort that would be! But all I see is the traces of fate and chance, only the mask of the unfathomable.

In the New Testament people are always demanding miracles of Christ. Even Satan attempted to incite him to perform miracles, to heal the sick, wake the dead, float down from the pinnacle of the temple and thus overcome gravity. I believe that we do the people of the New Testament an injustice if we see in this only the desire for sensations and thrills. There is surely more in it than that. These people are looking for God's autograph. They are troubled just as we are by the fact that God cannot be had directly. They see grief-stricken widows, they see human bodies rotting with leprosy, the hungry, the mentally disturbed. They see God in the distorted mirror of a world out of joint.

Indeed even in Jesus of Nazareth they do not "see" him. After all he himself is homeless, poor, without comeliness, and only one among many. And because they are so alone with their misery and God is silent or gone on a journey or nonexistent, it gets them down and they say: "Why do you make it so hard for us? Don't let us sink into a sea of madness. Please perform a sign: let the lame walk, let fire fall from heaven, let the dead rise! Not just to make things better for a few people or to punish a few rascals—not for that reason, Jesus of Nazareth! That would only be a drop in a bucket, and we know that others must die, that multiple sclerosis will go on, and that the world will remain unjust. Oh, no, we do not ask you to upset the world, Jesus of Nazareth; we are not that unreasonable. But just at this *one* point, this one cripple or this one dead man let us, just once, hear that divine 'Let there be' that sounded forth on the first day of the world. At just *one* point let your Father break forth from his anonymity! Let the heavens be opened just one crack and let your Father say to us, 'Here I am!' Then we would be content."

We understand this well enough, don't we? Haven't we all said the same thing at some secret moment or other? Give me just *one* sign, one single sign! Give me only one hint that the thing I cannot cope with comes from *thee*. Just give me one small indication of what I should do and where you want me to be.

And yet Jesus always refuses. When he was hanging upon the cross, and meaninglessness and absurdity gathered into one sheer malicious mass, he did not pray that the heavens be opened and twelve legions of angels appear. There he submitted and suffered to the end without a sign of God's intervening and acknowledging him. God went on just as always. It was not God's autograph but a lampoon that was nailed to the cross: Christ, the king of the Jews. The soldiers around the cross yelled loudly. But God was very still. A pin dropping would have been louder than God.

Why does Jesus always refuse to give a sign? Why cannot God appear for one moment as directly as he did on the morning of the world's creation? Is he only trying to torment us?

This is the real question we have to work on.

For, naturally, he does not want to torment us. He only wants to make us understand that he cannot be had as cheaply as a cigarette offered to us as an omnipresent service to be had anywhere, day or night, from a vending machine. God cannot be had just anywhere.

Many people think, for example, that he can be found in nature, in a sun-drenched clearing in the woods, a sunset in the mountains, the sublime expanses of the ocean. But the strange thing is that even here there immediately arise two difficulties which hide the face of God from me.

In the first place, the phosphorescent beauty of the sea does not tell me that I must change my way of life and that I have been unfaithful in my marriage. Nor does it ask whether I am wasting my life with pure trivialities or whether I have found the one thing needful. The mountain peaks and the ocean are beyond good and evil. But the face of God has in it something consuming for all who must stand up to it; for here we are seen through and challenged and destroyed.

But God veils himself in still another way in nature. What did the ocean look like to those young men on the doomed "Pamir" as their ship was driven with tattered sails before the hurricane? Do you think they still cherished elevated thoughts about the beauty of the sea or did not God instead threaten to become a ghastly specter?

James Whittaker, the English pilot, has described this same situation for us in his book, *We Thought We Heard the Angels Sing*. The story is about the occupants of a four-engine plane which went off course owing to a failure of the compass, made a forced landing in the ocean, and sank. The eight occupants were driven about for three weeks in rubber boats, without water, without provisions, in blazing sunlight and deadly loneliness. The book gives an account of the inner history of these three weeks. All of them, weatherbeaten men who loved the elements, begin to hate, really hate this torturing space between the ocean wastes and the blazing sky. All love and worship of nature completely evaporates. Nothing is left but a body- and soul-destroying desolation.

Suddenly one of them begins to pray the Lord's Prayer. He is the only one who knows it. In the evening they pull their rubber boats together and begin to pray to God for help. They swear vows for the day when God would save them. And because they never had any practice in talking with God, they do not know how to address him. The words "dear Father" or "Lord Jesus Christ" are still beyond their reach. So they address him, somewhat helplessly, but yet infinitely movingly, as "Old Man." And strange to say, suddenly the desolate, destructive elements are transformed for them. They know that God has pathways even here, that he has *one* pathway to lead them to their earthly or eternal home. And they are filled with a great peace, even though their skin is peeling and thirst is repeatedly driving them to the brink of madness.

What has happened here? It was not the grandeur of the ocean that revealed to them the image of God; on the contrary, here there were only visions of dread and mocking hallucinations. No, it was the Word of the Lord in the Lord's Prayer that suddenly drew near to them and transformed the ocean. It is not nature that opens the door to God. It's the other way around: God opens the door to nature. Because these men were suddenly near to the heart of God as they said the prayer of the Lord, this cruel sea became for them, in Gorch Fock's words, "a pool in the palm of their Savior."

To understand this we must sit down sometime and read Psalm 104 for ourselves. It speaks of all the glories of the earth just as the creation story does, of light and water, mountains and clouds. And yet there is more here than mere joy in nature. Its utterances are rather in the style of worship: "O Lord, . . . who coverest thyself with light as with a garment; . . . thou makest springs gush forth in the valleys; . . . thou hast made the moon to mark the seasons; . . . O Lord, how manifold are thy works!" And is it any different in Matthias Claudius' poem, "The moon has risen"? But how good is the softly shimmering moon to us, if we do not know the protecting Hand behind it? Then it would be nothing more than a cold, inanimate light in which the proud children of men perform their silly tricks, in which they vegetate in empty light and only end up farther from the goal.

The moon is therefore not always moon; it depends on whose name we see it shine in. And to him who knows this name, to him who knows the heart behind things, everything becomes a sign, really everything. He sees in the waves of the sea the power of God, in the moon his gentleness and the preserving order that sets the limits of the seasons. He sees in the spring and autumn rains the good, sustaining hand of God and for him death itself will become a homecoming in which he will see what before he believed.

And that brings us to the innermost secret of the creation story. Only as we take seriously the words, "God said," and understand that here someone is actually *speaking*, that here a heart is expressing itself, will we have the key to creation in our hand. For the man who is a hearing man all things become new. And I do not hesitate to say that then our enjoyment of nature will take an entirely new form. There really is such a thing as a Christian enjoyment of nature, because for us it becomes the garden of God and thus our native home. Then *everything* becomes home: the beach and the sickbed, the mountaintop and the old folks' home. But we must have the Father in order to know the Father's home. Otherwise the familiar will become an alien country and our home a labyrinth.

But this is so not only with nature but also with our *life*. Here too we are always wanting to see signs and to be able to detect the direct working of God in what happens to us.

Long ago I was ill for seven years and I still remember well what it was like. I saw other healthy young people jumping about and here I was chained for a long time to a wheel chair. I asked myself, "Why should this be so?" and I thought if I ever found the answer to that question the worst would be over. For then I would know the meaning.

So I set up a definite theory: perhaps God desires to make me more mature, more obedient, and more agreeable through suffering.

But the theory did not work. For there is a degree of physical suffering that simply prevents any kind of reflection and demands that one expend all his energy merely to endure it and get through it.

Moreover, after a while one begins to think that finally he has been tested and refined enough. Now he has graduated from the school of suffering and secured his certificate of maturity. Then the suffering goes on anyhow. And then there is no meaning at all and even time and endlessness speak against God.

So it is by no means true that affliction teaches us to pray. Just as truly it teaches us to curse. Even suffering does not lead us to God. Otherwise we should see the peace of God on the faces of all who are sick with cancer, of all the insulted and injured, of all who are broken and bankrupt. But who would seriously assert such a thing? No, not even suffering leads to God, any more than does nature. It is just the other way around: for him who has found God, his suffering and his pain will also become his native place, a visitation of God.

For at the very point where I cannot understand, at the very point where the world "divided by reason never comes out even," as Goethe once said, the urgent question arises whether I can simply trust that God has a purpose in mind for me, that he is realizing his higher thoughts in the very thing which in *my* thoughts must necessarily be meaningless.

This is why Jesus held up little children as an example for adults. If a father says to a child, "You are not old enough to drive a car; therefore I can't give you the car you want," the child is not likely to understand this decision of the father. For, after all, "Father can do everything" and he can buy a car too. But nevertheless the child will not think that the father is cheating him by refusing to give him a car and that he is heartless. Rather the child will trust that his father means well. For he knows his father.

And that brings us to the hardest question of all. Do we know our Father? We *must* know him if we want to feel at home in life, if the rebellion or the hopeless resignation in the face of that which torments us is ever to cease. Isn't it just cheap clerical clack to say, "In his Word you will learn to know him, in this very Word which at the beginning of the world declared, 'Let there be,' or which took form in Jesus Christ"? And you want to bang your fist on the table and say, "I hear the Word all right, but what I can't do is believe." In a word, God cannot be had directly; even in the Word he is hidden beneath seven seals and veiled in pure enigma.

"So let up on your pious pulpit dialectics! First you say you will not find him in the moonlight and the mountains. The world is not a parable that points to God. Nor will you find him in suffering, for there you will find only the sphinx of fate or the leering demons. You must look for him in the Word. Good heavens, I can't find him even there! Where would he be among those old miracle stories and nursery tales? I'm sorry, but don't tell me I must 'believe.' Please, anything but that. I'm sick of this eternal egg-dance around the great unknown called God. I don't care a pin for this windy answer: You must believe! Why does God make it so hard for us? Why doesn't he send a dead man from the beyond to tell us about it, so we would have in black and white what's going on there? Why doesn't he set up a loudspeaker in the sky and shout down to us: 'I am the Lord'? Why doesn't he give us a signal? Why all this windy talk about faith? Why does God make it so hard for us?"

Yes, why does he? Why does Jesus refuse to give a sign—and how we yearn for such a sign, for one little murmur, one little hint that he is there. . . .

We can also put the question in another way. Why did not Jesus accept the kingdoms of this world when the devil tempted him in the wilderness? If he had accepted them, the emblems of his sovereignty would have been planted on the highways, then his banners would wave over the earth, then we would know where we stand. And the everlasting doubt whether he is the Son of God, and whether there is a God at all would come to an end. Why doesn't God love clear-cut propositions and neat equations? Why does the whole drama of Christ end in the silence and bankruptcy of Golgotha?

If Christ had become the open and visible Lord of the world, he would now be separated from us by the distance and barricades that always separate us from prominent people. And this is exactly what he did not want. After all, he was the transmitter of a message—and the very burden of that message is that God does not sit enthroned in the heavens like a so-called supreme being, but that he wants to love us and be near to us. But love can be exercised only as we are very near to the other person and suffer with him.

This is precisely what so appeals to us in Albert Schweitzer. He may perhaps have been able to help the dark people of Africa far more effectively if he had been content to be a famous man in Europe and founded a company of wealthy businessmen and captains of industry and persuaded them to contribute to a permanent fund for a "Medical Aid Committee for the Dark Continent." Might not such a rationalized large-scale welfare enterprise have been established? An enterprise that would draw up a precise plan of strategy, plant innumerable little flags on a gigantic map of Africa, send out doctors and nurses—properly salaried, of course, so there would be some material incentive—and spread a network of modern clinics all over the continent? Would not that have been much more effective than going out to Lambarene all alone and confining his radius of action to a single Negro village? Would not that have been more profitable, more economical?

But now the counterquestion. Is it not this very thing, that Albert Schweitzer, instead of acting in a general staff based in Europe, actually went to the *front*, gave up all the comforts of civilization, shared life in the primeval forest with his patients, and became one of them—is it not precisely this one thing that makes him so credible and restores, at least a little, the distorted image of man?

Naturally, I do not intend to compare Albert Schweitzer with Jesus Christ. But at this point he followed him at least part of the way. For this Jesus Christ so loved us that he was willing to bear the whole of our misery. It is like a mother who knows that her boy is in a prison camp and in her heart she is with him from morning till night—so much with him that *his* hunger is her hunger, *his* homesickness is her homesickness, his trials her pain. One who really loves ceases, as it were, to be himself, transforms himself into the other person, becomes a part of him, and bears his pain with him.

And so it is with Jesus. He allows himself to be tempted as we are tempted; he endures our hunger, our thirst, our illness, our social bankruptcy, our death, and finally also our sin and guilt.

But may not all this have been only a sham maneuver?

Tolstoi once told us that for love of the disfranchised peasants on his ancestral estates he worked along with them for a time, shared their food, and slept with them in their primitive, stinking cottages. It was a shocking thing to him when one day it came out that what they were saying was: "We don't take your socialistic, humanitarian fad seriously. For you always have your rich father to fall back on. You can stop this social asceticism any time you want to. But this is just what we cannot do. You just *act* as if you were one of us."

May it not have been that way with Jesus too? Was it not for him a monstrous masquerade to be a human being as we are? Could he not have pressed a button and, behold, twelve legions of angels would have marched in and all our misery would be ended?

But this consideration is the very thing that lets us see the greatest fact about Jesus. The point is that he did *not* summon the twelve legions of angels. So utterly was he one of us that, according to the oldest account, his last cry was, "My God, my God, why hast thou forsaken me?" So completely did he become one of us that he went with us to the abyss of God-forsakenness and the dread of total nothingness.

If we are so loved, so uncompromisingly and unreservedly, then surely we dare to utter the word "Savior" without being pious in an untruthful sense.

And now I say that here lies the solution of the problem of why God apparently makes it so hard for us, of why he does *not* shout down from heaven: "I am the chief of the cosmic general staff; don't get excited when a tactical situation in your life is incomprehensible!" If that were so, the kingdom of God would be like the apparatus of a welfare state. Everything would click, everything would be taken care of; but then we would not need to bother about the *thing* that took care of us, *because* it would only be an anonymous apparatus and an apparatus has no heart. Instead of a loving heart there would be nothing but a filing cabinet.

But God does not want to be like that. He wants us to be near to his heart and therefore to believe what his heart says. That's why he became one of us. And because he became one of us in Jesus Christ, he can be mistaken for one of us, and then perhaps we say, "This Jesus really is a noble example of the human species. And the same thing happened to him that usually happens to unselfish people: he got trampled."

And this misunderstanding God has to endure. He takes it upon himself for love's sake, because he made himself so like us that he can be mistaken for a man. But one who sees him in his brotherliness, sharing our dread, our guilt, our loneliness, and our exposure to God-forsakenness can only fall to his knees beneath the power of that love and say: "My Lord and my God!"

He who comes near to the heart of God at this point really sees the world as it was on the morning of creation. For he has gained as his Lord and Brother the one who uttered the "Let there be" at the beginning. And he who thus extends his sovereign hand above the mountains and the firmament to summon them into being knows me and my needs too.

This great vaulting arch between the creation of the world and the lonely hour on Calvary, between the determination of all history and my little personal lot which I endure in my own little corner, this great arch, which the wise cannot comprehend by their logic, nevertheless has its place in the hearts of babes. For a children's hymn that re-echoes from the early morning of our youth sums it all up in a single, unspeakably comforting phrase: The Lord who numbered the stars in the blue vault of heaven and holds the universe in his arms "knows you too and loves you."

Do you understand? He loved "you" even while you talked

with the good Lord about your doll, and he earnestly listened to your every childish word. He loves "you" too who stand in the midst of hostile life; and "you" too whose eyes have grown dim and hands unsteady; "knows you too and loves you."

THE CREATION OF MAN

5

Man—the Risk of God

THE CREATION OF MAN—PART ONE

Then God said, "Let us make man in our image, after our likeness; and let them have dominion over the fish of the sea, and over the birds of the air, and over the cattle, and over every creeping thing that creeps upon the earth." So God created man in his own image, in the image of God he created him; male and female he created them. And God blessed them, and God said to them, "Be fruitful and multiply, and fill the earth and subdue it; and have dominion over the fish of the sea and over the birds of the air and over every living thing that moves upon the earth." And God said, "Behold I have given you every plant yielding seed which is upon the face of all the earth, and every tree with seed in its fruit; you shall have them for food. And to every beast of the earth and to every bird of the air, and to everything that creeps on the earth, everything that has the breath of life, I have given every green plant for food." And it was so. And God saw everything that he had made, and behold it was very good. And there was evening and there was morning, a sixth day.
—*Genesis 1:26–31*

I cannot believe that it is merely imagination to think that at this point in the story of creation where the subject of man appears for the first time there is something like a stoppage in the flow of the narrative. Up to this point the words came forth in monumental monotony: God said, God created, God made. But now the composition of the story shifts over, as it were, into another key. In other words, God halts and soliloquizes. He says, "Let us make man in our image, after our likeness."

One can almost detect something like a hesitation or even a recoil. In any case, it is the kind of bated breath with which we ourselves are familiar when we approach a decisive point in some piece of work on the success of which everything depends. We stop and stand off for a while. It may be the experience of a roofer who has covered a church steeple with shingles and then in one final, risky effort must set the cock upon the peak, or of a dramatist who sets out to compose the main and key scene in his play.

So when God pauses before he composes man into his creation, we sense that there is a risk connected with it: will the creation of man mean the coronation of creation or its crucifixion? Will creation reach its pinnacle when there is added to its creatures a being who rises above the dull level of reflex and instinct, who is endowed with mind and will, and is capable of living as a partner and co-worker of God his Creator? Or is the creation of this being called "man" the first stage in a tremendous descent that starts in the Garden of Eden and leads to a disturbed and desolated earth, that transforms the child and image of God into a robber and a rebel, and through him carries war and rumors of war to the farthest planets?

Coronation or crucifixion of creation—that is the question here. And we understand why God pauses and hesitates, for he is facing a risk. What a breath-taking thought! Is it not almost blasphemous even to think of such a thing?

And this is the way it was. In setting over against himself a being to whom he gave freedom and power he risked the possibilities that the child would become a competitor, that the child would become a megalomaniacal rival of the Creator. Then perhaps would come the moment, described in *Faust*, when man would no longer be gratefully conscious that he was privileged to be the image of his Creator but would rather rise up and cry, "I am the image of divinity," or, like Prometheus, even revel in his equality with God.

This venture of God in which he bound himself to man—and

exposed himself to the possibility of being reviled, despised, denied, and ignored by man—this venture was the first flash of his love. God ventured, as it were, his own self. He declared himself ready to suffer the pain the father endured when he let the prodigal son go into the far country, when he allowed deep wounds to be inflicted upon his heart, and still would not give up his child of sorrows. This line reaches its end in Jesus Christ. There God exposed himself to his rebellious children, put himself at their mercy, and let his most beloved die by their hand but for them.

So already we see how wrong it would be to talk too smugly about man being the crown of creation. Our text suggests backgrounds that will not allow us to use such a simple formula. And perhaps it is well for us at this point to take very seriously Gottfried Benn's disclaimer: "Man is not a higher being . . . . What we have achieved has been to a large extent the presumptuous, *hubris*, the stupid." Hence a "certain reduction of this arrogance" would certainly be more important than indulging in fanciful lofty goals.

Nevertheless, to me it seems wrong for us to chime in with the general and intellectually respectable decrying of man's failure. I think we must strike out in an entirely different direction, and I am convinced that here our text can become an important means of orientation.

If there is *one* rule that is given to us by the command to love our neighbor, it is that we must always judge a person by his optimum and not by his failures. I should like to illustrate this with an example.

Here is a woman who pours out the story of her broken marriage in tears. For her husband she simply does not exist, except as a lightning-rod for his temper and uncontrolled emotions. Everything she says indicates quite clearly that her husband is a brutal fellow, and one can understand why her love is almost extinguished under the constant pressure of his mental cruelty.

What should one say to her? That divorce would be best?

Naturally, this thought is bound to occur. But must I not say to her that then she might put him in a worse hole, that she might rob him of his last foothold? Or what else might be said in a situation like this? Perhaps that she should try to make herself love him? This would surely be rather foolish advice, for, after all, we cannot force ourselves to love anybody. This only results in forced, hypocritical tension. And sometimes we can see this in legalistic Christians.

But perhaps this is what I should say to her: "You loved your husband when you first knew him; isn't that true?" "Yes," she replies, "but then he was different." "True; naturally he was different," I allow her, "otherwise you would never have married him." "Yes," she interrupts, "you can depend on that." "But you did love him once," I continue, "and now I ask you who your husband *really* is? Is his real self what you loved *then* or is his real self the horrible being who makes you suffer so *now?*"

I shall not go any further with this conversation here, but simply say this: In Jesus Christ we learn that the love that once was there but has long since died had laid hold upon the real, the intrinsic nature of this husband. The way he appeared to his wife *back there* was the way God intended him to be. And his present state was a deviation and a fall from that former state.

When we stop to consider where Jesus gained the power to love harlots, bullies, and ruffians, we find only one answer and that is that he was able to do this only because he saw through the filth and the crust of degeneration, because his eye caught the divine original which is hidden in every man—in *every* man!

Jesus renews everything in us: he not only gives us a more sensitive conscience and mobilizes our will, but first and foremost he gives us new eyes. Then we see and recognize something else in our neighbor.

Now I think that we see that this account of the creation of man points in the same direction. For here is described the moment in which God "designed" man, and thus the moment when he tells us what he has in mind for him, what he thinks of him **as being.** He intends him to be his image, his friend, one to whom he wants to be faithful and to whom he wants to give a meaningful life. And if that is true, then all this is still there in every human being today, even in the wicked gossip-monger in my neighborhood, even in the young mugger and purse-snatcher, even in Khrushchev and Mao Tse-tung.

But if it is present in every human being, then I must take it into account, then I dare not simply react in fear or in hatred to such threatening figures, but rather learn to see them in the light of their optimum, in the light of what they were created to be.

I believe that a great sense of peace and serenity would result from this way of seeing. We would get away from our panic jitters, our everlasting anxiety, or even from our sterile contempt for human beings. "Is man no more than this?" asks King Lear. Yes, he is more, far more than that. He is the potential bearer of a crown, even though he may gamble it away a hundred times.

So, for a moment at least, let us wipe away from our eyes the vision of human folly, the vision of the Promethean, atomic rebel, and refresh ourselves with the vision of what God *meant* us men to be, that which even now belongs to every one of us—the captain and the lowliest stoker on our planetary ship—and belongs to us so truly that we can count upon it. I believe it would be something like a breath of oxygen, an undreamed-of refreshment, if we were to expose ourselves to this breath of the Spirit in our history.

This original design within us, on which I can count in myself and also in my neighbors, my colleagues, and my competitors, is described in our text from three points of view.

First, we are created to have dominion over the earth. Second, we are made to live in the relationship of man and woman and thus are not designed to be soloists, but rather to live together with our fellow men. And third, we are images and likenesses of the divine being.

I should like to speak about these features at some length in this sermon and the next one, for they represent something like a plan, a survey map of our whole human existence. When we have studied this map we shall know something about the meaning of our life. Then we shall know what the play is about and what role we ourselves have to fill. And this is not something one can make short work of; we must take some time for it.

Today I want to discuss the first of the three characteristics mentioned, namely, that man has been called to have *dominion over nature:* " 'Be fruitful and multiply, and fill the earth and subdue it; and have dominion over the fish of the sea and over the birds of the air and over every living thing that moves upon the earth.' "

It would be wrong to see in these words any suggestion that here man is conceived as a spiritual being who is elevated above nature, above the brute, and that he somehow hovers above all that is creaturely. The animal and man, the whales, the sparrows, and Homo sapiens are all created together on the same sixth day of creation and thus included in a whole. And I believe that it is not only true to life but also a great comfort that the Bible does not pretend that we are paragons of virtue, painted saints, and ideal figures of humanity. The Bible is well aware that the struggle of nature also determines our human life, that we too are controlled by instincts and urges, needs and desires, just as are the birds and the beasts of the field. Often our dreams, which we cannot control by our will, are an appalling reminder that we have our roots in the animal kingdom.

Isn't it really a comfort that the Bible sees us quite realistically as being higher animals? That God by no means thinks of us only as dwellers in the top storey of creation, as occupants of the penthouse reserved for the possessors of conscience and reason, but that he also knows the cellars, the dark and subhuman abysses of our being into which we allow no man to look? What would the gospel be if Jesus paid no attention to the cupidity of harlots, to our bodies with their urges and also their illnesses, if he were not near to us at our dying, where, after all, we are "like the beasts that perish" (Ps. 49:12).

I find it cheering beyond all measure that the Lord's Prayer does not pretend that we are only religious people, that is, people who occupy themselves wholly with high things and are completely absorbed in the wish that God's kingdom may come and his will be done. Oh, no, the Lord's Prayer knows that we have the urge to eat—again like the animals—that we must have our daily ration of bread, that we are indifferent to the most beautiful of picture galleries when we are coming down with the grippe, and that all sense of devotion trickles away when our feet are cold.

I find it simply wonderful that God does not treat us men as aristocrats of creation who are constantly living beyond their means and having to go to great pious expense in order to measure up to their certificate of humanity, but rather that we can come before him as people who are related to the fishes, the dogs, and the cats, in whom hormones and glandular secretions circulate just as they do in our fellow creatures; that we can appear before him as people who are lashed by the same libido as they are, and in whom—different from and worse than with animals—all these things are capable of condensing into inextricable complexes. We are acceptable to him just as we are, with all these characteristics, and this is precisely what Jesus took upon himself. And the Lord God is far less alien to nature and creatureliness than we are in our pious delusions.

So it is not beneath his dignity if we pray for a good digestion after an operation, or if a prisoner says grace over his watered soup. I believe that he even takes more pleasure in this than he does when we sit down with stomachs well filled by the "economic miracle," grunting a fatuous "Enjoy your meal," smugly enjoying our heavy silverware and gold-rimmed china, and gloating over how successful we have been. In any case, we stand before God as men of flesh and blood, and what is more, of frail flesh and unruly blood and with animality in our nature, and something of the effluvium of the earth blows upon us when the psalmist prays: "Man and beast thou savest, O Lord" (Ps. 36:6).

Is it then merely an ornamental flourish when ox and ass appear in the stable of Bethlehem and they all stand beneath the same Light? Is there no significance in the fact that the Son of God was born in an animal's manger?

It is not well when Christianity leads one to have contempt for the body and tries to be more spiritual than God.

It is a mistake for us to consider it pious to break out of the solidarity of the sixth day and behave idealistically and spiritually, as if we were only spiritual beings. The Utopians who dreamed of advancing into the superhuman and making the earth a heaven have always ended up by making a hell on earth. Jesus Christ keeps us close to the earth; otherwise he would never have come to this earth, but would have developed a method to lift us to superhumanity. But, no, he appeared in a stable and he was not estranged even by the beast within us. He saves man and beast. He encompasses both loft and cellar. He loves the *Arietta*, that utterly ethereal passage in Beethoven's Opus 111, and he lays his hand upon the wild and animal dreams of adolescents.

And again, when man is enjoined to be fruitful and multiply, this command appears in the same context with the multiplication of plants and animals. Here there is a very quiet allusion to the fact that we human beings generate progeny and are creative in a way that is different from God the Creator, that we are *only* men and therefore sharply distinguished from him. For God creates from nothing. We men, however, are everywhere bound to our creaturely condition and cannot lift ourselves above it. We are enclosed within limits we cannot break asunder.

Can we, for example, produce any kind of children we desire? After all, we have our genes within us and we must transmit them. As young parents, perhaps, we may tremble at the thought that this or that peculiarity imbedded in our being may be hereditary—yet we find it present in our children. The truth is that we cannot "create" children; we can only "propagate" ourselves with all our dubious characteristics. We do not, like God, create from nothing, but merely blunder about with the given conditions.

And so it is always in life. Even if we are educators, whether as parents or teachers or leaders of youth, we can only develop further what has been given, and where there is nothing we can create nothing. We cannot take an unmusical clod and make a Mozart out of him, even if we expose him all day long to the music of the spheres and stuff him full of the theory of music.

Or take the area of statesmanship. Even a statesman of genius cannot launch and "create" the world that exists in his dreams; he must rather practice the "art of the possible." He can move only in the narrow orbit of the given constellations. He cannot "create" situations as God creates them; he can only "exploit" the situations that are given.

So before we take due note of the fact that we are the crown of creation, we must first recognize that we are *only* men and by no means gods. Above these verses there hovers the dreadful majesty of the Lord, before whom we must perish and before whom we are as nothing.

And yet, despite all the questionableness of our nature, here is this word being proclaimed to us: "Fill the earth and subdue it." Now I do not believe that we can any longer interpret this to mean a tremendous glorification of man. For, after all, we are not to rule and subdue the earth because we stand *above* the other creatures, but only because we stand *under* God and are privileged to be his viceroys. But being a viceroy of the Creator is something different from being a creature who makes of himself a god or at least a superman.

If I am not mistaken, this also gives us the clue to the meaning of all *culture*. For, after all, culture is the conquest, the management, the cultivation of the world. When fruitful farm land is made out of a desert and when human settlements arise in the primeval forests, this means that the seal of man is stamped upon the world. Every sheltering home and every garden is a victory won by man over the surging elements.

We therefore dare not think that culture always arises only from strife and separation from God, that *hubris* and human autonomy are inherent in it by nature. No, on the contrary, it exists under the blessing and justification of a divine command. When culture becomes godless and finally produces its appalling symbol in the tower of Babel, then an *alien* element has been smuggled into the plan of God. I merely mention this here. We shall come back to this point in the coming addresses. At this point we are only registering the thought that one of the goals of God's creation is contained within culture and all that is great and aspiring.

We Christians, therefore, have not only to sing hymns; we must also pay attention to culture. God wants this too. But we cannot pay attention to culture if we are narrow-minded, stupid Christian philistines. Then we hand over the theater, music, literature, and politics to the so-called children of the world, and our somewhat belated agitation and concern that they may play hob with it, that they may make a cult of Eros or an atomic witches' sabbath of it, is completely out of place. "Is the plot of history to turn out in such a way," asked Schleiermacher in another connection, "that Christianity will go with barbarism, but science—and art—with unbelief?"

I believe that the church of Jesus Christ has not yet really grasped just *what* has been entrusted to us and the wealth that has been given to us. Often it seems to me that we Christians flounder about between heaven and earth, as if, down underneath, we had lost both, and therefore present a rather lamentable figure to the children of this world. We keep thinking about all the things "we can no longer do" as Christians, instead of enjoying the riches of creation and then accepting with open hands what God wants to give to us. Is God, then, a mistrustful miser who locks everything away from us so that we cannot get at it? Is he not rather the Father who is always giving with full hands and unparalleled generosity, always pouring out his gifts? I am afraid that the germs of a neopagan culture are being cultivated in our musty Christian incubators.

Today we are beginning our entrance into space and we are

about to subdue not only the good old earth but the cosmos itself. Is this *too* covered by the blessing of that command given at the creation? This is a question that may well get under our skin. Is God our Lord even in space and on Venus, or when we go there are we breaking away from the created home which God has assigned to us? Does this mean that we are reaching for forbidden fruit?

I can imagine what a thoughtful space-traveler might think on his first journey to Venus. Perhaps it would be something like this:

After the torture of the enormous acceleration was over, he might be overwhelmed for a moment with the triumph of this human conquest of space. But then as he looked back from his spaceship to his native planet, which was growing smaller and smaller, another thought would overtake him: "There you are, you tiny provincial earth"—he thinks—"far below me. Really? Have I actually left you behind me? Is the past, which I spent down there, really wiped out?"

But then that tiny thing, so small that it is no longer visible through the strongest telescope, suddenly grows near and great and oppressive: that stairway—so far away that it is hardly true and yet it *is* true!—where he bore false witness against his neighbor; that night on earth when he tossed and chafed with ambition and anxiety; his marriage in which he foundered and transgressed; and also the great triumphs and happinesses in his life. If there is a God, then all this is very near to him and pursues him with a swiftness compared with which his rocket moves at a snail's pace.

So he cannot strip off his past, no matter how swiftly he flies through space. And because he cannot do this, he cannot shake off identity with himself by flying into space. He must remain himself. For there are no wings of the morning that would carry him to some distant sea of stars and set him free from himself. He is bracketed by the day of creation on the one hand and the day of the Last Judgment on the other. Even in cosmic space his life remains within that discourse in which he is enclosed by the breath of God. And so he remains judged and secure at the same time. He cannot get away from himself and he cannot get away from Him who holds him to Himself.

This, I believe, would be the terrible thing for the space traveler: that his humanity is never left behind him and that he never gets away from his creatureliness and his sin.

No matter where he goes, whether it be Mars or Venus, immediately the same old story will begin all over again, the same old story that took place when the forbidden fruit was plucked in some mythical garden. Then Cain's fratricide will occur on Venus too, and the tower of Babel will rise on Mars. His chief, the commander of the space ship, perhaps already has in his portfolio secret plans concerning strategic measures on Venus.

Wherever man goes he takes with him his crepuscular light, the light of his reason, which his Creator gave him, and also the phosphorescent putrefaction of his anxiety and his greed for power. Dürrenmatt has evoked this vision in his *Unternehmen Wega*.

But perhaps still another thought comes to our space traveler. It may be that in his thinking the ant heap of so-called humanity was divided into two "races." The one "race" was composed of those who were fascinated by the possibility of man's seizure of space. Their imagination was directed toward the inconceivable remoteness of the cosmic horizon and they deified this fabulous being called man in his unlimited technological power.

But there was another "race," much smaller in number, and they were the ones whose thoughts remained on earth and upon men. They never tired of pointing out that the cosmic development of space was not the primary problem but rather that the problem was man himself, you and me. With dismay they saw this being, man, dreaming that knowledge is power and overlooking the fact that this knowledge had long since become a power *above* man and ceased to be something that his knowledge could cope with. They saw that everything must depend upon setting man straight and teaching him how to love and what we are here for. Otherwise he would forfeit his life, even if he gained the whole cosmos.

On this little earth way back there—this may be the last thought of our space traveler, as the earth has already become merely one planet among others in the immeasurable vault of the sky—there lived in the last decades a man who was a great scholar and artist. But the masses knew him, not as a great intellect—which he was—but only as someone who wanted to help other people, who went into the primeval forest and became a neighbor to those who were farthest away. The very presence of such a man created a tremendous sensation. When he came to Europe the people gathered in crowds. The Nobel Prize and many honors were bestowed upon him.

What a strange judgment on the earth that it should be considered an extreme sensation when someone turns out to be nothing else but—"a man," and that this phenomenon of a "man" is stared at like a wonder that outshines all the world champion boxers, football heroes, and film stars!

To be "a man," this is unique. But then what is "ordinary"? And yet it is a comfort that it is so, the space traveler may say to himself as he shivers with cold despite the controlled temperature of his ship. Yes, all the same it is a comfort, for it reveals in the language of signs what God designed us to be, that God is holding fast to his intention. We go stumbling or flying along by the grace of God. We must realize what is prepared for us.

So now Venus is very near and already its mountains and seas can be described. "Down there on earth," concludes the space traveler's meditation, "down there we say:

> 'Orient and occident
> Rest in the peace of his hands.'"

And Venus and Mars too are enclosed by those hands.

We cannot escape those hands, but we can be safe in them.

6

Creation and Evolution, Faith and Science

The Creation of Man—Part Two

These are the generations of the heavens and the earth when they were created.

In the day that the Lord God made the earth and the heavens, when no plant of the field was yet in the earth and no herb of the field had yet sprung up—for the Lord God had not caused it to rain upon the earth, and there was no man to till the ground; but a mist went up from the earth and watered the whole face of the ground—then the Lord God formed man of dust from the ground, and breathed into his nostrils the breath of life; and man became a living being. And the Lord God planted a garden in Eden, in the east; and there he put the man whom he had formed. And out of the ground the Lord God made to grow every tree that is pleasant to the sight and good for food, the tree of life also in the midst of the garden, and the tree of knowledge of good and evil.

And the Lord God commanded the man, saying, "You may freely eat of every tree of the garden; but of the tree of the knowledge of good and evil you shall not eat, for in the day that you eat of it you shall die."

—Genesis 2:4–9, 16–17

In his essay "In Praise of Mortality," Thomas Mann said, "In the depths of my soul I cherish the surmise that with those words, 'Let there be,' which summoned the cosmos from the night, when life was generated out of inorganic being, it was *man* who was foreseen...."

And the fact is that when we read the creation story we do sense that everything said about the plants and animals, the sun and the moon is only an overture and that the curtain does not rise, that the dramas and tragedies on this earth do not begin until that moment when man enters and begins to play his role.

But now, who is this man? Or perhaps we had better speak in the first person: What am I to think of myself and what role has been assigned to me, now that the curtain has risen?

It is a very strange thing: when a person goes to a movie of an evening—if he is not too hopeless a blockhead—he finds out beforehand what is playing, who has the chief role, who directed it. If I am not mistaken, however, there are only a few people who ask themselves the question: What is really being played out in my life? Who has the chief role? Who is the director?

But does not everything depend upon knowing these things? Can I tread the stage of my life without facing the question: What am I really going to play? Or do I propose to go blindly on stage and begin to babble away, depending upon the prompting of the moment to tell me what to say? If that is so, then when the curtain of our life finally falls at our last hour we can only make our exit with the vapid feeling that it was all a mistake: we have indulged in a lot of foolish talk, we have turned somersaults, lounged on sofas, rummaged in filing cabinets, we have engaged in quarrelsome dialogues, and even played a variety of love scenes, but it was all a disconnected tutti-frutti and had no direction and no style.

So in distress we ask ourselves: What is the meaning of it all? Is life just a journey into the wild blue yonder that never gets you anywhere—at best only to the station named Desire?

That's why it seems important to me to study more carefully this text concerning the creation of man. For these words of the creation story present something like a script for the role I have to play.

If we ask ourselves what man is, or better still, what *I* am, we shall be able to find an answer only if we adopt the method of defining man by the way he relates to other entities. I mention just a few of these entities which provide a point of orientation.

We can define man, for example, by determining how he relates to his *origin*. Then we say, "Man derives from the animal kingdom." If we make the assertion this way we tend to draw from it the conclusion that man himself is therefore a higher animal. Do not the same laws of the struggle for existence obtain in our human life as are observable in nature? We reproduce ourselves like all mammals and we finally die in the same way, either from old age and the desiccation of our cells or from violence.

But it is also possible to define the sustaining relationship of our life in quite a different way. We can say that our human life is determined by the way we respond to the *tasks* which life and vocation set for us. If we thus interpret man and ourselves on the basis of our task, we quite logically define him as a productive being. Then the meaning and purpose of our life would consist in producing something and filling our quota. Then inevitably Stakhanov or the high-powered executive become the model image of man. Then when the day comes that we can no longer produce, because we are in an old folks' home or have a coronary and can do nothing but walk around a bit, then our life becomes meaningless. Indeed we see often enough how sad and empty the lives of aging people become when they have chosen the productive principle as their god and then one day this god deserts them and casts them into emptiness.

I mention one last relationship by which we can interpret our life. We can also relate man to the *stars* which allegedly determine his life. If I do this, then I think of myself as merely an organ that carries out the will of the cosmic powers of destiny; then I am exempt from any decision and responsibility for my actions, because here it is astral fate that controls me and makes me a will-less functionary of the universal. How many people who reach for their daily horoscope find in it a kind of reassurance—not primarily because they find out something about their future (I do not believe that this curiosity is the primary motive at all!), but rather because they want to be led by the leading-strings of the stars and thus cease to be responsible for their own faults; and this is, of course, very comforting! We may borrow Edmund's words in Shakespeare's *King Lear:*

> "This is the excellent foppery of the world! that, when we are sick in fortune, (often the surfeit of our own behavior,) we make guilty of our disasters the sun, the moon, and stars; as if we were villains on necessity; fools by heavenly compulsion; knaves, thieves, and treachers, by spherical predominance; drunkards, liars, and adulterers by an enforced obedience of planetary influence; and all that we are evil in, by a divine thrusting on: An admirable evasion of whoremaster man, to lay his goatish disposition on the charge of a star!"

And now our text also defines man by setting him into relationship to another entity. But this entity is neither his animal origin, nor his productivity, nor his environment, nor his astrological destiny—but rather, God.

Now the thing that must strike one in this story is the fact that man, despite all his kinship with plants and animals, rain and sunshine, despite all his earthiness (which we spoke of in the last sermon) remains remarkably unique and solitary in his world.

Elsewhere the words always appear in the third person: "Let there be!" So the stars, the flowers, and the whales are summoned into life. All of these are without consciousness and they live out their existence under a Creator they do not know. But man is different and he is also created in a different way: he is addressed as a person, as "you." The squirrels and the lions receive no commandments concerning what they should do and become. They live, so to speak, by the automatism of their instincts. But to man a "Thou shalt" is spoken. "Of the tree of the knowledge of good and evil you shall not eat." "You shall fill the earth and subdue it."

And this is precisely what constitutes the uniqueness of man over against the animal world. This is what lifts him above his fellow creatures.

Schiller may have had this text of the Bible in mind when he said that animals and plants receive their destiny from nature, but not only this; they also fulfil their destiny without incident, for the way to their destiny is, as it were, "provided" for them by the Creator. Man, however, is only given his destiny; the way he fulfils it, however, he must find for himself. And therefore there is always the possibility that he may fail.

This can be expressed in another way. The embryo of a dog will always become a dog. This process cannot go wrong. But is it equally certain that a human embryo will become a man? May it not become "inhuman"? May it not become someone whom God intended to be totally different, someone who is constantly sabotaging these plans of God for his life, wasting his talent, and throwing away his destiny, until finally he ends in the pigpen with the prodigal son? May not this *too* be possible? And are we not burdened by the fact that sometimes this is precisely what does happen to us?

In our last address we said that man is a risk of God. And this is exactly what we meant. An animal cannot fail to fulfil its destiny; but man, you and I, can. We can play the wrong role. And at the Last Judgment there may be written on the margin of our life in red ink: "You missed the point." Fritz Reuter once expressed it in these words:

> The beginning and the end, O Lord, are thine.
> The span in between, this life of ours, was mine.
> Though I strayed in the dark and found no way out,
> With thee there is brightness and light is thy house.

But this terrifying possibility that I may fail in this in-between part, which is mine and for which I bear responsibility, and stake it all on the wrong card, that I may be straying in the dark and not safely lodged in that house—this is at the same time our chance, for it is, so to speak, the dignity of being human.

In other words, it tells us that we can have direct contact with our Lord and that when we have this contact *nothing else* can lay hold upon us and bring us under its power, that hence we do not need to make excuses by talking about the dictatorship of the stars or the compulsion of our heredity or our particular environment, but that we are directly responsible to him, the Lord *himself*, that we receive from him our orders and at the same time our royal freedom as children of God.

How many of us may have realized the truth of these things—namely, that everything depends upon the *relationship* to which we commit our lives—while we were prisoners of war, in a situation therefore in which hunger and creaturely fear and the struggle for the favor of the kitchen-bulls frequently enough turned the so-called crown of creation into a miserable bundle of nerves that responded only to its instinct of self-preservation, groveled before the guards, and servilely angled for a cigarette butt.

But again and again we have observed the other side of the picture, namely, how true it is that man does not live by bread alone and that he must have access to totally different sources of sustenance if he is not to perish.

For there were always some who even in such a boundary situation were not reduced merely to a relationship to their empty stomachs or their tortured nerves or their unrestrained animal instincts, but rather were sure of the nearness of their Lord in all these scuffles and in the hopeless darkness of their cells and were mysteriously lifted above the pandemonium. This support provided by the security of God really did hold, whereas the artificial supports of civilization and even culture broke down. Whoever heard the eternal Word and knew that He—who Himself became a prisoner and died for his sake—was with him, whoever lived in the dialogue of prayer with Him, was beyond the reach of the law of bestiality. He was lifted above it all and placed under another protection. In a word, he was able to remain a man, a child of God, and in that experience was preserved that moment of creation when God called him into life and said "you" to him.

Therefore in this uniqueness of man, which distinguishes him from the animal kingdom, there lies not only our peril (namely, that we may miss the point of our life) but also our royal dignity. When God calls us to be his children, when he speaks to us as he spoke to Adam and as he never speaks to an animal, then in this dialogue, in this relationship, we are safe and secure under a protection from which nothing, neither hunger nor fear nor atom bomb, can snatch us away.

Recently I came across a very comforting anecdote that speaks of this faithfulness of God.

In the conversations of Frederick the Great with De Catt there is an account of a gathering in which a famous Tory leader was telling about the shortest prayer he had ever heard. It was uttered by a simple soldier at the Battle of Blenheim and went as follows: "O God, if there is a God, save my soul, if I have a soul." The company at table took this as a joke and burst into laughter. Then the Bishop of Rochester who was present said earnestly: "Your prayer, Sir William, is indeed very brief, but I remember one which is equally brief, but much better, and likewise uttered by a poor soldier. In the excess of toils and exertions of his service his faith threatened to break down; he had neither strength nor time to pray more than this, but finally he said: "O God, if on this day of battle I forget thee, do not thou forget me."

And so it is in fact; we live in constant forgetfulness of God and often enough our faith is a guttering candle. But there is One who faithfully remembers us, even when we stand in our presumption upon the tower of Babel or when we slink away into the far country or when we descend to dull indifference.

Now perhaps some of you may be thinking: "All this is very kind and soothing. And I would give a lot if I too could base the role of my life on this script as the man in the pulpit seems to be doing so much as a matter of course. But can I really say in all seriousness: 'The beginning and the end, O Lord, are thine,' can I really talk this way about the faithfulness of God without doing violence to my intellectual conscience? For, after all, it says that man is made of a clod of earth. But can I believe that God created me, that he wants to be my Lord, and that I can be secure in his protection, if it is communicated to me in the form of such myths? After all, I know that man arose in a different way. I know that life on earth is millions of years old and that man developed from animality over unimaginably long periods of time. Isn't faith, with its mythical, unreal conceptions, starting with a great disadvantage compared with science, which has long since replaced these old and superannuated conceptions of creation with biological evolution (and done so with exact proofs too)?".

Even though this is a question discussed more in the lecture room than the pulpit, I know that many people are troubled by it and I intend therefore to weave some comment upon it at some point in this series.

The scientific doubt of our faith in creation, as we have just described it, is based, it seems to me, upon a wrong way of putting the question.

That is to say, I can ask where man comes from biologically, and receive the answer that he sprang from animal forms. Or I can ask why he is here, what is his destiny, what is the "role" assigned to him. If I put the question in this way, the answer I get from the Bible is that he was designed to be a child of God, he was intended for fellowship with God in Jesus Christ.

I must not mix up these two questions. Once one sees this, then the ill-famed question of "Faith and Science"[1] will look quite different.

I do not sin against faith when I say that man developed from the animal kingdom over a period of seven milleniums.

[1] The author has dealt more fully and in academic form with the relationship between faith and science in his book, *Theologische Ethik*, Vol. II[1], 2nd ed. (Tübingen, 1959). Compare the chapter "Man and Animal," sections 1182–1275.

How could one truth (the truth of science) possibly contradict another truth (the truth of faith)? I sin against faith only when I dare to assert that I can "derive" the *essence* of man, his *destiny*, and the *meaning* of his life from this prehuman source. If I do this, the answer I get is that man is "only" a higher mammal, perhaps a predatory animal, but in any case he is determined by the instinct to devour, to breed, and to plunder. Then the history of the world becomes a special chapter in general zoology. So we see where that would lead us.

Nevertheless, I must express myself more precisely. Naturally, I do not deny that from the biological point of view man is only a mammal, but—only from the *biological* point of view! In his essential being he is something else. Or would we be so bold as to say that the love of a mother for her child is no more than a monkey's care for her young and that man's death is the same as the perishing of an animal? Is not human sexuality also something totally different from that of our fellow animal creatures? Naturally, human sexual life *also* has its biological side. But it is still something more, and something different. For in man this biological receptacle which is the instinctual process, the process of procreation and birth, is set in a totally different context. After all, here my relationship to the person who is closest to me becomes a reality. I love him and serve him in a sexual way. In a sexual way I do him wrong, come to grief, experience fulfillment and defeat; in short, I am acting in a completely *human* way in all my loving and hating, in all my delinquencies and all my faults.

The biological is, as it were, only a receptacle that harbors a completely human I-thou relationship, and which therefore is full of love and devotion, but also full of guilt and rejection, exactly—though here we are stressing the biological—as everywhere else in my life where I have to do with my neighbor, no matter whether it be my boss, my employee, my colleague, or the person next door.

When I stop treating this receptacle, this *bios*, as a mere container and proceed to make it a content in itself; in other words, when I say that this biological, this instinctual thing is the end itself, then sexuality becomes unhuman; it becomes a blind urge. Then sexual intercourse becomes nothing more than the attempt to quench one's sexual thirst in animal fashion. Then my partner is no more to me than a glass of water which I pour down my throat and then put away or shatter against the wall. Then, strictly speaking, this my partner would no longer be a "person" and certainly not a "neighbor," but only a thing, a mere instrument.

These are the consequences which accrue if I do not use science merely as an information bureau to find out how man came into being biologically but make it instead a substitute for faith and expect it to tell me the meaning of my life and my destiny. This is precisely what it *cannot* tell me.

This is the reason why the Bible, even when it speaks of the creation of man, speaks in its parabolic images less of man's origin than of his goal, his destiny. Psalm 139 makes this clear in words of monumental simplicity:

> Thou didst form my inward parts,
>   thou didst knit me together in my mother's womb.
> I praise thee, for thou art fearful and wonderful.
>   Wonderful are thy works!
> Thou knowest me right well;
>   my frame was not hidden from thee,
> when I was being made in secret . . .
> Thy eyes beheld my unformed substance;
>   in thy book were written, every one of them,
> the days that were formed for me,
>   when as yet there was none of them.

One thing is very clear here. The psalmist is speaking about the biological formation of man in the womb. One might say therefore that here he is pointing to the mammal aspect of man and extolling the mystery of the meeting of sperm and ovum. And yet all this is only the biological receptacle within which something altogether different is going on, in which God is actually speaking his creative "Let there be"; and behold: there it is—there *I* am! In his heart I lived as a completed image when I was still a microscopically small, unformed seed; already he had called me by my name; already he had anticipated my coming days, my life history, my talents, my role. Already he had called me to himself. *That* is the point of the psalm—in spite of all its parabolic biological imagery!

And fundamentally, isn't this very simple to understand? After all, what are young parents doing when they send out a birth notice: "God has given us our first child"? When they say this, they do not mean that God let this child fall directly from heaven. They know very well the processes of generation and birth, the ecstasies of love and the biological processes which brought this child into being. No, when they send out such a notice they mean to express something altogether different. What they are saying is: "God in his goodness has given us this child by way of 'biological' processes." Indeed he has given the *bios* itself! "It went through our hands, but comes from God," sang Matthias Claudius. God's gifts also come through our bodies, through the endocrine glands and physiological laws. There is Someone there who bestows gifts upon us through the medium of nature—just as he signals the signs of his grace to us through the sunshine and the dew, the rainbow and the wind.

And now I should think that on this basis (insofar as it has been understood) it ought not to be difficult to see that faith and science do not contradict each other at all—simply because the assertions they make lie upon completely different levels.

Now, can we not take what we have just said about the birth of one child, one exemplar of "man," and apply it to all mankind? Can we not paraphrase the words of Psalm 139 and say: "Thou didst know man when he was still an unformed seed, or perhaps primeval slime or *euhomininen* or the ancestral form of Homo sapiens"? For at a specific point in these millions of years of development thou didst call him by name, make thyself known to him, summon him before thy majestic face, and bestow upon him that unique dignity of personhood which thou didst not give to any animal.

It is this one point at which God caused man to rise above the ranks of the other creatures and made him something special that our text describes when it says: "The Lord God breathed into his nostrils the breath of life; and man became a living being."

This is the decisive point in man's becoming man. Here is an earthy creature, still bound to ordinary creatureliness—which the Bible refers to by the symbol of "dust from the ground"—here this prehuman, still unformed germ is suddenly breathed upon by the breath of another world and transferred to that realm which we call specifically human existence.

I have always felt that Michelangelo's depiction of the creation of man on the ceiling of the Sistine Chapel is a profound interpretation of how man became man. Adam the man is already present, but, so to speak, not as man in the real sense. He is still a candidate, a mere claimant of humanity. He lies half raised up, with a dull and dreamy expression, though his face is turned in inquiring expectation to God the Father, who hovers over him, clothed in a great mantle and sheltering coming creatures. Adam's leg is already drawn up to rise; all is in readiness that in the next moment he may rise and meet God. But between these two instants a miracle must occur—the miracle of the spark of the Spirit leaping from the outstretched finger of the Creator to the man. Without that spark he would remain a creature of the soil, an earthbound clod. He might be a *higher* kind of creature—for this man is beautiful even before he becomes a man!—but he would still be something other than a "man," who can be God's child and partner. Michelangelo portrays as it were the last moment of the "pre-man," the *euhomininen*. Not until the next moment does he become man and child, brother and neighbor—an image of God and at the same time one to whom it does not yet appear what he shall be (I John

3:2). For God's dealings with man continue on to the Last Day and beyond it to eternity.

Thomas Carlyle once cried out at a congress of biologists who were discussing the theory of descent or evolution: "Gentlemen, make man a little higher than a tadpole. I hold with the ancient psalmist who said, 'Thou hast made him little less than God'" (Ps. 8:5).

This statement of Carlyle expresses in fine and pregnant form all that we have been saying. For what Carlyle was saying was this: "I have no objection, even as a Christian, to your deriving man from previous animal forms and declaring that the monkey is his grandfather and the tadpole his great-great-grandfather. Why should I? This is something for science to inquire into.

"But I have objections to something else. I object to your saying that therefore the nature of man, that your nature and my nature is like that of a tadpole. No, if you are going to define the mystery of man, if you are going to define what God has in mind for man and what he breathed into him, then you *cannot* say: 'He is only a little more than a tadpole.' *Then* you must say: 'He is little less than God.' In other words, you cannot define man on the basis of his biological origin; you must define him in the light of his destiny, his goal.

"Actually, you must enter upon another level. The mystery of man can be understood only if you put him into relation to Him who gives him his life, calls him by his name, sacrifices His most beloved for him on Calvary, and never rests until He has drubbed him out of his alienation, his madness, his fear, and his guilt and brought him back home to His peace."

When Luther spoke of this deepest and most comforting determination of our life, he was fond of calling it the "alien dignity" of man. This dignity does not rest upon his "own" human qualities, but rather upon the relationship with which God dignifies him. He makes him His partner, He addresses him, He allows him to deal with Him. This dignity is not an attribute of man, something he has *inside* him, but rather something that comes to him from the *outside*.

In closing, I should like to try and set forth in even simpler terms what Luther meant when he spoke of man's alien dignity.

We are all familiar with those Gothic pictures in which we see a face painted against a background of gold. The background represents heaven, the glory of God; and a reflection of this glory suffuses the human face. The painters therefore do not express the uniqueness of man by means of a portrait with strong character, something that a better photograph can give even to a wheyface with the help of a few lighting effects. No, here the greatness and the mystery of man is portrayed through the *relationship* of his life: this life is related to the glory of God.

We are also familiar with the ancient symbol in which the world is represented as a golden orb in the hand of the Lord. And here again the intention was not to say that the world is golden and we must think of it optimistically. It was not meant to express anything in the nature of an "attribute of the world." For these men were well aware of the miseries and the seas of blood and tears upon this earth. Rather they were saying: "No matter how hard life may and how cruel the world, it nevertheless rests in the hand of the Lord; it is related to the providence and the gracious goals of God. Therefore, with all its dubious elements, it shimmers with the glow of gold."

And finally, I am reminded of what Gorch Fock, that seaman in the First World War, wrote in a letter to his family: "If you should hear that I have fallen, do not weep! Remember that even the deepest ocean in which my body sinks in death is only a pool in the hand of my Savior." Gorch Fock knew what a cruel thing it is to drown and be strangled in the dark, cold vortex of the sea. But he also knew where he was going as he sank. He knew the ever-present loving hand that would catch him. Even that which is dark and murderous cannot be outside the jurisdiction of that hand.

So everywhere we are determined and defined by Him who breathed into us his breath and called us by our name. And when all grows silent and empty about us, when we are restless and lost in a gloomy maze, when we cry out in the dark and none seems to answer, let us remember that saying of Pascal: "I would not seek thee, O God, if thou hadst not already found me. Even my restlessness and my longing show me that thou art at work upon me." Or we can pray: "If in the madness of my passion and the wild commotion of my life I forget thee, do not thou forget me."

God is always greater than our faith, because the breath of his Spirit is stronger than the dust of the earth. And with this certitude one can live. Truly this is something you *can* live by. If I know this, then I know the theme, the point of my life; then my life can succeed.

7

The Meaning and Order of the Sexes

Then God said, "Let us make man in our image, after our likeness; and let them have dominion over the fish of the sea, and over the birds of the air, and over the cattle, and over all the earth, and over every creeping thing that creeps upon the earth." So God created man in his own image, in the image of God he created him; male and female he created them. And God blessed them, and God said to them, "Be fruitful and multiply, and fill the earth and subdue it; and have dominion over the fish of the sea and over the birds of the air and over every living thing that moves upon the earth."

Then the Lord God said, "It is not good that the man should be alone; I will make him a helper fit for him." So out of the ground the Lord God formed every beast of the field and every bird of the air, and brought them to the man to see what he would call them; and whatever the man called every living creature, that was its name. The man gave names to all cattle, and to the birds of the air, and to every beast of the field; but for the man there was not found a helper fit for him. So the Lord God caused a deep sleep to fall upon the man, and while he slept took one of his ribs and closed up its place with flesh; and the rib which the Lord God had taken from the man he made into a woman and brought her to the man. Then the man said,

> "This at last is bone of my bones
> and flesh of my flesh;
> she shall be called Woman,
> because she was taken out of Man."

Therefore a man leaves his father and his mother and cleaves to his wife, and they become one flesh.

—*Genesis 1:26–28, 2:18–24*

A concern for man has become something fashionable. At every anniversary celebration observed by a business organization it is definitely stated at the climax of the main address that in the last analysis the only thing that counts is not volume of production or profits but rather human beings. Even the technologists and atomic physicists tell us that man and not technological progress must be the chief concern of our time. Atomic power should serve man, instead of dominating and delivering him over to fear. Always we talk about "man." Who is this "man" anyway?

It is noteworthy that in the Bible this term "man" hardly occurs at all. Perhaps because it is far too general and weak. It is a distillate which is extracted in philosophical retorts. In the Bible, however, man almost always occurs as a special case.

Here there are rich and poor men, frightened and self-assertive men, masters and servants, old and young, men and women. And each of them has his special talents with which he must face life. But each one also has his special sins which rob him of peace with God in his particular situation. The poor man threatens to collapse because social injustice and the superabundance of his cares alienate him from God. Job, the afflicted, pours out his woe before God and cannot understand why he is so unfair to the devout, why he deceives and cheats them while the godless scoffers whose bodies are "sound and sleek" are given a place in the sun (cf. Ps. 73:3 ff.). But the rich and powerful too have their special peril: Mammon threatens to become their god; great lords easily forget that they too have a Lord and that he will not be mocked.

So the Bible presents only a vivid abundance of highly diverse, individual men, each of them with his own individual destiny with God; therefore each one of them also dies his own individual death. One who is old and full of days dies his death differently from one who is young and is summoned away in the midst of his hunger for life. Herod, who was eaten by worms, dies differently from Moses, who was still permitted to see the Promised Land from afar as he died upon Mount Horeb.

Now I find it tremendously comforting that the Bible does not speak of "man" and "sin" and "death" in general, abstract terms, but deals with them always as special cases which are taut and pulsing with life. And I find it comforting and fine and significant because this makes it clear that everywhere in our life, even in the remotest corners (the place where we work, our bedroom, our business trips, the night club, at a concert, or watching television), we are confronted with the presence of God. There is no corner or curve on our journey through life, no stage in our life story, in which God is not there, confronting us with the question whether we belong to him here and now, whether we are willing to obey him and grant him our trust here and now.

It is therefore certainly important that right at the beginning, when man is spoken of for the first time, the Bible does not speak of "man" but of a man, a particular, special man. God created him male and female, or more precisely, as man and woman. There is no such thing as a human being apart from a man or a woman.

This is far more than a matter of mere biological difference. Obviously, the polarity of the sexes affects all of the ultimate mysteries of life. It cannot be ignored in either the spiritual or the secular realm. We must realize, therefore, how far-reaching and consequential is the fact that here the Bible does not speak first of the creation of man in general and then *afterwards* of the difference between the sexes, but rather from the very outset speaks of man only in the framework of the polarity of the sexes.

Today let us do some thinking together on this mystery of the sexes. Besides hunger and the lust for power there is nothing that so fills our life and impels, torments, and delights us as does the mystery of our sexuality.

I should like to start out with a way of approaching the question which I believe affects every one of us, but naturally *young* people above all.

Every one of us, if he is not utterly dull and stupid, has at some time or other asked himself the question: "How can I gain the greatest satisfaction in my life? How can I achieve my greatest development and get the maximum from my potentialities?"

This question by no means applies only to our vocation in which we want to get as far as possible. It also applies to what we may generally call "human happiness." Then we would put the question this way: "How can I attain the greatest wealth of experience, the greatest happiness in sex and love, the greatest fulfilment of body and mind in my life?" "How can I," asks Françoise Sagan (the young French novelist who has in many respects become the spokesman of our skeptical youth), "how can I find freedom from satiety and boredom? How can I become deeply 'engaged' to the fullest? How can I participate in something with every fiber of my being, be filled and brought to ecstasy by something?"

Now, for me it is of utmost importance to make it absolutely clear that it is gravely wrong to put the question in this way. The basic question which we all address to life: "How can I be happy and find fulfilment?" is really a question put the wrong way around. Why?

This question emanates from the assumption that I am alone in the world. I conceive of myself, so to speak, as an organism or—to speak in Goethean terms—"as a molded form" which is supposed to develop in a living way and be brought to the fullest possible development. Naturally, I am generally not conscious of this. But even unconscious presuppositions are capable of exercising power over my life. Now, over against this view of things, which is inherent in us all, our text presents this word of the Creator: "It is not good that the man should be alone." It is not good, therefore, that he should be a self-contained organism which proceeds to develop itself; he must rather have a vis-à-vis, a partner, a companion, a thou.

And here the text touches upon one of the fundamental mysteries of our life.

That is to say, it is a remarkable fact—and this has become

my personal conviction, confirmed at every step of the way by life itself—that I do *not* attain the greatest possible development of my personality when I consciously try to develop myself, when I am constantly considering: "where will I have the best chance to live to the fullest? How can I gain prestige in society? Where can I reach the maximum of accomplishment and where can I experience the greatest pleasure?" On the contrary, I arrive at this fulfilment of my personality and my life as a whole only when I do not think about it at all, but rather when I forget myself and devote myself to something else, to another person or to a task, in short, when I serve and love and in both do not think about myself at all.

I have often asked myself what actually happens when two people love each other. When another person enters into my life am I, as it were, thrown off the track—like a billiard ball which collides with another and thus must change its course? Am I *remolded?* Or is it my real nature which is brought out?

I once knew two elderly ladies who were sisters. One of them was the mother of a family who seemed to have within her all the fulness of life. She had poured out her life in service to her family and sacrificed herself for them, but in the process she had become a vivid, vital person who had developed all that was in her to an amazing extent. Her sister, on the other hand, was a highly cultivated old spinster, who all her life had thought of nothing but the development of her personality and had absorbed all the benefits of culture she could obtain. And it was she, the very person who wanted to develop herself and made her personality an end in itself, who seemed dried up and one-sided compared with the other who had forgotten herself and lived for others.

Now, I do not mean at all to say, and I want to emphasize this expressly, that this formation of my own personality is possible only within marriage. Life presents such a wealth of possibilities to love, serve, and suffer with other people that even the person who lives his life without a married partner is given the same opportunity to find and fulfil himself in devotion to others. Marriage, to which the text refers, constitutes only a kind of model for the fulfilment of love in our life. So even the person who lives a single life can find his orientation in this text.

The point is that there are things in life—and one of them is the fulfilment of one's personality—which cannot be attained by going after them directly, but which come to us, as it were, incidentally, really as "byproducts." Only the person who loves and does not think of himself actually finds himself; and inversely, the person who seeks himself is always cheated.

Jesus was pointing to this remarkable secret of our life when he said: "Seek first his kingdom and his righteousness, and all these things shall be yours as well." This means, surely, that one who is really, seriously, and basically concerned about God is given everything else besides. To him God gives bread and friends, opens doors in his vocation, and showers upon him the abundance of life. The man who pursues his task in self-forgetfulness, who, disregarding loss, serves and is lovingly close to those whom God has given him to be his neighbors, that man receives joys, merriments, and riches which he never would have found if he had sought for them directly and with egotistic desire. Whoever would save his life will lose it, but whoever gives it away and does not seek himself and his life is precisely the one who finds himself—and along with it the beautiful in life, indeed, the interesting and attractive in life. God always bestows the greatest things incidentally. This we must bear in mind.

I should say that this is meant to show itself in the very way in which we live our lives. The person who gets up in the morning with the thought in his mind: "How can I make as much money as possible today; what can I do to promote my career, my security, my vitality?"—and then, incidentally, says to himself: "Later when I have achieved it all, I'll take time to be religious (and donate a large contribution to charity)"—I say that the person who thinks in this way has set up a false calculation from the very outset. He is the very person who will *not* find the fulfilment of his life. And even in the prospective happy ending of his life, the planned rendezvous with God in the green pastures of satiety he will be the one who is fooled. When God is not the first, the primary thing in our life he vanishes altogether—"*Dieu se retire,* God withdraws," said Leon Bloy—or we are aware of him only as a kind of spectral restlessness that keeps invading our life from its margins.

That's why I think that we must begin the day with him (simply because the most important things, the scheduled things belong at the top), that we must commit to him everything we have to deal with today: our marriage, our children, the people we have to associate with and work with, and our sick and lonely neighbor who needs our help.

In any case, we hold on to this: only those who do not seek themselves find themselves. Only those who love quite simply and do not think of themselves also attain the fulness of their own lives. God gives the best things with his left hand; "he gives to his beloved in sleep."

This fact that the best things in life cannot be sought for but are given also becomes clear in the command that is given to *marriage.* That command says: "Be fruitful and multiply." And that at once warns us away from the cult of our own personality and also the cult of seeking happiness just for two.

How many marriages are begun with both parties saying to each other: "We want to live out our love for each other. We want to arrange our life for work and vacations, for being at home and going on trips. We love nature and music and we are going to build a love nest. And children would only be a burden to us. If we had them, as far as time is concerned and financially too, there would be too many things we could not do that would enrich our life."

There are also not a few who say—and this they call rational marriage—"We are going to have a community of interests. We believe in marrying for money and keeping it in the family; we hope to make the most profit from this financial and business alliance."

And now the Bible tells us that both—the people who cherish this idyl of love *and* those who make a shrewd business proposition of marriage—are simply satisfying themselves and are therefore not entering into marriage but sidestepping it. In other words, marriage does not exist only for its own sake; it also exists for the sake of children. And here again the same thing applies in marriage as applies to the individual.

The love of two persons who live their lives together never reaches its fulfilment when the two make their companionship an end in itself and are completely taken up with each other, whether it be erotically or economically. It fulfils itself and is filled with pulsing life only as it is faithful to the command of creation and pours itself out in the service of children.

Naturally, there are situations—brought about by shortage of living quarters, illness, or financial stringencies—in which one must wait to have children. There are also not a few cases in which this blessing is denied to us altogether, and then God sends other fulfilments to his own. (For he is always the Giver, the one who pours himself out, and we need only to find packages addressed specifically to us and meant for our situation.)

But when young people, to whom the talent of possible parenthood is entrusted, assert their self-will contrary to the purpose of creation and heedlessly or even on principle renounce the blessing of procreation, then in time even their inner relationship to each other will be injured. Even this inner relationship to one's life partner cannot be desired as an end in itself. It too is bestowed upon us only incidentally; it is "added unto us." All parents know this who have accepted their children as "dew from the dawn," as Luther's translation so beautifully puts it. This dew has also refreshed their own relationship and matured it to fulfilments they never anticipated in their youthful dreams of love.

Our story touches upon still another mystery. The parabolic

reference to Eve's being created from the rib of the man points to the fact that they belong together, that one is a part of the other and both are a unity. "This at last is bone of my bones and flesh of my flesh," Adam cries out. Between the lines one senses something like the wonder of recognition: "Here is my *alter ego,* my other self." And the fact that it really is a wonder, a mystery, is indicated by the text in its reference to the fact that God caused Adam to fall into a deep sleep. How it comes about that two persons are created for each other—that such a thing should even occur!—is concealed by the wings of mystery, this cannot be seen by human eyes and can be spoken of only in a parable.

In any case, the biblical text here gives us to understand that in our life we are not only joined to our particular neighbor as such, the associate who needs a good word from me, the woman beside me in the trolley who is tired of standing, and the youngster in my class who is having trouble with something —but that he quite specifically gives to me *one* person who is good for me and for whom I likewise have a purpose to fulfil, and therefore a person who is in fact something like my other half and whom he has appointed precisely for *me.*

And here we must listen very carefully; otherwise we shall not get the point. God has given me a *human being,* not merely someone who performs the *function* of a human being. So in marriage it is not merely a matter of another person's performing certain functions for me, perhaps the function of erotic satisfaction or physical intercourse, or perhaps also merely the function of providing for me as a money-earner, or of acting as a contributing honorary member of my family or—from the husband's point of view—of furnishing a cheap housekeeper. If the other person is only good for performing such functions for me, then I really have no fellowship with him of the kind that God wants. And then too, he is "finished" as far as I am concerned as soon as he can no longer perform his functions.

How many marriages there are which end in divorce for this

very reason, because the other person has become unattractive to me and his erotic "function" no longer clicks. Then I look for a younger partner who can better perform the function.

God does not will that this should be so and he binds me to the *person*, not merely to his functions. This is clearly expressed in the ancient order for marriage, for in the vows it employs the words: "till death us do part."

Now, I can be willing to belong to another person till death —and therefore not allow myself to be separated from him by any period of separation, any stroke of illness no matter how severe, any other infatuation or even deeper engagement of the heart—*only* if I accept him as *himself* and not merely something *in* him. God has committed to me another *person;* he has lent to me something that belongs to him. "God gave you to me," said Matthias Claudius, "no other hand pours out such blessings."

But perhaps for us moderns, particularly when we are relentlessly honest with ourselves, this message sounds like something from the remote past. Isn't it true that we think that life is far more complicated than it appears to be in these simple lines of an ancient but perhaps naïve story?

Is there any certainty at all that this particular man or this particular woman is the only possible choice given to me by God? Is this so sure after all? If man must not put asunder what God has joined together—yes, but *was* it God who joined them together or was it not all too often just two deluded persons, who for a moment were filled with a lot of airy dreams and thought they were Romeo and Juliet, but after a short time simply choked with boredom and disgust whenever they looked at each other? "Marriage reminds me of a sugarplum," said Matthias Claudius in one of his letters to Andy. "At first it tastes sweet, and people think it will go on that way for ever. But the bit of sugar is soon licked off and then inside, for most of them, there comes a piece of rhubarb—then they pull a long face."

But even if there are not such rude disillusionments, are there not in almost every fateful relationship between two people moments when the question arises whether I should not have made a different choice, and thus whether the other person is really the hundred-per-cent complement for me, the flesh of my flesh of which this simile of the rib speaks.

In my lifetime I have learned to know many troubled marriages. Perhaps the crisis arose only because—and this is definitely not the most trivial situation!—the mildew of boredom and jaded monotony has settled down upon a relationship which began with gushing protestations like, "Every thought I have is of you, dear." For now they know each other, there is nothing new to say, and the enchantment ends in banality.

Or perhaps the crisis may come because another fascinating person crosses our path and sets to ringing sides of our personality which we never knew were in us. And then the question always arises: "Was it really true in my case—what according to this ancient story ought to be true—that I was assigned by a higher hand to the one person who really is suited for me? Or when I chose him back there did I make a wrong turn and am I now doomed to travel for the rest of my life in a direction which is alien to me and which leads me farther and farther away from my real self and all the fulfilments I dreamed I would have?"

Now, this question cannot be dismissed with a wave of the hand or with a cheap pious consolation. The preacher who has nothing more to say on this subject than the fact that he is "against sin" is undoubtedly taking the easy way out. Nevertheless, when I make two brief comments on this human difficulty and allow myself to be guided by the healing power of what Jesus Christ has taught us about love, I do so because I am convinced of one thing, and that is that nobody who is caught in this difficulty and does not know whether he should find his way back or be divorced, dares to ignore these two thoughts. One way or another he will get it all wrong if he does not face them.

The first thought is this: It is in any case utterly foolish to brood over the question whether the other person is the one conceivable partner for me. Perhaps I *really* could have married another man or another woman! That this particular person is the only person for me is not the thing which creates the foundation of marriage. It is the other way around: it is marriage that makes him or her the only one for me. Let me give the reason for this briefly.

Now that God has brought me together with this other person I have a life and a history with him. The other person has revealed to me his secret in his psycho-physical wholeness. We have gone through many trials and vicissitudes together. Perhaps we have been refugees together. Perhaps we have been hungry together, been homesick for each other in long years of military service, built up an existence for ourselves together, seen our very being reproduced anew in our children—and so put our stamp upon each other, each has become a part of the other. Has *become!* We no longer are what we were in the beginning; we each bear the mark of the other.

This is what I meant when I said: That the other person is the only person for me is not the thing which creates the foundation of marriage; it is rather the other way around. For this uniqueness of the other person, this unrepeatable belonging together, this business of your being cut out for me is not all something that is there beforehand. Rather we *become* unique and irreplaceable for each other only when God brings us together, gives us a life and a history together, and blesses us, if we will only trust him and watch for his directions. Anybody who does not trust that in everything God works for good with those who love him, and that his life partner is also included in this plan for his good is a poor wight indeed. For then there is nothing left but to try to puzzle out with his reason whether or not he has caught the right man or the right woman. (I say "caught" intentionally, because he is delivered over to chance or his own dubious calculations and now he must constantly compare his partner with others, incessantly comparing and never getting away from his uncertainty and his everlasting testing.)

And then the second thought. It is the more important and serious of the two.

In order to determine whether my life partner is really the right one for me, I would have to be able to ascertain objectively—in a clinical diagnosis as it were—who or what this other person is, and besides this, who or what I am, in order to compute by exact calculation whether we best complement each other.

I should think that one would need to go through this experiment of thought only once to find out how absurd it is. And if we stop and think why it is so absurd, and why it will not work, we shall discover a profound spiritual secret.

I once knew a very old married couple who radiated a tremendous happiness. The wife especially, who was almost unable to move because of old age and illness and in whose kind old face the joys and sufferings of many years had etched a hundred runes, was filled with such gratitude for life that I was touched to the quick. Involuntarily I asked myself what could possibly be the source of this kindly old person's radiance. Otherwise they were very common people and their room indicated only the most modest comfort. But suddenly I knew where it all came from, for I saw these two speaking to each other and their eyes hanging upon each other. All at once it became clear to me that this woman was dearly loved. And it was as if she were like a stone that has been lying in the sun for years and years, absorbing all its radiant warmth, and now was reflecting back cheerfulness and warmth and serenity.

Let me express it this way. It was not because she was this kind of a cheerful and pleasant person that she was loved by her husband all those years. It was probably the other way around. Because she was so loved, she became the person I now saw before me.

This thought continued to pursue me and the more it pursued me the more it lost all its merely edifying and sentimental features, until finally they were gone altogether. For if this is true, then I surely must come to the following conclusion. If my life partner or my friend or just people generally often seem to be so strange and I ask myself: "Have I made the right marriage, the right friendship; is this particular person really the one who is suited to me?"—then I cannot answer this question in the style of a neutral diagnosis which would list the reasons for and against. For what happens then is that the question turns back upon myself, and then it reads: "Have I perhaps bestowed too little love upon this other person, that he has become so cold and empty? Have *I* perhaps caused him to become what perhaps he really has become? The other person, whom God has joined to me, is never what he is apart from me. *He is not only bone of my bone; he is also boredom of my boredom and lovelessness of my lovelessness.*"

And it is exactly the same with our relation to God. If a person is steeped in emptiness and boredom and is tired of life, the reason for it is that he has not allowed himself to be loved by God and has not put himself in his hands. One who does not love makes the other person wither and dry up. And one who does not allow himself to be loved dries up too. For love is a creative thing.

Perhaps it may really be hard to love another person because we have become estranged and an oppressive coolness has settled down upon our relationship. But then we should remember that love never waits until the other person has *become* worthy of love, but that love which is ventured (expressed perhaps through some little, diffident sign, a flower, or a look) is creative and awakens the other person to something that we have long since failed to perceive with our appraising minds and no longer counted upon at all.

After all, God did not wait until we were worthy of his love. He loved us long *before;* he ventured his love upon us (Eph. 2:11–13). Did Jesus love the publicans, the harlots, the beggars, and the lepers because they were so attractive? No, they were in great darkness, withering and dying in their utter inadequacy. But then the glance of the Lord fell upon them and they were touched by a ray of his love. That's how they became new persons. It was the creative, the resurrective power of love that wrenched them out of nothingness and for the first time in their lives made something of them.

The other person is waiting for my love, for the creative breath which God has entrusted to me too. And only as I love with that creative breath will I learn what the other person is at all. Otherwise he remains an undeveloped negative and I have no idea what image lurks within him. Perhaps I have never yet realized who it is that walks beside me. The other person is what my love makes of him. For we too are what God's love makes of *us*.

8

The Great Sabbath

Thus the heavens and the earth were finished, and all the host of them. And on the seventh day God finished his work which he had done, and he rested on the seventh day from all his work which he had done. So God blessed the seventh day and hallowed it, because on it God rested from all his work which he had done in creation.
—*Genesis 2:1–3*

"Abide with us at the evening of the day, the evening of life, the evening of the world. Abide with us when the night of tribulation and fear, the night of bitter death comes upon us." These are the words of an ancient prayer of the church and they remind us of those primeval words of the Scriptures which are our text. For here too the theme is that of an evening and an end.

Heaven and earth and all its hosts are now complete. And as the young world in all its dewy freshness exults in the surge of life—the whales romping in the sea, the trees blooming and fading, the stars circling in their courses, and man roaming through the Garden of Eden—the Creator withdraws into a solemn, celebrative stillness.

The gaze of the church has always passed from this sabbath after the completion of the work of creation to the last day of the world when the sabbath of eternity will conclude and resolve the restlessness of history. We shall venture not to "pace off"—that would be presumptuous—but perhaps just to find some presentiment of the monumental, soaring arch this text flings across the space between the first and the last sabbath of the world.

Many of us may be familiar with the great monologue of Faust in which he speaks of his yearning for revelation "that nowhere glows more fair, more excellent, than here in the New Testament," and of how he sits down in his study to translate "the hallowed original" into his "well-beloved German."

But the very first words of the Gospel of John stop him short and he can go no further. The sentence reads: "In the beginning was the Word." But Dr. Faust thinks that the Word cannot possibly have such high value that the world could be founded upon it. "It is impossible the Word so high to prize, I must translate it otherwise." And finally, after several bold experiments with the biblical text, he comes through with the conviction that "In the beginning was the *Deed*."

With this formulation it became Goethe's fate to provide the refrain for countless distinguished speeches. Everybody quotes it: statesmen when they have won a war, building associations when they dedicate a new waterworks. "In the beginning was the Deed"—it always fits.

Why is it that this refrain should be so universally applicable? I believe it is because it touches upon a profound secret of life. Are not nature and history in constant, surging motion, producing ever new structures and forms? Do they not seem to point to a constantly active and creative God? After all, everything we see is actually undergoing constant change and presenting an everlasting succession of forms. Life is one constant blooming and dying and blooming again. New potentates emerge from the womb of history and supersede former hegemonies and they in turn must traverse the fateful curve of rise and fall. It is one continual, unremitting coming and going, one unbroken dynamic, which seems to be expressed exactly in the phrase, "In the beginning was the Deed," or, if you please, "In the beginning was the Dynamic."

And is not the image of the man Faust also drawn from the model of this unceasingly creative ground of the world? He too is always busy, always absorbed in the deed, the act. He is constantly striving. He is the man with two souls, incessantly surging and striving against each other. He rushes from philosophy and jurisprudence to medicine and theology and finally to the mysterious zone of magic, "dissatisfied every moment"—a human image of that world and its ground, which are likewise engaged in everlasting activity, reflecting a constant process of becoming and perishing.

We understand very well what Goethe means. We all have a sense of the restlessness of life, its teeming, fecund dynamism. This is why the parable of the Faustean wanderer will always have its profound appeal for us.

But now, how different is the world portrayed in these ancient words of the Bible that ring like bells above us today! They too pour light upon what was in the beginning and illuminate the mystery of the source and origin of all things. But they direct our attention, not merely to the creative impulse in the processes of life, but rather to the Creator himself, and behold—this is the tremendous and yet unutterably heartening thing—the Creator stands *above* all this restlessness of life and enters into the celebration of stillness.

So here there is something more than mere life that goes on reproducing itself in constant, creative unrest. Anybody who has only life and its laws in view would expect something different to happen at this point. He would expect that now the completed creation would immediately go on running—like a machine which must be set in motion as soon as it is erected in order to be profitable. He would expect that the harmony of the finished paradise must immediately dissolve into the dissonances of the Fall and that immediately there would ensue what Hegel and the Marxists call the dialectic of history, that the noise and clamor of human drama and tragedy would seize the stage, that the comedy of errors would begin, that the bloody scene of fratricide would be enacted, and war and rumors of war would reverberate. In short, he would expect that world history would begin with a rush and a roar.

Instead, something altogether different happens: it is not the unrest of nature or the human heart that prevails, but rather a great intermission ensues. On the border between the completed work of creation and the noisy alarms of history there is a great silence, the resting hush of the Creator.

What is the meaning of this strange message for us? Is it a beautiful, pious dream of worship that would enwrap and lull us to sleep, a lovely but quite unrealistic sentimentality?

No, I think that something altogether different is being proclaimed to us here. This is what it is saying: No matter how overwhelming the riches of creation may be—the profusion of birds and beasts and beautiful flowers, the spectacle of rising and setting stars, the wonder of seeds and fruits and unceasing growth—overwhelming as all this may be: a sublime hand grasps us for a moment by the shoulder, turns us around, so that all these glories lie behind us, and makes us look at the Lord of creation *himself*. Otherwise, you see, we might *over*look him.

If we examine ourselves very carefully, we soon discover that God very often disappears from our field of vision. We simply do not think of him. The letter we have to write, the appointment we have to keep, the scare we had a moment ago that still upsets us—these are all much closer to us than God. And beyond this, often we do not know what to make of him and we say that he doesn't exist at all. Often we must undergo suffering and we feel terribly deserted. Then we have the feeling that if there were a God, he would not permit this to happen at all. But it happens anyhow—so the report that there is a God must be a pious fraud.

Often it is simply that pure delight and love of life prompt us to forget him for whom all the glory of earth is but a parable and who is trying to speak a message to us through these glories. At evening we see the gentle moon and it touches us to the heart because it is so beautiful. But which of us then hears the message of the moon and sees it as Matthias Claudius did:

> Look up; the moon tonight
> Shows us but half her light,
> And yet we know her round and fair.
> At other things how oft
> We in our blindness scoff'd,
> Because we saw not what was there . . . ?[1]

Which of us reads all the beauty of the earth that keeps thronging in upon us, as we would read a letter actually addressed and sent to us by someone? Which of us on our vacation sees the secret greeting, written especially for us, beneath the picture of the mountains or the sea? Which of us descries in the starry sky that secret streamer unfurled in the most beautiful of all children's hymns—in this context too it forces itself into my mind—: there is One who has numbered all these millions of stars and holds them in his arms, and he "knows you too and loves you"? Which of us thus hears in all this the knocking upon his *own* door, the calling of his *own* name, and knows that therefore He is *more* than the enchantment of distance, the radiance of light, and the infinite vastness of space? Which of us hears in all this the message of a heart that remembers and knows us individually?

Ah, I really do not honor him at all if I see in him only the Creator of the Milky Way, the solar systems, and the microcosms of the world of the atom. What does this God of macrocosm and microcosm matter to me when my conscience is tormenting me, when I am overwhelmed with loneliness, or when anxieties revolve in my head like millstones, and I am a poor wretch and heap of misery but nobody cares, and they all sit there in the subway staring straight ahead and nobody sees me? The Father up above the stars sits there in some monumental headquarters while I sit here in my filthy hole somewhere on this cut-off sector at the front, somewhere in this awful dump, a lodger in a tenement or even in a villa, in this stupid job of mine that gives me the heeby-jeebies, or at my lonely executive's desk, armored by two receptionists.

[1] Translation by Catherine Winkworth, *Lyra Germanica*.

Those who complain in this way are basically right. In fact they are perfectly right. God's heart is really close to us only when we are given the certainty that he left the Milky Way, where I have little interest in him, and entered the stable of Bethlehem and went to the cross. He stops and talks to the poor woman whose daughter is mortally ill, the blind, the bug-ridden beggar, the sick man with the leprous sores, and the young man —called the rich young ruler—who is searching for the meaning of life.

When someone says to me, "There is a supreme intelligence that conceived the creation of the world, devised the law of causality, and maneuvered the planets into their orbits," then all I can say to him is, "You don't say so! A somewhat bold idea, but rather a nice notion . . . ," and then I go on reading my newspaper or turn on the television. For this is no message that I could live by anyhow.

But when somebody tells me that there is One who knows me, who cares a lot when I go my own way, who paid a great price in order to be the star you can gaze at and the stay you can rest upon—when somebody says that to me, I stop and listen. For *if* it is true that there is One who is interested in me, then this could mean a turning-point in my life, then this could put my worries, my pangs of conscience, my relationship to my associates, and my marriage in a wholly new light. Then this could mean a revolution in my life that would upset it, *happily* upset it.

But this in no wise means that I must say a farewell to the enchantment of a starry night or the wonder of a flower. For once God has taken possession of my heart, I receive all these things back afresh, just as Matthias Claudius was given a new vision of the moonlit night and the author of Psalm 104 received a fresh vision of the beauty of the clouds and the grandeur of the sea with its waves and its ships. Then, and only then, does all this become a parable I can decipher. Then I see in all this the creatures waiting for God "to give them their food in due season." I see him opening his hand and filling them all with good things. I see them all living by him—and I myself among them.

So *this*, I believe, is what we are being told here when this text says that God rested and celebrated the sabbath, when our attention is turned away for a moment from the great works of life and fastened upon the Creator himself. It is as if at this point a trumpet sounded forth the theme of the great symphony of creation: "It is I, the Lord, who was and am and ever will be at work, surrounding you with my care, searching for you, and am ever on my way to meet you." Only if I have learned this *theme* can I understand the wondrous fabric of sounds in my life, sometimes melodic and sometimes harsh and dissonant; only then will I not fail to hear the *cantus firmus* even though the confusing tones of life are sounding all about me.

After all, without this thematic key, I can so terribly misunderstand life. I can remain stuck fast in a merely esthetic or romantic enjoyment, because a full human life is so "interesting"—it really is interesting!—and because my blood delights in it, and because it is so engrossing and fills me with the love of life.

On the other hand, I can be shaken and frightened and utterly devastated when I am down on my luck. Therefore, if we are to gain the serenity of the Christian man, we must be constantly going back to measure ourselves by the one thing that counts, we must hear the theme that declares that an eternal heart is beating for us.

Some people experience the same thing in hearing Bach's "Christmas Oratorio." How many never got beyond the merely esthetic, the stirring vitality of this music, the feast of rhythm, or the measured proportions of its musical architectonics. Then they go out and for a few moments are transported—until the textured sounds are drowned in the clatter of the typewriter and the jangling of the telephone. For the world passes away with its lust—and also with its starry nights and oratorios—and when Dietrich Bonhoeffer stood beneath the gallows all this may well have expired before his eyes and vanished from his ears. The world passes away, and the lust of it, but the Word of God abides for ever. The message about this beating heart of God—that abides. And one day when for me it's all done and over and everything around me sinks, this one thing will still go with me, this "Christians, be joyful, and praise your salvation . . ."

Here again, as we hear the message of the great oratorios, must not that saving hand grasp us by the shoulder and turn us around, that we may be turned away from the wonder of structured sound, this earthly cosmos of tones—this supreme, majestic dust, but still the "dust" of mere sounds—and come to know, beyond the tumult of violins and harpsichords, kettle drums and trumpets, the ebb and flow of the *vox humana*, that *one* theme on which everything depends: that we may see and know the Lord in his stillness, the Lord above and beyond his creation and even beyond the angels singing *Gloria in excelsis?* That for a moment we may see *him*, beyond the soaring piers and arches of the sonorous stones of the cathedral? This is the only way that I shall ever go away blessed, as one who has received a message I can take away with me, a message by which I can live and die and rejoice and suffer. Only so shall we be more than mere waxen souls, impressed for a few moments by the fleeting spoor of noble sounds—sounds which are quickly swept away by the winds of the workaday world.

This, then, it seems to me, is the message that comes out of the sabbath rest of the Creator. The goal of creation is not the incessant activity of prolific life and the unceasing drama of history. "Subdue the earth" does *not* mean: "Create a rich, productive culture, create social perfection, transform unruly nature with your technology into the dwelling of civilization, conquer the assaults of nature, drive out the cold of winter, illuminate the nights, criss-cross the oceans, reach for the stars!"

"Subdue the earth" means this instead: "When you put your stamp upon creation, see to it that your human life and your culture do not become a sign of your eternal restlessness and your blind titanism, but rather a thanksgiving and a response to him who gave you this earth. See to it that everything you do does not miss its *theme*, but that it retains its part in him who created all these things, and that the reflection of his peace and repose falls upon it. Otherwise your gift of dominion over the earth will trickle away in your hands. You will become the harried slave of your own works. Your unrest and your greed will consume you, until, instead of subduing the earth, you make a hell of it, until, instead of turning to heaven, you build a tower against heaven—until, indeed, you provoke the Flood and in the end your earth is blown to pieces."

So, above all the restlessness of our human activity, above all the striving and devising, we must keep in sight the throne of God, where he calmly and peacefully observes the sabbath of creation. Only he who sees this throne of rest acquires the calm composure that enables him to look beyond the tumult to the world's horizon, to the place where the enigmatical world is grounded in the higher thoughts of a heart that is thinking of us, and where the world is summoned into being by these higher thoughts. And he will also look to that other horizon where on the Last Day this world will again return to Him.

Above all the devious, tortuous ways we walk—and stray!—between these horizons of the first and the last sabbath day of the world stands the great tranquility of God which embosoms all its unrest in his peace. "The Lord is in his holy temple; let all the earth keep silence before him." Let it keep silence before him in the hectic scramble of business, Christmas shopping, and competition. Let it keep silence before him in the drab wilderness of the dictatorships and the onrush of the Terror. Let it keep silence before him in the midst of the crash of rockets and atom bombs. God is in his sanctuary.

There is such a thing as tranquility in the midst of unrest, and peace in the midst of nervous activity. Then it is a reflection of this stillness of the Creator. "Past and pure Nothingness! . . . What boots us then creation's endless travail? Created but to nothing to unravel!" says Mephistopheles as Faust lay dying, referring to the restlessness that hangs even above this death as "the clock's hand falls." Where the stillness of the Creator reigns this Nothingness is conquered, because all *our* futile unrest is ended. For then we are co-ordinated into a peace and security in which never again can we be lost or lonely.

But the Creator's sabbath rest also gives meaning to *our* repose, *our* rest from work, and also to every Sunday's quiet. And this means that we are not bound to go on slaving like mad and succumb to the frenzy of an exaggerated sense of duty and work our heads off (preferably even in the name of God or of some sort of ethics of service). On the contrary, we are called upon to stop, to interpose pauses in the round of our work, and take a new look at the theme of our life.

In other words, this business of deifying our work and making an idolatrous cult of our vocation has nothing to do with any Christian idea of duty and service. We shall soon find that we are on the wrong track in this matter if we look at how the Bible speaks of the counterpart of sabbath rest, namely, of our work.

It is certainly of great symbolical significance that the problem of work is dealt with in, of all places, the context of the story of the Fall. This should set us to thinking. In any case, work is not simply associated with the world that was still sound and intact. There is something ambiguous in it that eludes us if we oversimplify and say that work is worship or work is merely vocation.

In order to understand this ambiguity we need to go beyond the creation story for a moment and note how God avenges man's profane seizure of the forbidden fruit. There we read of the pains of childbirth and the pangs of death; there the divine judgment suggests that our relationship to nature has been broken. Here something has broken into the accord between natural and personal life and robbed the house of creation of its harmony.

But the curse also applies to the ground. This means that even our *work* is marked with the sign of death, that it too has become ambiguous. The fact that judgment stands between us and the ground—symbol of our workaday world—reminds us that life is not only more than clothing (Matt. 6:25), but also more than our work. We do not live in order to work; we work in order to live.

I often think about what will happen to me when I can no longer work, perhaps when old age comes and hand and eye have grown weary, or perhaps in some other long period of enforced rest. None of us knows, after all, what lies ahead of us, what unexpected pages may be opened in the book of our life by a higher hand.

When that time comes will I awaken out of my work and my busy activity as from an anesthetic and not know where I am? Will I be at a loss to know what to do with myself and then begin to moan that my life no longer has any meaning or content? How empty life is for many old people when they retire!

Or will I be aware then of the high and holy hand that sweeps aside with a sublime gesture all that I have worked upon and created; will I hear the voice saying, "The things you have prepared, whose will they be?"

Then the money I may have earned will be consumed by moths and rust, and the success I may have achieved will sink into unsubstantial shadow. Then some altogether different questions will begin to stir: Are there any treasures in your life that have permanent value, that do not trickle through your fingers like sand, but remain in eternity? Have you believed and hoped and loved? Have you learned, even in the midst of utter loneliness, to listen to God and answer him, and thus to live in anticipation of the joy—Kierkegaard had this carved upon his tombstone—of "speaking eternally, eternally with Jesus"? Which of your neighbors have you helped? To whom did you speak a good word when he was down? For whom did you dig wells in the desert? Whom did you help with your love and who can testify for you in eternity?

The hour will come when these will be the only questions that count for anything, because then we will be alone with God and everything that has to do with work and achievement and success will lie so far back in the past that it will no longer be true.

Now we understand, perhaps, not only that God hallows our work and has promised to bless our vocation, but also that a judgment has been laid upon it. Death, the pains of childbirth, the ambiguity of our lifework—in all this there is a judgment and a hidden grace, through all this God is trying to confront me with the real theme of my life.

What good is the most thrilling romance of a life, yea, what good will it do if my life has been successful in secondary things and men heap carloads of wreaths upon my coffin, what good will all this be, if a higher hand writes on the margin of my life: "You missed the theme; you did not get the point. I sent you signal after signal in judgments and promises. But you did not see and did not hear. You saw only your barns which you wanted to fill, but not the Father's house where one day you would stand. You acted as if you would live for ever—as Adam wanted to do—as if there were no eternity on whose shore your journey would one day end."

But it is not only our personal life, "my lifetime" that ends upon that shore. *History* too is marching on to that final day. Its restlessness and torment, its glory and its shame, its tumults of war and its periods of peace will one day enter into the great sabbath, into the silence of eternity which will replace and encompass the shouting, the clashing of weapons, and the sirens of disaster.

Do we understand what this approaching midnight means— this end of the world which the foolish virgins drowsily approach thinking about breakfast, as if there would be no such thing, whereas the wise know it is the hour of destiny and therefore reckon with it in utter wakefulness.

To which group do we belong?

The faces of our clocks indicate only very imperfectly the mystery of the last day of the world.

The large hand tells us, of course, that the hours are slipping away. But it goes on circling in what looks like unending succession. And this cyclic movement creates in us the illusion that the clock will continue to produce new hours, that we shall always have a new beginning at our disposal.

The small hand, which revolves more slowly—but still revolves!—seems to say the same thing about our day. And yet it is preaching to us the first suggestion of a sermon: When it approaches twelve midnight, another day is past and gone.

Perhaps I have made a decision or a turn which I regret, but which nevertheless determines the path I must go. And now I go spinning along on a predetermined track. I cannot turn back and I cannot turn sideways. Perhaps I have hurt another person; perhaps something has snapped within me too, and certain rifts and cracks and wounds which I have inflicted or received have left their mark behind them. I cannot undo anything. I cannot revise my past; it is fixed.

And though the small hand revolves mechanically and always at twelve o'clock midnight releases a new day, in reality it never returns to the same place. I am no longer in control of my past. I am fixed upon it, like one transfixed to a cross.

After all, why is a person who is seeking a position required to submit particulars about his life; in other words, why must he exhibit his past? This is done, to be sure, because we all proceed on the assumption that a man *is* his past, that a man is *identical* with what he has done, his achievements and delinquencies, his good points and also his "previous convictions." And not a few know that one thing or another "sticks" to them and they can no longer shake it off, because people—the bosses, the neighbors, associates, and sometimes their own families—are cruel enough to crucify us again on the cross of our past, to nail us down to our past and recall it to us for good or for evil: Who you are? Well, you did such and such!

And so it is. We cannot turn back the little hand. We cannot erase or revise many of the passages it has traversed; they must remain for all eternity.

For all eternity? But this is the miracle—that now someone else has allowed himself to be nailed to the cross of my past, that there is one who took upon himself and carried away everything that I cannot alter! That there is one who provides a new beginning—really the only one who can erase the past, because he puts himself in the place where *I* would have to stand!

When on the last day of the world, at the Last Judgment, I am compelled to stand before the throne of God and he says to me, "Who are you?" then even before I can open my mouth the Accuser will answer and say, "Lord, I have the chronicle of his past in my hands. Here is the list of the secret things in his life that nobody knows about. Here are the words with which he maligned and hurt and killed. And here are noted the times when he said and did nothing while his neighbor was hoping for his help. And this, Lord, is a profile of his jealousies, his hatreds, his envies, and his greeds. This is what he was, Lord, this is his past, as only *I* and none of his fellow men, for whom he put on an act, know it. This is what he is, because he *is* his past."

And when the great Accuser has spoken a miracle will happen. For then God, the great Judge of the Last Judgment, will say:

"Stop your attacks! When I ask who this is, I do not want to know what he has done. For his past has been canceled."

And at that moment, I myself will be allowed to join in the proceedings before the throne and say:

"Yes, Lord, it *is* canceled. If you ask me who I am, I shall not tell you that I am the one who did these things. Instead I say to you: I am the brother of my Savior, Jesus Christ. He came to me, and I was not too base for him. And look, here he is beside me; he will vouch for me. It's not my sins, Lord, not this black list that will tell you who I am; that's out of date. I am ... well, I 'am' only the brother and companion of your Son, and therefore I am also *your* child. That's what I am, dear God, My feet are dusty, sure. But that comes from the far country where I strayed and erred. I have blots on my escutcheon and my record isn't clean. But what is that to you, Lord? You look at the heart. And this heart of mine has hungered and thirsted after righteousness. Even in the most terrible hours of doubt this heart has cried: 'I believe, dear Lord, help my unbelief.' And sometimes this heart has seen, beneath the mask of the neighbor and in the midst of all contempt for men, the face of the secret Savior. This is all I have, Lord, only this. I have lost my past, because I have found him who carried it away for me and now is with me always, to the end of the world."

Then God will say:

"Well done, good and faithful servant (I can hardly believe my ears—"good and faithful"—but that's what he says!); enter into the joy of your Master."

That's the way it will be on the last day of the world.

Will my knowing about the end change my life here and now? What do I really expect from life? Am I eagerly expectant to see what tremendous opportunities may still come my way? Or am I old and tired, looking ahead to nothing but death after a longer or shorter barren stretch of increasing loneliness and physical infirmity? Or am I worried about the atom bomb, the Red tide, or about the next night, which I dread because I cannot sleep? What am I waiting for?

Whatever it may be, a feverishly expectant hope of happiness or depressing dread, it is all changed, canceled, prevented, and transformed by something altogether new: the fact that someone is there, waiting for me, accepting me despite all my inadequacy, someone who leads me safely over the ridges and through the dark valleys to the place where out of the darkness comes a voice saying: "Ah, there you are, my good and faithful servant."

The fact is that we are not on a journey whose outcome is uncertain. We walk in the blessedness of Advent. We walk through the storms of change unafraid, because there is One who makes all things new.

It's true: I can become a different person, a new man. I can lay down the luggage of my past. I can become an expectant person.

Therefore, let us stop looking nervously to the future, always wondering *what* is coming. For we know *who* is coming to us.

And he who possesses the last hour need have no fear of the next minute.

THE STORY OF THE FALL

9

How Evil Came into the World

THE STORY OF THE FALL: PART ONE

Now the serpent was more subtle than any other wild creature that the Lord God had made. He said to the woman, "Did God say, 'You shall not eat of any tree of the garden'?" And the woman said to the serpent, "We may eat of the fruit of the trees of the garden; But God said, 'You shall not eat of the fruit of the tree which is in the midst of the garden, neither shall you touch it, lest you die.'" But the serpent said to the woman, "You will not die. For God knows that when you eat of it your eyes will be opened, and you will be like God, knowing good and evil." So when the woman saw that the tree was good for food and that it was a delight to the eyes, and that the tree was to be desired to make one wise, she took of its fruit and ate; and she also gave some to her husband, and he ate. Then the eyes of both were opened, and they knew that they were naked; and they sewed fig leaves together and made themselves aprons.

—*Genesis 3:1–7*

I still have a vivid memory of one night during the war. On a height near Stuttgart there were some twenty boys from a Latin school manning an antiaircraft battery. They were anxious to have me come and give them religious instruction. But since this was prohibited and their request was not granted, they went on to a higher commanding officer and finally, by their spirit and persistence, secured his permission. So I walked out to visit them regularly and we sat down among the guns and talked about the "last things."

But on this occasion they had called me for another reason. Their position had been hit by a low-level attack and the father of one of the boys, who happened to be visiting, was killed while his boy was manning the gun.

The boy carried his dead father away in a wheeled stretcher. The youngsters—for that's all they were—crowded around me deeply shocked, almost like chicks around a hen. They were completely broken up and they looked to someone older for protection from a world whose dark enigma had suddenly leaped upon them for the first time. I spoke some words of comfort to them, though I myself felt utterly helpless.

But then the thing happened that accounts for my relating this incident at all. On my way home the moonlight lay upon the quiet valley, the white flowers of the trees shimmered in this soft light, and an unspeakable peace and stillness rested upon the landscape. The world was "like some quiet room, where wrapt in still soft gloom, we sleep away the daylight's sorrow."[1]

I mention this, not to be romantic or to gain a sentimental effect, but rather because for me this hour was a parable of the dark threshold which, the account of the Fall says, man has crossed. Before me lay the seemingly whole and healthy world of a springtime night. But in that moment its very peace was like a stab of pain. For I knew that the peace of nature is delusive, and that I had just spoken, encompassed by a sea of blossoms, with boys whose eyes were filled with dread even though they bravely swallowed their tears.

No, this world was not sound and whole, because man had invaded it with his murderous instruments and despoiled it of its peace. And will it not grow even worse? How long will men be able to refresh themselves by looking at the starry heavens and their majestic calm? Will man disturb even *this* peace with his space ships and cosmic spies?

---

[1] The lines are from Matthias Claudius' poem, "The moon hath risen on high," translated by Catherine Winkworth. (*Trans.*)

The story we shall discuss today shows us how from this *one* point in the world—where man stands—evil streams out like an icy breath into the world, into a world that once was sound and whole, a world over which there rang the joy of the Creator: "Behold, it was very good; behold, it is very good."

That wonderful serenity of the first man under God that rings out in Joseph Haydn's radiant duets between Adam and Eve is suddenly ended. Their frank and open candor is shattered. Now they have something to hide, and they hastily make themselves aprons. And when they hear the voice of God as he walks through the garden, they go into hiding like culprits caught by surprise and with palpitating hearts watch to see what will happen.

We can only stand in amazement at this age-old story, for it summarizes in exemplary fashion what we see happening all around us and especially within ourselves. Surely all of us feel as I must confess I do when I hear these words. At first, as an intellectual living in the atomic age, one is inclined to take offense at many of the *mythical* features of this story—for example, the idea of a serpent that can speak. *But* scarcely has this skepticism begun to stir than we are so compelled to listen to *what* the serpent says that the feeble protest of our intellect is simply thrust aside.

Do not all of us know certain scenes in our lives that recur in this story of a temptation? Is it not something like a concentrate of the whole art of temptation? How can one capture in a few pages the great profusion of shapes conveyed in this story?

So I can do nothing else but deal with it several times, in order that in this way we may slowly work our way to the arch-question of all mankind—the question that even fourteen-year-olds ask and that still pursues people in their old age: the question of how evil came into the world.[2]

And the first thing that strikes us is this. The drama of temptation, which now begins and puts a sudden end to the vision of a

[2] The theme of this chapter is resumed in Chapter 11, "Guilt and Destiny."

sound and healthy world, begins not with the crash of the kettle drum but rather with the sound of oboes. One might even say that it has in it hymn-like motifs.

The overture of this dialogue is thoroughly pious, and the serpent introduces himself as a completely serious and religious beast. He does not say: "I am an atheistic monster and now I am going to take your paradise, your innocence and loyalty, and turn it all upside down." Instead he says: "Children, today we're going to talk about religion, we're going to discuss the ultimate things."

Well, something like that immediately inspires confidence. After all, blackguards and rascals do not dabble in such topics. When you talk about pious things you immediately secure for yourself the alibi of serious-mindeness and sincerity.

So he begins by asking, "Did God—this God whom we all revere; even I, the serpent, honor him dearly—did our revered God say that you should not eat of any tree of the garden?"

In other words, the serpent is trying to start a discussion, something like a theological discussion about the "Word of God." So there is not a trace of doubt—oh, no! The devil himself believes in God. He takes his stand on the fact of "God."

In any case, he seems always to plan his tactics from this quarter. The Tempter in the wilderness too did not say to Jesus Christ: "You are a fool to obey your heavenly Father." He too cited nothing but Scripture passages and pious sayings when he urged Him to make bread of stones, leap from the pinnacle of the temple, and accept the kingdoms of this world from his, the devil's, hand. The devil acts more pious than a nun and knows his Bible better than a professor of the Old Ttestament or a Jehovah's Witness. This reptile would even lift his eyes devoutly to heaven, if he had the eyelids to do it with.

So this is the first point that we must note here: the Tempter always operates in disguise. He hides behind a mask of harmless, indeed, pious benevolence. All temptations in life begin in sugared form. "The people never know the devil's there, even though he has them by the throat," says Mephistopheles in *Faust*.

Recently, I made an interesting experiment in this respect. My students performed volunteer service for several weeks in a camp for refugees from the East, and almost every day they put on a Punch-and-Judy show for the children. It was the greatest attraction in the camp. The hall would have had to have rubber walls to accommodate the crowds of eager children who came. It was my job to play the devil. I wielded a horrible, fiery red puppet in one hand and mustered up a menacing and horrible voice to represent all the terrible discords of hell. Then in tones brimming with sulphur I advised the children to indulge in every conceivable naughtiness: You never need to wash your feet at night; you can stick your tongue out at anybody you want to; and be sure to drop banana skins on the street so people will slip on them.

Now perhaps some worthy parents will be horrified by the fact that I relate this so openly. They may wonder privately how this man can act so unpedagogically and even talk about it publicly. But this is the remarkable thing—and this observation really does have a bearing on the exposition of our story!—the pedagogical results which I achieved in this role of the devil were enormous and generally recognized in the camp. The children suddenly stopped sticking out their tongues and they also washed their feet at night. They actually shouted me down with ear-splitting protests when I handed out my wicked suggestions. They would have absolutely no truck with the devil. If they had had anything to say about it, the Fall would never have happened. But then, too, the serpent in paradise could not have been the kind of devil that I was. For then he would have had to play the game openly, as I did. For in our Punch-and-Judy show there was *one* decisive point at which I was actually different from the serpent that spoke in paradise: right from the start I let it be known by my mask and my voice that I was the devil

Hence my seductions could never succeed; on the contrary they turned out to be positively productive as a pedagogical device.

The fact is that man wants no truck with the devil, any more than did the children in the refugee camp. Adam and Eve, you and I, undoubtedly plump for the good. In other words, no man really *wants* to be evil. I have often talked with hardened criminals in prison cells, but I have yet to find a single one who *wanted* to be bad. But many of them did say something like this: "When I committed that robbery or theft, or murder, I didn't think it was wrong at all. In any case, it never entered my mind. The old man I struck down wasn't an old 'man' to me at all; he was merely the anonymous possessor of a fat pocketbook. He was a guy living off the fat of the land and I was hungry. He may have seemed to me to be an abscess on the body of society, a profiteer enjoying his plunder, while *I* had strength and vitality that never had a chance to develop on the shady side of life." Dostoevski's Raskolnikov had the same kind of thoughts when he murdered the old moneylender. He, too, had no desire to be "evil."

Therefore it is really true that the decisive point in this story is the fact that the devil does not declare himself. He presents himself as a representative of the good, even as the advocate of God. The serpent in paradise is a good and faithful beast, an accepted member of the divine household.

So here we have made plain for us the first law of all temptation. And as I now proceed briefly to characterize this law, I ask one of us to visualize certain situations in his life in which this law operated in his own personal history.

The Tempter never whispers to us, "Come on, I'll teach you a sin." If he tempted us in this way, we would immediately recoil and feel that we had to declare ourselves. For, as we have said, we are not so depraved that we *want* to do evil!

Instead he says to us (if he is out to tempt us in the area of sex, for example), "Come on, I want to give you a fascinating experience. You have no idea of what life has to offer. Do you want to miss the best, the most exciting things in life?"

Here again we note this effort to strike a pious, soulful pose. And the Tempter adds perhaps, "Surely God doesn't want you to miss anything in your life. He wants you to avail yourself of all the potentialities with which the great Creator endowed your body. After all, wasn't it God who put this passion into your veins?"

Well, after all this is something that can be discussed! Actually, we *must* discuss it. And talk and discussion is the first point in the serpent's program. The Tempter is a spirit of discussion.

When he sets out to alienate young people from confirmation over there in the East Zone and tempt them to participate in *Jugendweihe*,[3] he does *not* say, "My whole satanic heart yearns to make you renounce the faith of your fathers, to soften you up, and make you a disloyal turncoat." Oh, no, the devil does not put on this red, satanic mask. He turns on the soft soap and warbles with a gentle voice, "My child, *Jugendweihe* is a purely political act; it has nothing to do with religion. We'll discuss it sometime and you'll see how tolerant I am; you'll see that I have no intention of taking away your faith and that I mean well with you. I am so eager—just because I love humanity!—to see you get ahead in your profession, to see that you get some higher education or some good trade. And, after all, you *can't* have all this, if you belong to the church. I only have your best welfare at heart...."

So, with the most friendly and ingenuous words in the world, he invites us to step on a trap door that looks like a parqueted floor. And not until much later do we realize that we have stepped into a trap that pitches us into a bottomless pit.

Just so harmlessly does temptation begin. It starts with the fact of "God." "Did God really say, 'You shall love your neigh-

---

[3] *Jugendweihe* is a ceremony instituted by the German Democratic Republic in which fourteen-year-olds pledge their loyalty to communistic socialism, a measure obviously adopted to break down the church's practice of confirmation. (Trans.)

bor'? But tell me, who really *is* your neighbor?" You can discuss that question for a long time, and the Tempter knows that as long as you keep making a problem of it and talk it to pieces, you will never lift a finger for your neighbor.[4]

"Did God really say, 'You shall not eat of any tree of the garden'?" "My dear people," says the serpent, "I certainly do not want you to start doubting God. Oh, no! Just stop and reflect for a moment—not by way of *opposition* to God, but in the *Name* of God—whether he *could* have said anything like that at all! After all, it would certainly be 'undivine' of him to forbid you to eat of these trees! Do you think that God is so narrow-minded and wrongheaded that he would not let you get near these unusually wonderful products of his creation in the midst of the garden? Is he the kind of God who does nothing but set up barriers, put on bridles, and post prohibitory signs? Does it take me, the serpent, to explain to you that God is a God of the unlimited abundance of life? Why should anything that he himself made be bad and forbidden?"

And he goes on to say, "Did God forbid you to live your life to the full and use all your instincts? Do you really think God would be so prim and pedantic? After all he created you and your vitality the way it is. So everything *you* do is covered by the Creator!"

The serpent goes on talking, with all kinds of variations:

"Perhaps you are a man who has machines, bank accounts, and influence at your disposal. It tickles you to make a regular cult of your social prestige, to have people bowing and scraping before you, and to make a big splurge. Don't worry, as a serpent I have a few soothing words to say to you too." Then, not without a few guttural heart tones in his voice, he goes on to say, "Did God forbid you to think about yourself once in a while instead of your neighbor? Do you think he really demands that you limit your opulent banquets and possibly even lose a

[4] Compare the exposition of the parable of the Good Samaritan (Luke 10:25-37) in Thielicke, *The Waiting Father*, pp. 158-69.

HOW EVIL CAME INTO THE WORLD

little weight just to contribute your hard-earned pennies to the hungry children in far-off India or the refugee camps in Europe? Nonsense, my good man, don't burden your conscience with such moral crotchets! After all, who gave you what you have? Wasn't it providence that blessed you with business opportunities and economic miracles? Didn't you hump yourself and work hard for it too?" And then another oily quotation from the Bible comes from the lips of this old serpent: "You shall not muzzle an ox when it treads out the grain." So in the name of the Bible, stuff all you can in your own mouth first. The ox comes first, says God, and you can be the ox!

So this is the *first* idea that the serpent insinuates into our hearts with all the arts of suggestion. God is different from what you think. He is not at all a narrow-minded, moralistic God who is always getting in your way. Rather he is the God of life, the God of abundance. Take everything you can get, for God is handing it out to you. Act according to the laws of life, even when they are cruel, for God made life. Take advantage of the rights of the stronger, for God is always on the side that has the heaviest artillery. Keep shoving down and climbing up; that's the way to get ahead. After all, that's what this life God created looks like! Take away the hidden irony of that famous song of Bert Brecht's and make it the principle of your life: "If anybody does the trampling, it's me; and if anybody gets trampled, it's going to be you." *C'est la vie*—life is like that—and that's probably what he who made it is like too.

It is quite apparent that the serpent has well-reasoned arguments. He is far too subtle to appeal only to the baser instincts. His ambition is not to persuade but to convince.

And yet we have not even touched upon the shrewdest point in this temptation. The serpent not only does not suggest to Eve that she rebel against God; he actually gives her the chance to champion God and break a lance for him, as it were, to become religiously active. The serpent actually fires Eve's piety; he activates her belief in God.

"Did God say, 'You shall not eat of the trees of the garden'?" So runs the question with which the serpent introduces this pious exercise.

"No," says Eve, thus becoming God's defender, "he did not forbid that at all. He even permitted a great deal and gave us a lot of choice. We are allowed—most generously!—to eat of all the trees in the garden. God excepted only the *one* tree in the midst of the garden; we're not even supposed to touch that one."

Now, this is really a pious conversation. One must be capable of distinguishing precisely between spirits in order to catch here certain undertones and see certain traps being laid.

Now, let us pause for a moment in our endeavor to recognize the strategic principles of temptation, and try to understand what God means by forbidding men even to touch the tree in the midst of the garden.

When God forbids men even to come in contact with this tree, he obviously means: "Don't even come close to it! Keep your distance from it!" In other words: "Don't even put yourself in this tempting *situation!*"

Significantly, the Lord's Prayer teaches us the petition: "Lead us not into temptation; do not even allow us to get into the critical situation in the first place." Significantly, the petition does not read: "Lead us *out* of temptation" (once we are in it); but rather, "Lead us not *into* temptation." Once we are near the tree, our pulse begins to stir, curiosity flares up, and passions are aroused. In such a situation our ability to make decisions is paralyzed.

That's why so much depends upon our not beginning to pray after temptation has already come, when rebellion is already raging within us. Nowhere are we promised that we can pray at all in that situation. Therefore everything depends upon our beginning to pray when we are still sober and prudent, at the beginning of the day therefore, before we are caught in the toils of our own passions and the day's transactions, when the day still lies ahead of us and our wishes and desires have not yet become the father of our thoughts.

Many of us who do not know how to pray and yet yearn to know ought to try this sometime. They should not wait until they have gotten into the high-tension zone of the perilous tree —and how often we are in the range of its radiation every day! —but rather pray in the first and last hours of the day.

In other words, you cannot take everything that has to do with God and squeeze it in just anywhere, accomplishing it by the way and if you happen to be in the mood. We must set aside in a planned way a few minutes for God each day, in which he is our *whole* concern. The person who reads the newspaper and listens to a radio service at the same time, or the person for whom God can be reduced to any old prayer that happens to come out in a bad situation, has heard nothing and said nothing and therefore dare not be surprised if he falls victim to the enchantment of the perilous tree.

I would even go further and say that we should not even touch that tree in our prayers. Let me indicate briefly what I mean.

Generally, we feel an urge to pray at the very time we are troubled by some concern or other: mothers worry about their children, businessmen worry about a slump in the market, politicians about the next election, students about their examinations. Every one of us carries about his burden of worries and cares. And this care can thus become a tree that we should not touch. When Jesus Christ says to us, "Do not be anxious," he is thoroughly aware that he is touching a dark spot in our life. For every care is a vote of no-confidence in God. Every anxiety tends with a serpentine cunning to prevent us from saying confidently: "Who points the clouds their course, Whom winds and seas obey, He shall direct thy wandering feet, He shall prepare thy way."

Now, my point is that even in our prayers this tree of care must be viewed only from a distance. We dare not touch it or handle it. I have repeatedly observed in myself and also in others that when we come too close to the tree of care it grows overlarge and dominates even our prayers. Then even our prayers become a means by which we get pinned down in our cares.

During the war I saw this illustrated repeatedly in the panicky prayers uttered in the air-raid shelters. Not infrequently, while the bombs were crashing down, even those who otherwise were never accustomed to pray would suddenly send up ejaculations of prayer to heaven. But basically, these prayers were not addressed to God at all. These people were seeing in their imagination only the deadly specter of falling bombs. And after it was all over, the praying stopped. Fundamentally, they were not talking to God at all; they were talking to the bombs.

And this means that we can set down this very important conclusion. In exactly the same way that the Tempter insinuates himself into Eve's pious and edifying thoughts he also sends his partisans—in the form of our cares—into the intimacy of our prayer life. Prayer alone proves nothing. One can pray in a way that is all wrong. As praying persons we can make the same mistake that an unskilled bicycle rider makes when he tries to avoid a collision with a tree. He is so transfixed by fear and care that he runs into it full force.

We learn how we are to pray from Dürer's engraving, "Knight, Death, and the Devil," a picture that I must repeatedly recall to your remembrance. Specters and hideous monsters lurk on the path of this gallant rider. But the knight looks above and beyond them all. Indeed, he cannot see them, for his gaze is fixed upon the castle in the distance which is his home. He is riding toward the castle. And just because he keeps his *goal* in view, he escapes the onslaught of the specters and their temptations. He does not even need to concern himself with them.

I should like to cite as an example a very special case that illustrates how we can get the Tempter out of our prayers.

When a young man is assailed by his unruly passions and if he is really in earnest about winning this battle, it would be a great mistake for him to keep staring at the tempting images in his imagination and then fight against or even to pray against them. The Tempter is all too willing to get us into wrestling match with our lusts and desires, for then we shall very probably turn out to be the ones who are defeated. And finally, the abhorred fantasies thrust themselves even into our prayer and fill it to the brim. The more we concentrate upon the images of our imagination, even as enemies to be fought, the more they gain power over us.

We must rather combat the temptations in our path in a *positive* way. We must not stare at them with hostility and suspicion. We must rather keep our eyes fixed upon the positive goal, the castle, the home place on the horizon. For the young man this means that he does not pray: "Lord, preserve me from this thing which is almost overwhelming me and tearing me to pieces; thou knowest my accursed passions!" Rather he should pray the other way around, positively: "Lord, I thank thee for the powers thou hast given to me; grant that I may use them in thine honor and for thine ends!"

God is always positive. He gives us nothing that we cannot accept from him with gratitude. As long as we accept it from God's hand, nothing can hurt us.

So now the woman in her conversation with the serpent has mentioned the critical point on which her destiny with God will be decided. It is really only "one point," namely, a single tree, and on that tree, only one apple. God put at man's disposal the whole breadth of his creation: the multitude of plants and animals are at his service, the laws of nature are there to be explored and technologically utilized, and the whole cosmos is offered as his dominion. Only one single spot in all this infinite expanse must remain tabu, inviolable, and reserved to God himself, namely, this one tree. And at this one point the serpent now begins to fire away.

Thus he is actually very careful not to try to tempt Eve with an atheistic suggestion. He does not say: God is an illusion; the only things that are true are what you can see and taste and touch. He makes only one modest, almost hesitant objection to Eve: After all, this *one* paltry point cannot matter that much! What is this one apple compared with the peaches and melons and strawberries and apricots, to which God has no objections! If you conform to God in 999 points in a thousand and more in the area he has assigned to you, surely, Eve, this one point in a thousand isn't going to upset your peace with God!

But that's the way it is; that's the way it really is—in your life and in mine. The fact is that all of us have sectors in the territory of our life which we are quite content to leave to God. But each of us also has a point which we will by no means let God approach. This point may be my ambition whereby I am determined to beat my way to success in my career at any price. It may be my sexuality to which I am determined to give rein no matter what happens and no matter what it costs. It may be a bottomless hatred toward one of my fellow men which I literally nurse and which gives me a kind of sensual pleasure which then comes between me and God and robs me of my peace. God can have everything, *but not this one thing!*

God can have my unselfish devotion and service. After all, I am an idealist! I will devote myself to a task unreservedly and without regard for loss. I am industrious and active. He can have it all—*except this one thing.*

God can even have my neighborly love. I am good-hearted, I like people, and I wouldn't hurt a fly. He can have my love for my neighbors, that isn't hard for me. He can have everything—*except this one thing.*

Now, the curious thing is that God lets me find him only when I offer to him this one, hardest thing in my life. In other words, God never comes through the door that I hold open for him, but always knocks at the one place which I have walled up with concrete, because I want it for myself alone. But if I do not let him in there, he turns away altogether.

Innumerable uncertainties, doubts, and difficulties, with which we torment ourselves, which rob us of our peace with God and hopelessly block our ability to pray, do not lie in intellectual difficulties at all. This we only imagine to be true. Has any one of us been bothered during this chapter by the fact that he is unable to imagine a serpent that can speak and think? No, the reason why we can find no peace, the reason why we cannot find God lies at this *one* point in our life, this *one* tree in the midst of the garden, which we refuse to allow to be forbidden.

What is this point in your life and my life?

We ought sometimes to read the story of the temptation of Jesus (Matthew 4) in order to find out. Everything, absolutely everything depends upon finding out what stands between me and God. Something is certainly there. And it is probably only one point, one single tree, one single apple, one single person, one single passion.

But there is something else that stands between us and God. Between him and us stands Jesus Christ. And he stands on *God's* side. It is not we, after all, who are the seekers for God. It is rather God who is seeking us men. And Jesus is the lamp, the "light of the world" by which he seeks for us.

But Jesus Christ also stands on *our* side. He knows what temptation is, for he endured it himself. He know what death is, for he tasted it himself. *He knows all about us.* And therefore he is with us, even when the darkness falls all around us.

This is the miracle of the gospel—that we can seek and find God, not in the heights, but in the depths. "I will not leave you desolate; I will come to you," he says.

Between me and every dark and evil temptation stands Jesus Christ.

10

The Bridgehead of the Tempter

The Story of the Fall: Part Two

Now the serpent was more subtle than any other wild creature that the Lord God had made. He said to the woman, "Did God say, 'You shall not eat of any tree of the garden'?" And the woman said to the serpent, "We may eat of the fruit of the trees of the garden; but God said, 'You shall not eat of the fruit of the tree which is in the midst of the garden, neither shall you touch it, lest you die.'" But the serpent said to the woman, "You will not die. For God knows that when you eat of it your eyes will be opened, and you will be like God, knowing good and evil." So when the woman saw that the tree was good for food and that it was a delight to the eyes, and that the tree was to be desired to make one wise, she took of its fruit and ate; and she also gave some to her husband, and he ate. Then the eyes of both were opened, and they knew that they were naked; and they sewed fig leaves together and made themselves aprons.

—*Genesis 3:1-7*

We remember that the Tempter asked Eve a catch question: "So you dare not eat of any of the beautiful trees here in the garden—God keeps a pretty tight hand upon you, doesn't he?" And Eve, we remember, was quite eager to be God's defender and she answered: "Oh no, God is very generous; we can eat of all the trees in the garden. We can freely enjoy everything that life has to offer. No, my good serpent, we need have no inhibitions about what comes from the hand of God." (So far God's approval still prevailed above this bright and wholesome world; there were still no dark, disreputable areas in it.) "There is only one point at which God is not to be trifled with," said Eve to the serpent. "We dare not touch the tree in the midst of the garden. There is *one* place where God wants us to realize that we are only men, that though we are like God, we are not equal with God, and that we must be content to remain within these limits, the limits of humanity! He has permitted us everything and given us free choice; except that if we violate this *one* point, if we invade this *one* place that is reserved to God, we shall die."

And hardly has Eve said this when the Tempter abandons his reserve, throws off his disguise, and lays his cards on the table: "You will not die. For God knows that when you eat of it your eyes will be opened, and you will be like God, knowing good and evil." Here the dialogue between the Tempter and man reaches its climax. What has happened?

In these words of the serpent there are two concealed charges which are exploded, as it were, by a time-fuse, at just the right moment.

The first explosive charge lies in the Tempter's effort to bring Eve to the point where she will not take God seriously. Up to this time she had taken him seriously. She knew that when we are dealing with God we are dealing with life and death, that one can die if one crosses him; then our destiny in time and eternity is at stake.

But now the serpent says to her: "Surely it is sheer nonsense to think that God would let you die and perish utterly just because you don't take him so terribly in earnest, but rather just partly seriously. You will not die. The question of God is not that serious, my dear lady! All honor to your respect for him. I take my hat off to your display of piety, but really now, he's not *that* serious about it!"

This sounds like sympathetic kindness: "Child, you take

things too hard." Who doesn't like to be told things like this and who isn't receptive when somebody tells him to take it easy!

Sometimes I think there must be countless people who have carried on just such a conversation with the serpent at some time in their lives. They have no intention whatsoever of abolishing belief in God. By no means do they want to go that far. After all, we need something like religion. You can say to the children: "God is watching you!"—so in God you get a free babysitter, a religious form of coercion and support in the raising of children. Besides, there are moments—perhaps when I look up at the star-spangled sky at the end of a beautiful day, or when a wedding procession moves up the aisle of the church amid the sound of organ music—moments when I feel a real religious thrill and I wouldn't want to miss the emotional value of it.

Naturally, I know that I cannot live by these emotional values. At most they are a kind of low-calorie dessert with a slight tonic effect. The main dish on which I really live is my monthly income, my weekly wages, or my bank account, or my professional success. If that were taken away from me there would be the devil to pay. This would really be an awful threat; this would really be a matter of life and death.

But what would happen if religion were taken away from me? Well, it certainly wouldn't be nice; but after all a man can live without dessert if he has to. Life would be a little poorer; but even the functionaries of godlessness seem to have a good time and do not feel that they are going to ruin. That a man can destroy himself by what he does about God, as Eve says here, is surely nothing but a bare assertion. Jesus' saying, "one thing is needful," is definitely a propagandistic exaggeration.

With a certain shudder, of course, one remembers something that seems to contradict this idea that religion is only a kind of dessert. One remembers that after all there were people who in the name of this God remained steadfast and refused to deny him in the cellars of the GPU and the Gestapo, that, like the nuns in Gertrud von le Fort's famous novel, they went to the scaffold singing and poured out songs of praise to God at the stake until the smoke choked off their voices.

Is it really possible to suffer like that for the dessert of life? Can one accept physical and mental torture, can one thus triumphantly conquer the burning desire to live, if one does not know with an utter certainty that the everlasting death I could incur from God is incomparably more terrible than the little bit of misery and fear which I must endure in the next few hours if I fall into the hands of men?

Just *because* God is such an elemental fact—this is the other side of the coin—I therefore possess in his peace a sovereign superiority over all dread of atomic destruction, over the apprehension of growing old and the horror of loneliness. When I am in the peace of this Lord, safe in the boat where Jesus Christ is sleeping, then indeed the sharks of life are no more than little fishes. Then suddenly there is a great regrouping of all life's values.

It is really a marvelous thing. When God is all in all to me, the valley through which I must walk may be ever so dark and yet there will be light. I may languish in a camp for war prisoners or as a confessing Christian in prison, and this will be the very time I can *live* by him, even without bread. Then his faithfulness builds a wall around me. Then the rod and staff of the Good Shepherd are there ready at hand, and mysterious bridges are flung over all the abysses I dread.

But the opposite is also true. If for me God is only a term for a bit of religion which I use as padding against the hard knocks of life, then this religious comfort will evaporate in my hands when the first real crisis comes. Then I shall not be able to pray; and no answer will I hear. I'll stand there utterly helpless, and the great silence will only be a refutation of God. "From him who has not, even what he has will be taken away." This is the sad end of the sad story of being only a little religious and wanting God only for a pious dessert.

And this is precisely the point to which the Tempter wants to bring Eve. First she must swallow this fact: "You will not die; nobody ever perishes because of God; don't be so stiff about this religious point of view; take it easy." Once this initial sparking of temptation comes off, the rest of the chain reaction goes off of itself, and the last phase, which is nihilism, is child's play.

But there is still a second explosive charge in this remark of the serpent. He says, "God has forbidden you to eat this fruit only because he knows very well that your eating it will endow you with a secret knowledge. But knowledge is power. And God is afraid of it. He wants to keep you on a short leash so you men will not get beyond his control. He is afraid that you will compete with him and that his little divine throne may totter if you discover the tremendous potential that lies in your human reason and the enormous leverage you could bring to bear if you call a general strike like Prometheus."

In other words, here the Tempter is engaging in a little well-poisoning. His action can be reduced to this simple formula: He is sowing doubt of God's goodness in Eve's heart. He is saying: God doesn't mean well by you when he forbids you to eat of this tree. His motives are rather jealousy and malevolence.

The serpent knows very well that, if this seed of distrust falls on receptive soil, it is only a short step from doubt of God's goodness to doubt of his existence.

We see this happening in ourselves. When we meet with a severe misfortune—an incurable disease perhaps, which slowly saps our strength, which is completely meaningless and does nobody any good and is only a torment and a burden for us and those around us—then a secret but highly penetrative suspicion creeps into us. We begin to think that a God who permits something like this to happen cannot be a good God. Perhaps this so-called God is only blind fate, possibly even a sadist. But does such a God really exist? Might it not in that case be better and more honest to speak of a personification of chance and get along as best we can alone—alone beneath a heaven that doesn't exist and in the face of an eternity which is nothingness?

THE BRIDGEHEAD OF THE TEMPTER

Such is the course of the chain reaction of our thought. That's how doubts come over us. And what can be done to stop it?

When we doubt the goodness of God the fatal switch is set for just such a precipitous slide. And the Tempter ensconces himself in the switch-tower and proceeds to manipulate the controls. His trick is to inculcate distrust.

This procedure has its very human parallels. Here is a boss who has a subordinate for whom he has a high regard. This man is devoted to his boss and untiringly available whenever the boss wants something of him. Somebody comes and suggests to the boss that the man is only doing this to curry favor and take advantage of him. From that time on a blight has fallen upon this relationship and a secret suspicion is always lurking. The boss no longer trusts his subordinate.

Or here is an employer who is concerned about the welfare of his employees and worries about each one of them like a father. But there is one man who starts a whispering campaign during the coffee break: "The old man is really smart. He treats you this way just to soften you up. He wants to get the last ounce of production out of you. He doesn't care about you at all; what he wants is to play on your good nature to increase his volume of production. Love your neighbor—it's a trick! Believe me, the old man knows what he's doing."

In a case like this confidence is shattered in an instant and suspicion, once awakened, soon discovers many symptoms that confirm it. The Bible knows why it regards slander and murder as being the same thing. The serpent is slandering God.

Faith, too, is destroyed by distrust. And therefore the Tempter begins to work on this most important strategic spot. Once I believe that God is not good, that he does not deserve my trust, then everything is poisoned, then everything argues against him.

This is the source of the myths about distrust of the gods. The myth of the ring of Polycrates has its origin here. And when this spirit prevails, life becomes a weird and sinister thing.

We have all had this experience. When I achieve something

fine in my life I can no longer enjoy it properly. For now I cannot look upon it as a blessing for which I may be grateful; instead I grow afraid that the gods may become jealous, that their distrust will devise some revenge. When I say in the company of friends that my business or my health is good, I immediately knock on wood to frighten off the jealous spirits. Any number of superstitious acts and sayings are simply expressions of this kind of fear—precisely this fear which is basically nothing else but the poisonous flower planted in my heart as a seed of distrust.

It is worth while to throw a bit more light on these remarkable processes that go on in our hearts. How do we come to be afraid of the jealousy of the gods and allow this fear to blight every lover's happiness we experience, all our joy in our children, and every success in our work? Why it is that this secret anxiety creeps in precisely at the point when we are happy and prevents us from cheerfully enjoying the blessing? Why is it that we are denied the happiness of gratitude? Is it because we have a sick and self-tormenting imagination? Is it just because we are melancholiacs?

No, the fact is that it is something altogether different. Again it becomes clear that there is no such thing as a religious sphere that can be isolated from the rest of life, but that everything we experience with God is closely interwoven with our relationship to our neighbor and with our life as a whole.

Let me illustrate what I mean with an experience of my own. I once knew a man who was exceedingly talented; even when he was in school everything seemed to come his way. He was a handsome fellow and popular with the girls. Later he achieved rapid advance in his profession, and he was constantly concerned with comparing his life with others. His house had to be more elaborately furnished than those of his associates; his name had to appear in the newspaper more frequently than those of his fellow inhabitants in the small city where he lived. When one got to know him better one soon became aware of a definite trait in his character. Strictly speaking, he did not enjoy his success and his fine home; he enjoyed all this only because people envied him. He even went out of his way to stimulate artificially this feeling of inferiority and envy in others, because he relished it. He ostentatiously displayed his success, he assumed a pose in order to make others wild with jealousy. (This, by the way, also occurs in less exaggerated forms. How many of us try to have a more exclusive type of automobile than our neighbor, and in many an apartment house a television aerial or a comfortable, streamlined, chromium-plated baby carriage is the mark of being better off for which people want to be envied!)

Everything I have just said could look like a bit of social criticism or moral criticism. But this is not at all what I mean. I am concerned only with one particular aspect of these manifestations.

My wrong attitude toward my neighbor, whom I may thus maneuver into the role of envy, must inevitably poison my relationship to God; indeed, when I do this I literally draw down the judgment of God upon myself.

In other words, it is my view that anybody who needs the envy of his fellow men in order to live, by this very token cannot imagine God either except as an envier, of whom one must be careful and whom one can by no means trust.

So even the successful man whom we mentioned above became a worrier. His heart's desire that he should become the most envied man in his town was amply fulfilled, it is true; but he also feared the envy of God, whose image was just as distorted in his imagination as the envious grimaces of his neighbors. That is to say, he became the victim of the compulsive idea. One day my life will come to an end, he kept thinking. Somewhere the ravens are already fluttering. Perhaps a disease is already brewing in my body. I have queer pains and sometimes my heart misses a beat. Or a war may come, the market may collapse. . . . So he kept running to the astrologers to avoid the misfortunes that lurked all around him. There was nothing in his life which he had not insured. He was in constant flight from the fiends that lay in wait in secret hiding places. He was hemmed in by visions of dread.

When we are thus hard pressed by the anxiety of life—and who ever escapes it!—we should realize what the real reason for it is, namely, that we no longer trust God and that we are victims of the compulsive notion that God is jealous of us. Then we should carry this painful diagnosis of ourselves a step further and realize that our relationship to our *neighbor* is disturbed. God is not mocked—nor does he allow himself to be mocked by our mocking our neighbor. For how dare we make an envier of *him* for whom Christ died and thus ruin the soul of *him* in whom Christ meets us every day?

At this point it again becomes obvious that I must never grow weary of emphasizing that, if we do not get into the clear with God and if for us faith remains a book with seven seals, the reason for this is not that we are unreligious by nature or that our intellect is tripping us up, but probably because there is something in our *life* that is not in order.

The point is that God is no pale product of the imagination; he is a real fact. Therefore God also has to do with the realities of our life. If there is something wrong here and if we are living in downright sin, this affects our faith, and we are blocked at the decisive point of our life. The chain of doubt to which we are shackled does not as a rule consist of intellectual difficulties but rather of sins. That we can depend upon.

That's why John the Baptist does not say: "Let me explain things to you; I will discuss your doubts away." No, he says: "Turn around, repent! Lay the ax to your roots; get the weeds out and set your life to rights. If you want to believe, you dare not start with the problems of religion; you must begin with your neighbor.

Anybody who looks for Jesus Christ in heaven will never find him, for heaven is the very place he left in order to come to us. But anybody who is close to his neighbor suddenly discovers that he is meeting the hidden Savior and that He is sending *him*, for whose sake He suffered, across our path to greet us. The neighbor is the "third sacrament." In, with, and under the form of the neighbor, Christ is seeking to meet us.

So the Tempter sowed two poisonous seeds in Eve's heart. First, he persuaded her that one must not take God too seriously, because what he says is by no means a matter of life and death; and second, he made her distrustful of the goodness of God.

It may surprise us—but it is typical of the course of every temptation—that at this point the conversation *breaks off*. We do not hear that Eve immediately reacted to these insinuations by saying, "Yes, you are right, I have been taking God too seriously. I have been relying all too naïvely and simple-mindedly upon his goodness." No, the conversation breaks off; the poison must be given time to take effect. Besides, the Tempter is never fond of a static war of position; he prefers elastic tactics and a war of movement. So now like a fencer he suddenly changes his position.

Up to this time he has been playing with ideas, entangling Eve in a religious, philosophical discussion of the severity and goodness of God. Now he turns to a completely different area of the self, namely, to the senses and sensuality. But he knows that he has made a considerable dent in Eve's intellectual resistance by the preceding arguments and that in this state she can be completely upset by a small sensual titillation.

So he simply proceeds—as we have said, *before* the discussion about God is finished—to dangle the forbidden fruit before her. There it hangs in all its luscious fulness and Eve's eyes are sucked fast to it. Her mouth begins to water. "The woman saw," the text says, which is to say: she meditated on the fruit, she turned it over in her thoughts.

But is was not only the sensual tickling of her palate that enchanted her. It was also the secret with which this fruit was laden: the eating of it would make one wise. So the fruit exerted a sensual and an intellectual fascination.

What happens here can be illustrated by comparison with

sexual desire. This too is much more than mere sensual stimulation. It also seeks to penetrate the *secret* of the other person. At the bottom of all sexual desire there is a yearning to know. "Let me know your secret," says a love song, and in the Hebrew text the word for sexual desire is exactly the same as the word "desiring to know" (*jadah*).

So, under the pressure of this twofold curiosity, the fascination of the senses and the mind, Eve reached out for the fruit. And only as she did this, as she performed this practical act of disobedience, did she actually answer the serpent's question whether she was really going to take God so dreadfully seriously and whether she was really going to trust his goodness so utterly—answering it almost without being conscious of answering it. Now she is going to do "*neither* of these things any more. And therefore she commits the forbidden act. So now she has given notice that she is quitting—not officially, not formally, and not by flinging an emotionally charged and defiant No toward heaven—like Prometheus—but through one very small gesture, through one very harmless snatch of a tidbit.

I believe that the biblical story is far more true than the legend of Prometheus. I have never yet met anyone who raised his fist against heaven as Prometheus did and defiantly severed friendly relations with God. What I have experienced and observed has always been what is described for us here in this text, namely, that a person removes himself from God through nothing but little nonessential things and that even today the serpent operates with simple little suggestions. Unfaithfulness to God always begins at the periphery, just as here it begins at the extreme ends of the gustatory nerves.

I should say that this is generally what happens in our lives. I may have a good friend perhaps, with whom I have been closely associated for decades. But now he has a dreadful disease; he is confined to a wheelchair and is suffering from depression. He yearns to have me come and visit him and he clings to his friendship with me. But I myself no longer get anything out

THE BRIDGEHEAD OF THE TEMPTER

of these visits; they are only a burden to me. On the other hand, however, there are so many nice and healthy people who stimulate and uplift me and I would much rather be with them. As I picture to myself that somewhat depressing sickroom—I can, of course, allow my thoughts to revolve about what is repulsive quite as well as about the attractiveness of the apple of paradise! —I find all kinds of reasons why I should *not* visit my friend. I have no time today, and tomorrow Marlene Dietrich is singing on television. Thus the image of my sick friend grows paler and paler, and finally the visits stop altogether.

Now, if somebody were to ask me: "Tell me quite frankly, do you really mean by your conduct to sabotage the Christian concept of loving one's neighbor? Have you decided against the biblical principle that Jesus Christ desires to meet you in your sick friend?" I would blow straight up and reply: "What do you think you're saying! Of course I hold the 'Christian point of view' just as I always have; I consider the commandment of neighborly love to be the Magna Charta of all Christian ethics!"

And Eve would have answered in exactly the same way, if the serpent had asked her: "Do you want to become an active atheist? Would you submit a notarized statement, calling it quits with God?" Eve would have thrown up her hands in horror and given the serpent a proper rebuff. She was not prepared to draw any such far-reaching religious conclusions or make such a decision of faith. She allowed herself to be inveigled into doing a very small, unimportant thing, namely, to look at the apple a bit and finally to grasp at the succulent bait. After all, it couldn't be *that* bad. Why should it be?—God himself was not at all as serious as she had formerly thought.

And it is exactly the same with me when I fail to visit my sick friend. I have no intention of rising up against God when I neglect this, not a bit! But still I have my reasons: I'm a little short of time; it's a long way to go; there are always too many traffic lights on the road, and most of them are red.

And yet—I am denying God at the periphery, at the point of

a small, incidental kindness. But this sore eats its way irresistibly to the center. And one day I suddenly can no longer believe.

But then when I can no longer believe, I also seek other reasons for it. "Good heavens, that old Book!" I say to myself. "No modern person who has any respect for himself can swallow all that stuff." I almost always look for the sore spot in my life at the wrong place, and the idea never occurs to me that my faith and my peace of heart began to disintegrate when I eyed that *one* apple and when I kept away from that *one* doorstep of my sick friend.

So it always is; I don't like to get up five minutes earlier to read a Bible verse and pray. It's hard for me to get out of bed. And naturally, this is because I did more than my duty yesterday. So, you see, I have a respectable reason. Besides, on my bedside table is not the Bible, but my appointment book, which I look at the first thing in the morning, and believe me, there's plenty there to keep me busy. Naturally, I take my stand "on the basis of Christianity." I'll take second place to no one on that. But the strange thing is this: the first thing we reach for in the morning, our appointment book—and, dear me, what a harmless act that is—is something very like reaching for the forbidden fruit. In just such small things decisions are made of which we never dreamed. My formal assertions that I take my stand upon the Christian position are of scant interest to God, because they do not commit me to anything. The oaken beams of my alleged Christianity quickly collapse when they are eaten away on the inside by the little woodworms.

So the message of our text is this: Watch your periphery! For God is always to be found in the details of things. I have to do with him—and also with the Tempter!—at every point in my everyday life. God is in a harmless apple, on my bedside table, and the doorstep of my sick friend. The serpent always wriggles about the periphery first, but finally he will choke off the center of the breath of life.

But now it would be quite wrong—I must say something

about this yet in closing—if we were to conclude that therefore the devil has his seat in sensuality. In the New Testament we find, not only harlots and sadists, and thus sensual sinners, but also mental sinners: cultured intellectuals and scribes whose thoughts are entangled in vanity and delusions of greatness. But the senses are the point of entrance. Eve's mouth watered. And that was the beginning. But the Tempter would not have found entrance into the oral cavity, if he had not already held a bridgehead within her, if she in her heart had not already been halfway doubtful about the severity and the goodness of God.

In Eve's *heart* too there hung by a very thin thread an overripe apple of doubt. Even before, when she was still in contact with God, she may often have admired the apple. Then it did not matter to her, however. But now that she was at odds with God in the depths of her being, now that she no longer took him in dead earnest, one little glance was enough to seduce her. When the substance of our faith has been corroded, a breath of air or a covetous glance overthrows us.

This observation leads us to the profoundest secret of the gospel. That is to say, the gospel does not practice what the physicians call symptom-therapy. It does not subject us to moral cures and it does not enjoin us to be nicer, friendlier, more responsive to human needs, more hard-working, and more upright. True, it does point us to all these things *also*. But before it speaks of this, it tells us something completely different. It says that every cure must begin at the innermost center. Then the moral improvements follow of themselves; they are only an incidental effect.

But what is it that should happen in our innermost center? And again it is basically only one thing, and this really is the central thing: I must be willing to be told that God loves me and that he grieves over me when I go other ways.

To understand this I need only to look to Jesus Christ, who pursues those for whom nobody else cares and who also sees the misery behind the facade of human greatness. But this my misery does not annoy him but instead attracts him. He did not come to the well and healthy, but to the sick. He knows what is wrong with me. And this is precisely why he seeks me out. He seeks me so single-mindedly that he gives his life in the search. Even when he was dying he was thinking with solicitude and kindness of the tough customers beneath his cross. While they were bawling and brawling in an alcoholic haze, with no conception of what was happening right next to them, he was grieving for their souls: "Father, forgive them; for they know not what they do."

Is there any discovery greater than the discovery that someone cares for me? And that he does not reject me, even though he has seen through me utterly?

Once this miracle has dawned upon me, once I have grasped that such a thing is true, then the ice encrusted about my heart begins to melt and something like love begins to stir within *me*. As I begin thus to cling to Jesus Christ, I can no longer find it in my heart to hurt him. For I know that I cannot play fast and loose with my body and my thoughts, because this hurts him just as if I were to lay violent hands upon him himself. For I am his, and it grieves him as if it were a part of his own self.

When I am made new at this point, when I take my stand on the ground of this unheard-of new fact, then the Tempter has lost his bridgehead and everything is changed. How rich is the earth and how the trees in the Garden of Eden beckon to me, what joys, what merriment and mirth are given to me! I don't need to be a Puritan. I don't need to be a timid, anxious worrier. "All are yours," says the New Testament—really all, everything!—"and you are Christ's."

And when a person has a new heart he also sees things differently. When I discover the secret of being a Christian it is like a revolution of joy that sweeps over me. And—it is a thing that goes to the roots, not merely a passing breeze that fans the treetop. The ax goes to the roots, but the joy also sets in at the roots. Pain and bliss are woven together. Becoming a disciple is a whole thing and a fully rounded thing. It is simply great and thrilling and gladsome that there should be someone in this world who wants us, wants the *whole* of us and also makes us *wholly* new.

Cheap things can never do anything like that. The gospel is not cheap merchandise which you can take or not, or take along with something else. God really begins to move in my life only when I venture myself *wholly* upon him. A divided heart can only kill me. Faith divided by two equals fear and anxiety.

11

Guilt and Destiny

The Story of the Fall: Part Three

And they heard the sound of the Lord God walking in the garden in the cool of the day, and the man and his wife hid themselves from the presence of the Lord God among the trees of the garden. But the Lord God called to the man, and said to him, "Where are you?" And he said, "I heard the sound of thee in the garden and I was afraid, because I was naked; and I hid myself." He said, "Who told you that you were naked? Have you eaten of the tree of which I commanded you not to eat?" The man said, "The woman whom thou gavest to be with me, she gave me fruit of the tree, and I ate." Then the Lord God said to the woman, "What is this that you have done?" The woman said, "The serpent beguiled me, and I ate." The Lord God said to the serpent,

> "Because you have done this,
>   cursed are you above all cattle,
>   and above all wild animals;
> upon your belly you shall go,
>   and dust you shall eat
>   all the days of your life.
> I will put enmity between you and the woman,
>   and between your seed and her seed;
> he shall bruise your head,
>   and you shall bruise his heel."

—Genesis 3:8–15

Still there lingers in our ears from the preceding chapter the sound of the serpent's voice saying: "You will be like God, knowing good and evil." And we recall what he meant to imply by this—namely, that God doesn't want you to know anything. God wants to keep you ignorant. In other words, God is afraid of your knowledge. For knowledge is power. If you become powerful, God will fear your competition. He knows very well: "Once men wake up to the potentialities of their reason and once they explore these potentialities, it is all up with my being God. Then my time is up as Lord of creation. Then man will use what I have given him *against* me. He will burst all boundaries and set himself up as the dictator of the universe. But me he will relegate to retirement. He will make of me a fairy character of the world of childhood, he will make me the opium of the people or turn me into a religious ideology. He may turn me into a pathetic old man whose helplessness is so extreme that it is macabre, as in Wolfgang Borchert's *Outside the Door*."

All this the serpent implied by way of every possible innuendo. And I think that when he did this he touched upon a problem which nobody who thinks about the problems of faith with any intellectual alertness can ignore.

If I were to state the decisive problem without beating about the bush, it would run something like this: Is God really afraid of man's knowledge? Does faith in this God mean that I must forgo knowledge, that I must suppress knowledge? Can one then have faith—I am expressing this somewhat drastically—only if one is a bit dim, only if one is somewhat short on intellect? Is there something right about Marxism's thesis that religion has been dethroned by science and therefore the enlightenment of knowledge, once it has dawned, must necessarily banish the dimness and darkness of faith? *Either* faith *or* knowledge—is that the alternative?

But this is putting it much too generally and simply, since obviously there are two completely different kinds of knowledge.

There is a way of knowing which remains *under* God; and there is also a knowledge which is actually loaded with danger, a rebellious knowledge which is directed *against* God. The builders of the Gothic cathedrals had a knowledge of the laws of statics and the secrets of stress and tensions in their soaring arches. They allowed their architectural knowledge to "serve." For them it was the technical prerequisite for the fact that they were able to point symbolically—that is, by means of the glory of their cathedrals—to the ground and the goal of the whole world order, to that which is "above."

The builders of the tower of Babel also had the same knowledge. But *they* used it to build a this-worldly bastion, to secure man with a Maginot Line, and thus to keep God outside and far away.

There is also a medical knowledge of the health and diseases of the human organism. The physician who serves the Creator uses this knowledge in order to heal. The medical robots, however, of the kind enlisted by totalitarian systems, employ this knowledge to exterminate the enemies of their system or to devise subtle, psychiatric methods of torture.

Are we not aware of this ambiguity, this duplicity of knowledge everywhere today?

Is there any one of us who is so stupid that he has not yet remarked how true it is that there also exists in this world a rebellious, a plundered knowledge, a knowledge which is aggressively hostile to God? It is true that in times past—but how long ago that was and how naïve it seems to us now—it was thought that knowledge is power. The idea was that he who knows the laws of nature and understands how to utilize them can rule the world, that he is mightier than others who are ignorant. It was possible to hold entire colonial peoples in check with a few rifles and cannon. After all, the white man "knew" more than the colored peoples. Therefore he had power over them.

In the meantime it has become clear to us that this dogma "knowledge is power" is not *that* true. For our knowledge can become more powerful than we ourselves; it can actually make us impotent.

We see this in atomic science. Do we not know more about the atom than we are able to harness? Knowledge of the laws of nature enables man to bring down the energies of the sun to the earth and to build atom bombs. We have become so powerful that we can blow up our planet and deflect the moon from its cosmic orbit. We are afraid of what we can do.

So one can no longer simply say that man has gained power through his knowledge. On the contrary, one must say that our knowledge has become mightier than ourselves. Today we are even afraid that this knowledge of ours will kill us.

Why then do men build atom bombs when they do not really want them and are afraid of them? They do so because their fear of *one another* is still greater. And this fear of one another increases in proportion as they know that the other, the potential enemy, is powerful. That enemy can exterminate my country by pushing a single button. Therefore I too must have such terrible weapons as a counterbalance. So each keeps outbidding the other. This is what is called the arms race. Nobody knows where it will end. Nobody wants it, but everybody thinks they have to do it.

I have mentioned this because it makes clear a very important insight, namely, that the statement "Knowledge is power" is obsolete. Knowledge itself is no longer a problem to us. It keeps on advancing constantly—almost automatically—and we know how to secure it: by seeking and learning.

Nor is power a problem to us. We know the way to gain it, how to make nature subservient through technical means, how to change society, how to gain erotic power or social precedence. All this is no longer a problem, at least not a fundamental one.

But in its place a different and totally new problem has arisen. And this is the problem of the knower, the knowing man *himself*. He is afraid of his knowledge because he feels he is not equal to it, because he is too fragile and brittle to carry such a weight. And he is also afraid of his own kind. He has the uneasy feeling that all his knowledge and power is leading him into the unknown and that there will be no stopping there, no turning back, and no certain direction.

Formerly, men had dreams and visions of the future development of humanity. They envisioned a coming kingdom of peace and justice in which there would be no more need to work and in which technology would eliminate the drudgery of toil. These visions were called utopias and they constituted a foundation for optimism.

Today our writers are devising horrible nightmares: destruction of the world through atomic technology, dictatorships—as in George Orwell's *1984*—in which the wielders of power control the lives of their subjects by television, a world of artificially generated test-tube children and robots—as in Aldous Huxley's *Brave New World*.

Knowledge and power are no longer a problem. But the knowing man is an enigma *himself*. He is afraid of his own potentialities. We might even say that we live in an age of complete knowledge, but at bottom we no longer know *what* we know.

For, ultimately, what do we know—even though we know enough sociology to erect a welfare state and co-ordinate man into a system in which he is completely provided for—if we do not know why man exists, to what end he lives, the *meaning* of his life, and where his temporal and eternal fulfilments lie? Without such a commitment will not the end result be like a perfect machine, idling endlessly and producing nothing, a perfect emptiness that betrays itself in boredom and anxiety?

What good does it do us to have the medical knowledge of how to decrease infant mortality, prolong life expectancy, or even produce human beings artificially, if we have forgotten—in other words, if we have lost the knowledge of—the *theme* of this life which has thus been snatched from death or nonexistence? Without this knowledge, must it not inevitably become dead and empty again, must it not become purposeless and peaceless? Knowledge without faith creates anxiety; it is graceless. We have really lost the ground and goal of knowledge. Why is this?

Quite certainly because we are no longer bound to God and therefore have gotten ourselves into an incalculable adventure from which there is no exit. Quite certainly because we no longer know the One to whom we can entrust ourselves, the One who desires our good and thinks his higher thoughts concerning us. And this means that we have lost the theme whose variations our life was meant to contain and carry out.

The alternative "faith or knowledge" is therefore false to the very core. It would be nonsense to say that knowledge is evil. No, only *pirated* knowledge is evil. It all depends upon in whose name I want to know. Do I want to know in order to stage something like an eighth day of creation by launching Sputnik and thus quite literally supersede the Creator? Do I want to know in order to secure life at every point—against death, against care, against every eventuality? In other words, do I want to know in order to take charge of my own life and no longer have any need to trust God? Do we no longer want to sing:

> We plow the fields and scatter
>   The good seed on the land,
> But it is fed and watered
>   By God's almighty hand.

Do we want instead to produce also the growth of the seed ourselves, in order to boast: "All this we have accomplished, and this hypothetical 'God' has become obsolete"?

Do we want to know the laws of nature only because we want television sets, refrigerators, and automatic washers, indulging in the treacherous illusion that then life is complete? Take your rest, O my soul, now you are provided with comfort and diversion for weekdays and Sundays; the goal of your life has been achieved! Have we overlooked the ghostly hand, writing upon the wall of our life: "Weighed, weighed, and found wanting; missed the point—knowledge without grace"?

Have we failed to hear the voice saying, "This night your soul will be required of you. Who are you and where do you stand?"

That's the way it is with knowledge.

And our story describes exactly the same thing. The serpent insinuates to Eve: "I offer you more than God does, if you will only reach for the forbidden fruit of knowledge. I offer a knowledge that will make you independent and autonomous. Then you will no longer be dependent on God's patronage. Then nobody need tell you to 'commit your ways to him.' Nor will you need to say 'Thanks' when you partake of the fruits of the Garden of Eden on your table. You don't need to be obedient any more; nobody can put a curb upon you. Your knowledge will make you free and you will learn the tricks of this old Lord of creation. You will learn to concoct his recipes, and then you will run things the way *you* want them to go."

The serpent therefore did not simply offer Eve knowledge as such, but rather a particular kind of knowledge, namely, the knowledge that one can live without God. It was *this* poisonous fruit that Eve ate.

So the history of man's fall from grace began with something very small and quiet. The first acts of the drama are enacted only between God and man. The question at issue is whether man will remain within the limits set for him or whether he will be rebellious, whether he will commit himself trustingly to the hand of God or whether he will be suspicious and want to run his affairs by himself.

But now we see how the stage of events is widened, as it were, in the next chapters of this tale of the beginnings. We see that it is divided into two storeys, one above the other.

Whereas at first the action takes place in the upper storey and concerns what happened between God and man, in the intimate sphere of the religious life, in the next moment a dramatic episode begins to unfold on the lower stage where men are dealing with men.

And yet the play on the human level is precisely synchronized with the drama on the upper stage. When things go wrong between God and me, they also go wrong between me and my neighbor. (We have encountered this interrelationship before and we shall do so again.) These people in paradise lost their lack of embarrassment not only before God, but also before each other. They made themselves aprons and were ashamed. And soon Cain will slay his brother, soon the world order will be shattered and the Flood will come.

The first thing that happened on this lower stage of the theater was that Eve also proceeded to give her husband to eat of the wicked fruit.

And this again is the primal pattern of the sinful act which is constantly being repeated among us today. For the adulterer cannot do otherwise; he must seek to seduce others also to take this step or at least be intent upon certain manly conversations in certain companies. The thief secures accomplices. A human swine procures the magic wand of Circe in order to transform others into swine. A secret necessity inheres in sin: it must seduce, it must spread its evil seeds to the soil of other hearts.

Why is this so? Why does the compulsion to seduce belong as much to sin as contagion does to diphtheria or stench to filth?

My answer would be that it is because sin and separation from God always make us lonely and isolate us. We cannot endure this depressing loneliness with our conscience. And therefore we seek out the perverse companionship of others who are like us. And we strive for this companionship either by seeking out the company of dubious companions—and with the instinct of vice we are dead sure to find it—or we seek it by "seducing" others and thus making them too what we already are.

There is a very simple explanation for this. When I, as an individual with a blot on my escutcheon, live in a clean company, I feel that I am constantly being called in question; then this constitutes a steady attack upon my conscience. Naturally, I want to put an end to this state of affairs as quickly as possible or preferably keep it from occurring at all. On the other hand, if I live among my own kind and the others are just like me, then I feel I have some support. The dictum, "Others are no better than I am," is the consolation of all scoundrels. That's why I am compelled to drag the others around me down to my level; in other words, I must seduce them.

In this perverse way I hope to escape from my tormenting isolation, for in one way or another I *must* live in fellowship with others. If I have lost real and clean fellowship, I am compelled to make a pact with the devil or look for accomplices. If I am corrupt, then others must be corrupt too. For only so can they confirm me in the position I occupy, instead of calling me into question.

This is exactly what happened here in our story. Eve sought in Adam an accomplice.

It was frightening to walk about with the forbidden fruit in the garden all alone. Every branch of every tree whispered its question: You no longer belong to us, you have excluded yourself from the rest of creation. The accusation sprang at her even from the eyes of the beasts. "But if I have an accomplice, it will be easier; then my situation will be relaxed. Then I can say to God, 'Why do you reproach me? To err is human, all too human, God. Look, Adam fell into it too, he is no better than I am.'" Then the Father—so Eve probably imagined—would knit his brows thoughtfully and reply: "Yes, if such a breakdown occurs twice, then there must be some defect of construction in my creation. And if this is really so, well—I surely can't sell these two people down the river; I must be liable myself for this fault in construction."

This is precisely the calculation which Eve set up here. And fundamentally, this is the way we all figure. For example, if more than 5 per cent of a class fail an assignment, it is the teacher's fault. It can be reduced to a simple formula: 'Sin is a "breakdown." And the cause of the breakdown is a defect in the construction of creation which has gotten into it through no fault of my own. I personally am only an innocent victim of this breakdown. At bottom—but, of course, one dare not say it out loud—God is mainly at fault.

> To earth, this weary earth, ye bring us,
> To guilt ye let us heedless go,
> Then leave repentance fierce to wring us;
> A moment's guilt, an age of woe,

says the aged harper in Goethe's *Wilhelm Meister*.

This is the theme of the scene that now begins to be enacted.

At first, of course, it commences somewhat shamefacedly. As God walks in the garden in the cool of the day and calls out, "Man, where are you?" the pair hide themselves. At first they are by no means in such an arrogant mood as to dare to say: "Dear divine Father, there has been a breakdown, there is an error in your apparatus of creation. You've gone and let a beast like the serpent, like the impulse to evil, get into paradise. Besides, you've made another slip in putting into our hearts, not only good thoughts, but also little flaws like curiosity, distrust, and doubt. And now look at the mess: the apple is gone and here is the stem of it! We disclaim all responsibility. After all, *you* created the laws by which we must live our lives, you alone. So there you are!"

This is just what the pair do *not* say at first, though one might not put it past Eve, holding the philosophy she did. (I myself have slipped quite unconsciously into the slang of our everyday speech, because we are so dubiously familiar with this business of talking ourselves into and out of things.) Oh, no, at first they know very well that what they should really say was: "Before thee alone have we sinned; we cannot answer thee once in a thousand times; Lord, have mercy upon us." And they also know very well *why* they are slouching along and taking cover.

But, instead of confessing their sin and thus gaining a chance to experience in this way the mystery of grace, they set out on the age-old path of self-vindication; they settle down to play the classical game of passing the buck.

Adam comes up for examination first and he answers glibly; "The woman whom thou gavest to be with me—understand, the woman *thou* gavest to be with me—so it's quite clear who really pulled the trigger and who is the chief culprit—this woman who sprang from thy source, she gave me the fruit. What part in it did I play? I simply drew the consequences; all I did was to put the dot on the 'i' and bite into it—*c'est tout*—that's all!"

So the great game of passing the buck begins. Adam—you and I—we keep shifting the blame upon others, our neighbors, the conditions in which we grew up, or the opportunity which, as you know, makes the thief.

Eve does the same thing, she makes the next move in this game. "I didn't start this either, dear heavenly Father," says she. "It was the serpent whom thou didst put into paradise, he started the ball rolling and set off the chain reaction."

If God had pursued the questioning further, I have no doubt that the serpent too would not have been at a loss for an answer. He certainly would have replied: "Why should you call *me*, of all people, to account? Why talk to me at all? Weren't you, the Almighty, the one who made the devil and set him loose on earth? Wasn't it in your name that I became a devil? Wasn't I just carrying out your orders? After all, *you* are the one who is later going to have me harry Job and Dr. Faustus and make me play the role of Mephistopheles. But, if that's the case, *you* are the one who is responsible. Then you can't call either me or my victims to account. You, God, and you alone are the cause of the mischief. You're the one who pulls the strings in this wicked game."

It is rather illuminating, is it not, that here the serpent, of all people, should become the defender of man? Doesn't this in itself show that there must be something wrong with this game of passing the buck?

Well, we ourselves have made every move in this game. Every one of us at some time has said: "This *one* cursed passion, this *one* appetite that I can't control, this *one* blemish in my character —the fact that I am 'by nature' envious, jealous, sexy, or furiously ambitious—this *one* thing lies in my heredity or in the environment in which I grew up or in the constitutional character given to me, it lies in my erotic disposition. This *one* cursed, faulty power that is constantly getting me down lies in all these things, not in my own self. Certainly, in the last analysis I didn't make myself what I am. I didn't choose my parents, my genes, my blood. I complain against the unknown; and *if* there is a God, then he is this Unknown One, who is responsible. But as for me, I wash my hands of it."

And then come the tragic poets and the environmental theorists and the sociologists and the students of heredity and even some jurists, and they all blow the same horn: God sits in the dock, and man, this poor victim of a bungled creation, is the chief witness for the prosecution. The Garden of Eden becomes a tribunal. God has played out the role of accuser; now he must defend himself.

How, then, did evil come into the world, if it is God who made the world and if he made it rightly? This is the question that keeps troubling us.

We have already observed earlier how the myths solve this question. They say—we call to mind the story of the giant Ymir—that God made the world of curse-ridden matter. Even before the curtain rose upon the history of the world, prehistoric dramas were enacted. Murder and homicide went on between gods and men. These prenatal fatalities, these myths say, are actually inherent in the world as such. And these mischievous forces which are inherent in the very matter of the world—and thus not God's failures in construction, but rather the basic defects in the raw material of creation—are now constantly emerging and creating new faults and new mischief.

But we said, it may be remembered, that from the beginning Christian theology radically rejected the attempt of the myths to explain the fault in this way. Christian theology declares that God created the world from nothing and therefore that it was not created from curse-ridden matter.

But this only makes the problem of evil more enormous. For if evil is not to be traced back to the matter from which creation was made, what other conclusion can be drawn except that God himself, the Creator, is the cause of evil? For, after all, it cannot very well be charged to the nothingness from which the world was made. So God is the accused in Christian theology itself. What else?

One certainly cannot get out of this difficulty by saying that the devil, the serpent is there *too*, existing alongside God. In philosophical terms, this is to say that the ground of the world is dualistic. The evil in the world does not go back to God but rather to this underived principle of evil *alongside* of God.

But even this way out is barred to us, for the biblical text expressly says that the serpent was "more subtle than any other wild creature that the Lord God has made." So, according to the biblical view, the serpent is not the devil at all; the serpent simply turns up among the creatures, and thus within what God had "made."

But isn't this a dangerous conception? Doesn't this mean that evil came into the world through the act of creation itself? Did not the biblical writer get himself into a terrible corner here? Did he not cut off every possibility of going back and arriving at a mythical explanation of evil or of explaining evil by means of the idea of the devil, the Satanic principle?

Consequently, do not all the ways lead back to the dock where God is the accused? Do not all fingers point at him, is he not surrounded by a serried chorus of revilers who keep repeating this one refrain over and over again: " 'To guilt you let us heedless go,' you, and you alone. You, not man, should hide yourself in the woods of Eden. You are the one who should be accused by the mothers who lost their children in flight, the widows whose husbands molder in mass graves, the orphans who are growing up unprotected; you and you alone should be accused. You would do better to call yourself a bungler or just blind fate. Then at least we could play out our lives as a tragedy which we can do nothing about. Then at least we could drop this convulsive lying gesture of having to beat our breasts and keep crying out: 'Wretched man that I am! Who will deliver me from this body of death?' You are the one who made death and evil, you alone!"

I believe that we must pursue this line of reasoning to its bitter end and that we must not allow ourselves to be stopped by any pseudo-Christian dodges or pious stop-signs. Only when we drink of doubt to the last dregs will we be able to perceive the real message of our text.

The very point of this ancient story is that it shows us that we put the question wrongly when we ask how evil came into the world. That is to say, when anybody asks the question in this way he is diverting attention away from himself.

We had an impressive illustration of this after the collapse in 1945. Then the question was: Who was responsible for the millions of exterminated Jews, who was responsible for the brutalities of National Socialism in our own country and in occupied countries, who was responsible for Anne Frank, for the concentration camps, for Theresienstadt? Was not a people who would allow this bestial government to gain ascendancy among them dreadfully compromised? Was it not the fault of all of us that these hideous things could happen among us?

But then we began the game of passing the buck again and we asked the question: How did this evil come into our people? And we replied: It was the dictated treaty of Versailles that gave us the unemployed and the economic depression, that's what did it. . . . But back of that was the Wilhelmian militaristic big talk that evoked concern and finally the will to destroy in the Entente. And back of *that* again was the envy that others had of our German efficiency and back of *that* was the alleged or real national imperialism of the Bismarck era which drove others to feel that they were threatened. Back of *that* was the Prussian tradition and back of *that* was the Reformation with its submissiveness to authority. Luther, Frederick the Great, Bismarck, Hitler—this was the line of the game of passing the buck which was popular at that time.

So one might trace the game farther and farther back to Adam and Eve in paradise. Everybody else was guilty, everybody else had brewed the mischief except us, and certainly except me. So everybody set out to catch the original culprit, because nobody wanted to be the villain.

The historians combed the terrain of history with whole troops of scouts in order to discover earlier and earlier causes of the development of evil and to show that we are merely victims and not the principal culprits—in other words, in order to transform guilt into fate.

This is the crucial point: here "guilt is transformed into fate." In other words, anybody who raises the question of how evil came into the world is turning the question away from himself. He wants to find the *original cause* of evil. But an evil that is caused is no longer an evil; it is only a fate, an inevitable process.

So in the last analysis I am *not* looking for the cause of evil at all, though I may pretend to do so. I am rather trying to do away with evil by asking a question; I am saying that it just "happened." But if it just happened, then I am no longer the cause, but merely an effect of this fatal process, a victim of a tragic concatenation of events. I want to justify myself and divert attention away from myself.

There is only one condition under which I shall take seriously my own guilt—and therefore all evil—and that is when I am willing to say: "I and I alone am the original cause of it. I am the one who vented his spleen upon his neighbor. I am the one who lies and kills. I am the one who gives free rein to his wild passions and is ready to sacrifice his neighbor for a bit of advantage. I and I alone am the one."

In other words, when I face my heredity, when I contend with the bundle of nerves which I may be, I must be able to say: "This is I." This is the *mystery of our humanity*.

So there can be no answer to the question of how evil came into the world, because the question itself is wrongly put, and even more, because it is a shrewdly biassed question by which I hope to get myself off the hook. I want to "derive" evil from something else, and thus turn it into fate. I want to be a victim and not the accused. I want to shout "Stop, thief" and meanwhile go on stealing in happy innocence.

Therefore the most genuine moment in our story is not that scene in which Adam and Eve seek to "derive" their guilt, in which they keep fishing for causes and manipulating causality. By trying to derive their guilt in this way they are only searching for a lightning rod to deflect the judgment of God.

No, the most genuine moment in our story is that moment when the pair are hidden behind the trees, covering their shame and suffering the pangs of bad conscience, and knowing down in their hearts that they, and they alone, are the ones who are meant when God calls, "Adam, man, where are you?" We, and we alone, are worthy of the judgment. The great game of passing the buck which we try as a final act of despair is lost from the very outset.

But there is still one last important question. Was it not asking too much of them to expect them to give up this game of passing the buck and instead come to God in all frankness and confess: "Yes, it was I, and against thee only have I sinned"? Would it not have been foolhardy of them to abandon all self-defense from the start and simply come out from behind the bushes in the cool of evening and surrender unconditionally to God: "Do with us as thou wilt"?

The fact is that none of us could do this. We would have to resort to this trick of passing the buck just as our first parents did, we would have to go on lulling ourselves with dishonest, "tragic" illusions—if these words, "Man, where are you?" had not been spoken *again*, and this time in a totally different way.

For Jesus Christ too is calling to us, saying the same words. He too is searching for us behind the bushes and calling, "Man —my brother and my sister—where are you?" And at the same time he says, "I seek you, not to condemn you, but to save you."

And there they stand before us, the figures of men and women in the New Testament who simply fling aside this chessboard of the game of passing the buck and dare to say: "*I*, poor and unhappy man, I have caused thee pain and sorrow. *I* wrought the nails for thy cross. *I* fashioned the beams of that cross. *I* denied thee thrice. *I* did not visit thee when thou wast in prison. *I* did not give thee a cup of water when thou wast thirsty." There they are, all of them, standing before us, saying this—or something like this—to us: the publican, the woman who was a sinner, Peter after the miraculous draft of fishes, and Paul, who dared to confess: "I persecuted and killed thy disciples." And even as they said it they were already wonderfully free, for now they no longer needed to cherish any illusions, now there was no more need to pretend.

For they knew to *whom* it was they could say this and to whose hands they could entrust themselves; they knew it was the Savior. They could be honest with him, for they knew that he would never despise or reject them, no matter what they might be.

He who loves can heal, and this Man loved us. I can confidently put myself into hands that are kind and good. In the Garden of Eden were two people who defended themselves because God was their accuser.

But wherever Jesus Christ appears, everything is changed. Then it is my own conscience that accuses me, and Jesus Christ is my defender (Luther). And because he is my defender I no longer need to defend myself and make excuses. I no longer need to have any illusions about myself and I can give up the game of passing the buck. He protects me from my own conscience, for he says to me: "All that lies behind you and all the charges laid against you I have torn to pieces. I have nailed the tattered shreds of your life to my cross. Your past simply does not interest me any more. I am interested only in what I want to make of you. Accuse yourself, but trust that I will stick to you *even* when you despise yourself. When one dies for another, one will never give him up."

Here is where the game of passing the buck in our life *really* stops. And here too the question of how evil came into the world ceases to be asked. Not that the question is "solved." There can never be a solution to a question which is wrongly put. But I am delivered from having to ask the question.

Now all I can ask is: "Who is this mysterious Figure, who tears up the bill of indictment against me, who beats down the accusations of my conscience, who grants me a new, unburdened future, and lets me breathe freely again? Who is this Figure, who gives me courage to come out from behind the bushes and be honest with myself, who makes it possible for me to get along without tragic illusions?" "Dost ask who that may be? Christ Jesus, it is he."

"For I am sure that neither death, nor life, nor angels, nor principalities, nor things present, nor things to come, nor powers, nor height, nor depth, nor anything else in all creation, will be able to separate us from the love of God in Christ Jesus our Lord."

12

The Mystery of Death

The Story of the Fall: Part Four

And they heard the sound of the Lord God walking in the garden in the cool of the day, and the man and his wife hid themselves from the presence of the Lord God among the trees of the garden. But the Lord God called to the man, and said to him, "Where are you?" And he said, "I heard the sound of thee in the garden, and I was afraid, because I was naked; and I hid myself." He said, "Who told you that you were naked? Have you eaten of the tree of which I commanded you not to eat?" The man said, "The woman whom thou gavest to be with me, she gave me fruit of the tree, and I ate." Then the Lord God said to the woman, "What is this that you have done?" The woman said, "The serpent beguiled me, and I ate." The Lord God said to the serpent,

> "Because you have done this,
> > cursed are you above all cattle,
> > and above all wild animals;
>
> upon your belly you shall go,
> > and dust you shall eat
> > all the days of your life.
>
> I will put enmity between you and the woman,
> > and between your seed and her seed;
>
> he shall bruise your head,
> > and you shall bruise his heel."
>
> To the woman he said,
>
> "I will greatly multiply your pain in childbearing;
> > in pain you shall bring forth children,
>
> yet your desire shall be for your husband,
> > and he shall rule over you."
>
> And to Adam he said,

> "Because you have listened to the voice of your wife,
>   and have eaten of the tree
> of which I commanded you,
>   'You shall not eat of it,'
> cursed is the ground because of you;
>   in toil you shall eat of it all the days of your life;
> thorns and thistles it shall bring forth to you;
>   and you shall eat the plants of the field.
> In the sweat of your face
>   you shall eat bread
> till you return to the ground,
>   for out of it you were taken;
> you are dust,
>   and to dust you shall return."
>
> —*Genesis 3:8–19*

There is probably not one among us who has not now and then had the experience of being suddenly confronted by the dark enigma of life.

For long stretches, of course, we go on living our lives fairly innocuously, with no particular problems. Life simply pursues its course. We observe that evil does not pay, that success comes to the diligent, and that idlers finally come to grief.

But suddenly something happens that sounds like a broken axle in this smoothly rotating machine of life. We are confronted with a contradiction which we simply cannot explain. We read in the newspapers that an airplane has crashed with ninety persons aboard, fathers, mothers, and children. Among them is a great musician, an irreplaceable scholar. Some ridiculous little bolt or screw that came loose—it may perhaps have cost only a dime—was capable of silencing beautiful music, annihilating the promise of increased knowledge, destroying human happiness, and shattering the ties of love.

Are we not surrounded on every side with these dark enigmas, which are so hard to shake off, once they are discovered? Why is it that just when life reaches its supreme moments we should suddenly be overtaken by the dread of mortality and the fragility of life? Why do folk songs always link love and death? Why must the tragic poet always repeat this one refrain, that greatness in the world must go down to defeat and that glory must be crushed between the millstones of guilt and fate and end in sullen gloom?

> Are you proud of blooming cheeks,
> Aglow with milk and crimson?
> Ah, the roses die and fade away.

Why is this?

Is nature an exception to this rule? A lovely, wooded valley with a stream running through it may strike us as idyllic, but we have only to look a little closer or fetch a microscope to see that here too there is devouring and being devoured, the dread of death, and the groaning of creation. Ecclesiastes and Job, Sophocles and Heinrich von Kleist, Wilhelm Raabe and Gottfried Benn, and you and I too, each in our own way, have wrestled with this enigma. Everyone of us bears wounds and scars inflicted by the claws of this enigma.

Our text for today, which concludes the story of the Fall, paces the whole area of this enigma: Why should toil and the drudgery of labor exist at all? (On my trip to the Far East where I saw thousands of Egyptians on the Suez Canal and later Chinese coolies toiling in the scorching sun, I suddenly realized how immediate and real this question remains and how very superficially it is covered up by certain technological and social facilities.) Why should death exist? Why should the fate of men be like that of the beasts (cf. Eccles. 3:19)? Why cannot even the strongest love hold on to another when his hour has come? Why is the birth of new life accompanied by pain and dread and peril of death? Why do thorns and thistles encumber the fields? Why does frost fall upon the springtime blossom? Why should we be at enmity with nature, which, after all, was once the Garden of Eden? Why should the horror of infantile paralysis exist alongside of the miracle of new life? Always, always the question: Why? Why?

And this text of ours deals with these hard, harassing questions of life. It points to the background of it all, to the rift in the framework of the world and the contradictions we cannot reconcile. Many of us, perhaps, may say that it is useless to think about *why* life is as it is. They may advise us not to bore too long in the depths but rather get busy and stick to what is given to us to do each day. Goethe repeatedly counseled himself in this way and summoned himself to "action" whenever he was appalled by the fathomless depths of life.

But would not this be escape? After all, it is possible not only to be a coward physically—when a person fails, for example, to jump in to save a drowning man—but also a coward about certain thoughts and, as Goethe once expressed it, to "blink" them. But it will not be so simple to evade our text by blinking it, once it catches us and has us in its clutches.

To begin with, these primordial words of the Bible do something that is really tremendous. They take all these riddles of existence—from the mystery of death to the throes of a young mother and the misery of toil—and set them down within one mighty key signature, and then interpret them according to this one signature, which declares that all the contradictions and absurdities of life are manifestations of the creature's disobedience to the Creator. They reveal that the world is no longer whole and sound and that it has lost its peace because it has lost its peace with God.

In other words, the Bible does not simply say: "Well, that's the way life is!" Nor does it say: "Nature is cruel and that's all there is to it." Nor does it simply fall back upon the natural law of mortality, polarity, or the struggle for existence. Nor does it belabor the tragedy of contradiction. It says very simply and with an almost shocking straightforwardness that back of the suffering and back of the death in the world lies human *guilt*, and that therefore the only way I can come to terms with my lot is to come to terms with this *guilt* or else learn to know a court of judgment that will relieve me of it.

All this is, of course, a tremendous, breath-taking assertion.

It is a good thing that the Bible does not express this assertion in philosophical propositions. This would only result in endless discussion. It simply sets before us a few monumental facts of life and says, "Just look at these for a moment. Don't withdraw from the affair by saying that they are just myths. No, look at them for once!"

The greatest of these facts is *death*. And by speaking of it this primordial story confronts us with nothing less than the thesis that "the wages of sin is death" (Rom. 6:23).

Let us recall certain details of the story of the Fall.

God said to Adam and Eve, "You shall die if you eat of the forbidden fruit." And when they wickedly ate of it nevertheless, God said, "Behold, the man has become like one of us, knowing good and evil; and now, lest he put his hand and take also of the tree of life, and eat, and live for ever," God sent him out of the Garden of Eden.

So the curse of mortality settled down upon man.

This may strike us as nothing more than crude, embarrassing mythology. Perhaps all this leaves us quite at a loss. But before we interject and declare our doubt, let us force ourselves to listen for a moment longer and try to understand what is being said here.

The disobedience of man consists—we are given to understand—in the fact that he wants to be *superman*. He wants to "be like God." He is the notoriously Unbound One, and by no means only in certain peak examples and high fliers, like Prometheus or Napoleon or Hitler. No, he is *always* the Unbound. He establishes the welfare state and abolishes—or at least thinks he abolishes—the misery of human existence. He undertakes to provide for every life situation and plays the role of the divine father of all.

But is it not utter folly that he should imagine that he can really burst the bounds of afflicted humanity? Does he not merely shift the misery from outward poverty to inward poverty? Does he not cause men to be debauched inwardly with excessive prosperity, comfort, and boredom by inculcating the illusion that the peace of his soul is to be found in cars, television sets, freezers, and other miracles of civilization?

Man also desires to be unbound in his technology. He breaks the bounds of this ancient earth and reaches for the stars. And as he launches cosmic expeditions and grasps at realms which earlier generations considered reserved to God, he takes with him into the universe his peacelessness, his anxiety, and his hunger for power; perhaps he may still upset the stars.

So, since that dark hour in the Garden of Eden, this has been the story of us all. We want to be untrammeled. We want *more* than God the Lord has allowed to us. We want *more* success, *more* power, *more* money. If we are workers, we want higher wages. If we are employers, we want higher profits, if we are publishers, we want larger printings. Expansion must never cease. The first limit we encounter—it may be the limit of our physical strength, the limit our heart trouble allows us, the limit of some sudden disillusionment with people we trusted—staggers us. For we no longer take any limits into account, simply *because* we are unlimited. "If gods exist," said Nietzsche, "how could I bear not to be a god?"

Therefore I must also prolong my life; I believe all the humbug that any magazine blathers about some new hormone or cosmetic product which will make me live to a hundred and preserve the appearance of youth.

And then what happens—and this is the dramatic point in our story—is that this arrogant man who wanted no limitations put upon him, this man who wanted to snatch God's eternity for himself, who wanted to be immortal and like God, *has his limitations cast into his teeth.* "The man has become like one of us," the story says, "knowing good and evil." After he has nibbled at the tree of knowledge, he will also reach out for the tree of life and plunder the fruit of immortality. He will want to be unlimited in time, he will want to be eternal.

And therefore he is driven out of paradise and the burden of mortality is placed upon his back. In other words, the unlimited one is shown his limits, and the chains of time come clanking down upon this man who wanted to snatch eternity. He is hurled back into the realm of the finite, where there is such a thing as "finis," where one day my last hour comes and it's all up with me.

The fact that we must depart and that our life has a terminus is therefore a reminder that we are *only* men and not God. The fact that we must die and leave everything behind that we have made and loved and perhaps also idolized is a part of judgment. In this judgment there flames the reflection of a divine flash of lightning that says: "Thus far shall you come, and no farther, and here shall your proud waves be stayed!"

In Japan one can always see from tremendous distances the majestic, snow-capped pyramid of Fujiyama. And so it is with us: the death we are approaching stands like the landmark of Fujiyama above the landscape of our life and makes life a "being unto death."

This "being unto death" is far more and also something different from our last hour, which we Christians talk about perhaps far too much. For death is present not only at the end of our life but is there long before, in every moment of our life.

Why do we keep hastening at our work? Why do we say: I must make the most of my youth? Why do we think: Now we are in our best years, now is the time to get it done? Why do we use calendars and clocks? Behind such very ordinary phrases and facts stands the appalling circumstances that hour by hour we realize that we must die, that we have only a limited time. Today will never return again. "Everything passes, everything passes away," says a popular song, and for once it is right. " 'Tis but the time and drawing days out, that men stand upon," says Shakespeare. Even the physician who struggles to preserve life fights this battle in the shadow of death. He may fight a delaying action but he cannot conquer death, and in the end he himself will be snatched away.

So it is indeed; we see the Fujiyama of our death wherever we stand. This flaming barrier, at which the cherub stands with his flashing sword, cannot be overlooked. Arrogant, unlimited man, who would seize eternity, is hurled back behind the barrier of time.

Only now that we have spelled out the text to this extent dare we come forward with our doubts and objections. Let me repeat these doubts once more quite boldly and revert once more to the questions we asked before. Is what we have just said sheer mythology or perhaps even very sinister mythology? Is not death, instead of being a judgment, a purely biological process? Is it not caused by the dehydration of our cells and the natural wear and tear of the organism? Are not birth and death expressions of exactly the same rhythm of life which we observe in spring, summer, autumn, and winter? And is not death merely the final beat in this rhythm of life?

At first sight this looks very plausible. And yet it must strike us as significant that a physician hardly ever dares to tell a dying man that he is now facing a very natural process. If these things are really so terribly "natural," why not call a spade a spade? Why must one stage these camouflage and diversionary maneuvers? Is there perhaps something more than—and something quite different from—this natural process behind the act of dying?

Not long ago I read again the following account in the diary of a young flier who fell in the war.

He was gathering a bouquet of lilacs. As he parted the branches he saw beneath the flowering bush the half-decayed body of a soldier. He drew back in horror—but not because he had never seen a dead body before. On the contrary, in his young life he had seen far too many. He recoiled because of the screaming contradiction between this dead man and the flowering bush. If he had only come upon a withered lilac bush he would not have been horrified. After all, a blooming lilac bush sooner or later will become a withered lilac bush—this is really an expression of the rhythm of life. But that a *man* was lying there in a decayed state, was something that would not harmonize with blooming nature. That's why he recoiled. He sensed that this dead comrade was something contrary to the Creator's plan of life. He felt that this dead man was a foreign body in God's flowering world. There came over him the feeling that the death of man is an unnatural thing. And this young flier with his shock of horror was certainly nearer to the world of the New Testament and its message than the people who are always driveling about the "naturalness" of human death.

When Jesus Christ heals the sick and raises the dead the fundamental thesis behind these acts is that sickness and death should *not* exist. These things are physically unnatural—in a deeper sense than the purely biological sense; they are contrary to the intention, the conception of creation; they are not order but *disorder*.

So for the Bible death is not simply a part of nature. Rather the natural processes—which, of course, the Bible does not deny —are only the vehicle in which the "last enemy" drives about. Therefore all this unnaturalness, this disorder, this "wrongness" in the world must give way when Jesus Christ comes and lays our hand again in the hand of the Father.

Then, of course, the biological processes of death still go on. But the judgment is gone. Then death acquires, so to speak, a different quality; it ceases to be a hostile barrier let down between time and eternity which violently hurls us back into our finitude. Now death becomes a bridge, a transition.

To understand this one must sit down and read the funeral hymns of our church:

> Through sin and death he strides,
> Through this world's grief he rides,
> He strides through hell's dark tide;
>   Where'er he goes,
>   I too abide.
> He keeps me by his side.

So sang Paul Gerhardt. This is what is meant by the statement that death has lost its sting. Then death is no longer a judgment that compels us to leave all; then it becomes the joy of going back home. For now my Lord awaits me on the other side of the dark grave and he leads me from faith to sight, from this world where we see in a dim mirror to the table of the Father.

> Could the Head
> Rise and leave his members dead?

That's the way it is with death now.

When I say "I have to depart," then the values and the things of my life—my house, my garden, my stamp collection, my vocation—are the standard by which I measure the departure. But when I can say, "I am going home," then there is a point in my life where even the greatest things become an insubstantial shadow and I see only the shore of home where I am awaited.

True, this presents many questions and here I cannot even attempt to make the roads of thought any easier to follow. The power of this truth is so great that there is no way to approach it except by bowing in reverence before the mystery of it.

And yet I might ask: even when we look upon death as being primarily a natural event which we can reduce to biological formulas, do we not perceive that this leaves an insoluble remainder, a mysterious unknown factor? Must we not agree with what Alfred E. Hoche, the psychiatrist, says in his well-known autobiography[1]—and he certainly is not saying this in defense of any biblical texts: "Man cannot understand his death. To him the thought is intolerable that this whole world of love and friendship, this world of work and devotion should be simply wiped out, intolerable simply to fall by the wayside, while others go on, chattering as if nothing had happened. . . . This mocks all logic."

As a matter of fact, it cannot be reconciled with any biological categories either, for here we encounter the unknown factor of which the Bible speaks when it points to the judgment which constitutes the background of our finitude.

[1] *Jahresringe*.

Always, when I stand at the grave of a person whose life was filled with meaning, who loved and was loved in return, a rebellious feeling descends upon me. Here is a person who was bound to human fellowship with every fiber of his being, he may also have been at peace with God, and here he must depart hence "like a beast." Must death be? *Must* this limit, *must* this abyss continue to exist, if one is in the hands of a living God? This is the protest against death that rises up within us, if we have any conception of what man was *really* destined to be. We can understand Hölderlin's complaint in *Hyperion:* "May God pardon me, but I cannot understand death existing in his world."

None of us can understand the exultation that rings in the New Testament accounts of raisings from the dead and of the resurrection, none of us can comprehend the splendor that hovers over the fifteenth chapter of I Corinthians, if he has not seen this dark foil in the background.

To be sure, even here in this story of the beginnings we can already perceive the first flickering of the promise, which the message of the resurrection will later make explicit, and we find it in a very discreet, almost hidden thought. God had forbidden man to eat of the tree in the midst of the garden with the threat: "In the day that you eat of it you shall die." And now man *had* eaten of it, and the lightning bolt of judgment struck beside him in the ground which would henceforth bear thorns and thistles, and it also struck the serpent. Thus the sentence of death did *not* overtake man on the spot. Instead of dying at once, the fate of mortality was imposed upon him. He is thus allowed to go on living, though in the *shadow* of death. He was granted a reprieve.

So in the midst of judgment the hidden mystery of grace is at work.

And again the promise arches over to the New Testament, where all this is enlarged and where it becomes more graphic and vivid. The barren fig tree is not immediately hewn down, but is given another year of probation. The clock of our life is turned back once more, in order that even today we may "know the things that make for peace." "This night your soul is required of you," says the Lord in the story of the Rich Fool. Who am I, where do I stand? The point is: In the *coming* night will my soul be required of me. Today I am still allowed to live. Today I can still answer the question whether I am content with my filled barns, my success, my comfort, my reputation and prestige—until suddenly it all forsakes me!—*or* whether I shall make my peace with God and set the whole course of my life toward homecoming. Today I can still watch for him to whom one day, when I shall have to depart and yet will be going home, I shall be permitted to say: " 'If one day I must depart, depart thou not from me.' Thou art he who came in to this passing world of mine and endured for me the powers of sin and suffering and death. Thou wilt be my comrade and brother now that my time is up and I must go through the gate, alone and without any baggage, where not even my most beloved can pass, except thee, who art the Lord of both time *and* eternity."

So Adam must leave paradise. For every one of us it's in the past. And only fools think that it can be re-established on this earth. As a rule, those who have promised men a heaven on earth have made of life a hell. No, the cherub stands behind us and there is no road back. We were never promised that the burden of mortality would be removed from us.

But Adam, all of us, you and I are permitted to go on living for a space. In the midst of the darkness of suffering and death, which we ourselves have conjured up, God will let his sign of grace shine, to proclaim to us: "Behold, I have not forgotten you; I have loved you with an everlasting love, and I will be the star for you to gaze at, the spring from which you may drink, and the peace that will cover you like a protecting mantle in all the strife of earth." So he made the rainbow of reconciliation to shine above the storms. So he gives to us the laughter of a child, the encouraging word of a friend, the healing of an illness, the return from prisoner-of-war camp. Again and again the towers of the Father's house suddenly light up as we tread the dust of the far country. The Savior walks beside us on the refugee's road, for he himself was homeless and had nowhere to lay his head. He lies beside us in the hospital ward, for he too was stricken and smitten. And yet at the same time he is the Physician who heals us.

That's the way God's judgments always are when they bring hardship and darkness into our lives and we "have to depart." Even in the deepest darkness the kindly, beckoning hand that is calling us home can be seen.

The other judgments of which our text speaks point to the same mystery, for the question of death slumbers in every experience of life. When a child is born this is accompanied by pain; these are sore moments and death is not too far away. What was once wrapped in the Creator's blessing of fruitfulness and a symphony of joy, this too has become an ambiguous thing, shifted to the boundary of darkness. Whenever new life comes into being there is pain and dread and the beating of the wings of death is heard. Thus Eve is told: "In pain you shall bring forth children." And in the symbol of the subjection of the woman there is also a reference to the servitude and slavery which will prevail in our world.

But here too there slumbers a hidden blessing wrapped in darkness. The pangs and oppressions of our life keep reminding us that "this poor earth is not our home" and that we are waiting for a new heaven and a new earth in which there shall be neither mourning nor crying nor pain any more, and every tear shall be wiped from our eyes and the last enemy has been robbed of its power. How many of us would give up the darkest hours of suffering in our lives, now that we look back upon them; the hours of utter hopelessness as prisoners of war, the hours of failure in our work, the hours of painful farewell? Would we ever have learned how God can comfort, how faithfully he remembers us, and how punctually he fulfils his promise? ("When comes the hour, comes help with power.") Would we ever have learned this, if we had not sat in darkness and the shadow of death? God's stars are seen only from the deepest wells, and we learn that he hears us only when we cry to him from the depths.

So we are surrounded on every side by signals and beacons. They keep flashing the message that there is One who is determining the course of our life, that he is guiding us home, and that we shall never be left alone in the fog that veils the coming day and in the storms we dread.

Often we do not know the meaning, but we believe in Him who does know the meaning. This is the secret of our Christian life. And with it we walk straight through the enigmas of life.

Never can we say: "*Because* certain conditions are such and such, certain things happen to me." We'll never get by with that answer. It sticks in our throat, doesn't it, when we think of the millions who died in the last war, the subterranean terror in the cellars and bomb shelters, the stricken women and children? The fact is that we do *not* know why this had to be; but now we can say: "I will abide with Thee."

For just as our own death is not merely a biological process, so the great mass deaths are not mere historical processes which mechanically unfold according to pitiless, eternal laws. No, there is a heart that watches and cares, and everything must pass in review before that heart before it comes to me. There is a secret censor and no stroke of fortune which would strike us can get past without being examined to see whether it will be for our good.

Therefore *what* we meet with in our life is not so terribly important; the *only* important thing is whether we accept it as coming from God's hand and whether we dare to trust that it was made to measure—your measure and mine—and therefore is exactly right.

> Lord, send whate'er thou wilt,
> Joy or sorrow, either one;
> I dare to trust that both
> Come from thy loving hand.

Is it not strange that the Christians on the sinking "Titanic" sang, "Nearer, my God, to thee," and so lost their fear of drowning in the icy Atlantic? The point is that they did *not* sing, "Farther away are now the golden jewelry in my cabin, the precious documents in the ship's safe; farther away are my loved ones at home, farther than thousands of geographical miles—for now I must leave you for ever." No, this is not what they sang or thought. It was not sad leave-taking and passing farther away; it was a coming nearer: "Nearer, my God, to thee."

It is not necessary to go down with a ship or to be mortally sick or to find ourselves in a "boundary situation" or to be on our last legs in order to make this avowal, "Nearer, my God, to thee." We still live in the light; perhaps life still lies before us. We rejoice in our home, the splendor of autumn leaves, a beautiful picture, the sound of music. It would simply be pride and pious snobbery to want to brush all this aside as "worldly pomp." This would be not to honor the Giver of all good gifts but rather to offend him.

But we must not cling to these things and get caught in them. Instead we must find our way through the things which can be so fascinating and delightful in life—but *also* through the burdens and trials we have to bear—to Him who gives us all things, both good and hard, and in both is saying: "I know you. You no longer need to depart hence 'like a beast'; you can come home 'like a child.'"

So he blesses the flush and flower of youth and comforts the loneliness of age. He lays his hand upon the little ones, and upon us too when the end draws near. He sends us the happy, starry hours of life, but he is *also* beside us in the dark valleys with his rod and staff and the marvel of his consolations. He always blesses. He is always near; and he changes everything—everything.

THE STORY OF CAIN AND ABEL

13

The Cain Within Us

The Story of Cain and Abel: Part One

Now Adam knew Eve his wife, and she conceived and bore Cain, saying, "I have gotten a man with the help of the Lord." And again, she bore his brother Abel. Now Abel was a keeper of sheep, and Cain a tiller of the ground. In the course of time Cain brought to the Lord an offering of the fruit of the ground, and Abel brought of the firstlings of his flock and of their fat portions. And the Lord had regard for Abel and his offering, but for Cain and his offering he had no regard. So Cain was very angry, and his countenance fell. The Lord said to Cain, "Why are you angry, and why has your countenance fallen? If you do well, will you not be accepted? And if you do not do well, sin is couching at the door; its desire is for you, but you must master it."

Cain said to Abel his brother, "Let us go out to the field." And when they were in the field, Cain rose up against his brother Abel, and killed him.

—*Genesis 4:1-8*

The sound and healthy world of creation now lies behind man. The cherub with the flaming, slashing sword sees to it that there is no returning. The logic of events which follow from one great, initial wrong decision goes on ineluctably working itself out. From the plucking of the forbidden fruit there now develops Cain's fractricide, and already the first stones of the tower of Babel are being gathered together.

What now commences—at precisely the point which marks the boundary of the intact world and closes it off to the rear—

we call "world history." It is the space into which we are "thrown"; the space in which Cain lifts his ax and Abel falls lifeless to the ground; the space in which creatures fight to the death for a place in the sun, in which the stronger triumph and right is threatened by power; the space in which, according to Goethe, the battle between belief and unbelief is fought out and in which the miracle men of history, the "world-historical individuals" rise from the abyss to "conquer half the globe" and then fall back again into the depths from which they came.

The history of the world is the space in which Cain's ax finally becomes dynamite and phosphorus, hydrogen explosions and space rockets.

One must pay very careful attention in order to catch the precise second in which world history began to unfold. This initial impulse, the direction the first movement takes will determine the curve of all future events. This terse, age-old story of Cain and Abel is the pattern for everything that we can see in ourselves and all around us. He that is able to find the key to this extremely concentrated extract of history will find that nothing human and also nothing divine is any longer alien to him.

Therefore we must proceed with utmost caution. As in the case of the story of the Fall, we shall not be able to dispose of it in one onslaught and we shall have to make several attempts to find a path through the primitive rock of the story of Cain and Abel. But once we have traversed this massif, we shall know ourselves better than before and more easily find our way through the terrain of our own lives.

If you read the story of Cain and Abel only halfway through, you expose yourself to a shock. For, without any reason being given, we are suddenly and abruptly told that "the Lord had regard for Abel and his offering, but for Cain and his offering he had no regard." We search in vain for what the lawyers call a "basis for judgment." There must be some reason, some motive for God's strange reaction of approval of Abel and rejection of

Cain! Was Abel perhaps a highly moral and religious man? Was Cain a questionable character, a secret rebel?

Perhaps, but we are not directly told that this is so. We have only this account written in the tersest telegram style. Only the skeleton of events is indicated and this bony structure is not clothed with even a modicum of narrative flesh, much less a fatty deposit of epic breadth. And search as we may in this archaically spare account for clues which might explain God's attitude, we find none at all at first, for everything said of both the brothers seems to be run on precisely parallel lines.

Both come from the same parents, and thus have, to express it in modern terms, the same heredity. Both pursue a solid, steady, we might say, elemental, vocation: the one is a farmer, the other a shepherd. Both approach an altar and perform a religious act of worship. One may also assume—though this is not explicitly stated—that each of them brought the choicest offerings from their own spheres of work, Abel the best sheep of his flock and Cain the richest fruit of his harvest.

But all this is only suggested by dotted lines and is not emphasized. It is only the overture to the first scene we see when the curtain actually rises: the one is accepted and the other rejected. Abel departs with a blessing. But Cain's countenance falls and he begins to brood and devise mischief.

At the altar of God, in the midst of devout worship, the threads of fate became entangled in the first knots, and the process never ceased until nets and snares were formed. Later on it will be said concerning the end of history that judgment will begin "with the household of God" (I Pet. 4:17). The unfaithful church and the idolatrous altars, from which curse instead of blessing, confusion instead of salvation has gone forth, will be the *first* to be visited by the wrathful judgments of God.

Anybody who has any instinct at all for what is weird and uncanny senses that something appalling is being said in this ballad of Cain and Abel and that here allusions are being made to the deep hinterlands of the world. There is the sound of some dark strain here which we must pursue and examine.

In the first place in any case, when we think of the absence of any basis for God's judgment, we are faced with the question whether everything depends on whether a person happens to suit or not to suit God. Was there some reason why Cain did not "suit" God?

There is a voice within us which is inclined to agree with this melancholy question. After all, don't we see it being confirmed all around us in life?

There are people who are good and decent in their way, but they have no luck. In examinations they get the very question for which they have not prepared. When they drive a car they are always hitting the red lights. And of all the nice girls they meet, they always get stuck with "plain Jane." They are always out of luck. Could this be the type that does not suit God and whom he allows to flounder about?

And then again there are other people for whom everything runs smoothly. Their children get only A's in school, they never have to go to the dentist, and all they have to do is smile and everything falls into their laps. Apparently they are the good Lord's Sunday-children who suit him very well. "For some are in the dark and the others in the light." *The Three-penny Opera* has plenty to say about this sad way of dividing things up.

But is this really all the Bible has to say about the freedom of God, that freedom which supposedly permits him to do as he pleases and thus indirectly suggests that God is merely capricious? Do the manger in Bethlehem and the cross on Golgotha, do the Lord's Prayer and the Lord's high-priestly prayer really have nothing more to proclaim than this one hard, distressing fact that God can do what he wills, that he chooses Abel as his favorite and has a grudge against Cain? This is hardly possible. But then what is the case?

A first bit of light upon the mystery of this strange circumstance may lie in the fact that the names Cain and Abel have meanings which are revealing.

Cain means "I have gotten a man." Thus Eve, the proud mother, suggests that this son will bear the dignity of being the first-born and that for her he is to be the quintessence of power and strength.

Abel on the other hand means something like "nothingness, frailty." The younger brother is thus overshadowed by the elder from the very beginning. He is destined to play second fiddle. He is the representative of those who get the short end of the stick. He is the typical *declassé*.

Everything that subsequently builds up into dramatic tension and finally explodes in the catastrophe of fratricide ultimately derives from this inequality of the roles in which Cain and Abel and all others find themselves: the fact that some have favorable chances to begin with and like Cain are provided with the privileges of the first-born, whereas others grow up in the shadows and are nobodies.

Did Eve do right in thus determining the unequal destiny of these two in the very cradle by showing favoritism and discrimination? Well, the fact is that now Eve is acting outside of paradise; she is the mother of world history—and, after all, this is the way of the world. Even the greatest deeds have a hidden dark side, and the seeds of horror spring up with others in the dreams of every budding life.

So from the beginning Cain grew up with the suggestion that first rights in everything were his due. The will to power and the egotistical self-assertion which were in his blood and ours too—for we are all the children of Cain!—appear to him to be perfectly legitimate. For him Abel is by no means his neighbor, who has his own rights in life. For him Abel is neither a partner nor even a brother, but simply exists to be used: "I, Cain, am the star, the privileged one; but Abel is simply an extra on the stage. Abel is of interest to me only in so far and as long as he serves my career, as long as I can make a profit out of him. Apart from this—that is, as a 'man'—he is nonexistent, he is a 'negligible quantity.'"

The figure of Cain really speaks volumes. It is actually a

symbol. It blabs out all the callousness, contempt, and cynicism toward our neighbor that lies hidden in *my* heart too. For I too have within me the Cainitic urge to make myself the center and appraise all others only by whether they are useful or harmful to me. I am a small-scale Machiavelli, for whom all men are classified as either friends or enemies and the face of my neighbor threatens more and more to disappear.

Of course, at first all these feelings take place in secret. Apparently Cain himself did not realize what was happening inside of him. It took time until these secret tongues of fire in his heart burst into open flame.

At first the two still went together to their altars. Even Cain was not a godless man; he was a man who attended to his cultic duties. But what does that count for? Were not the scribes and Pharisees in the temple too? Did not the Renaissance popes celebrate mass? May it not be that many a regular churchgoer, who says "Forgive us our debts, as we forgive our debtors" when he utters the Lord's Prayer, really does not want his sins forgiven, because he has no desire whatsoever to recognize his sins? May it not be that he is by no means prepared to forgive the person who has injured or cheated him, that on the contrary he is actually pouring more oil on the flames of his hatred and thus even desires this fire in his heart and in a perverse way enjoys it? There is such a thing as getting a sensual pleasure from hate!

So what does it mean, after all, that Cain should come to the altar! Our wicked heart is quite capable of devising mischief even in holy places, and as we sing hymns the wolves may be howling in the cellars of our souls.

While Cain is making his sacrifice he may perhaps have been far away from God.

He considers it quite natural that God should recognize him, that he should confirm him in his role as the stronger one. He thinks, perhaps, that it must be so that God is on the side of the heaviest artillery, the biggest cars, and social superiority. And likewise it is no problem to him that *God's* scale of values should also assign this Abel to the category of an "also ran." For just as Cain expects that *Abel* will dance to his tune, so he also expects the same of *God*. God is supposed to dance when Cain pipes. For somehow God has become for Cain a kind of celestial functionary who must execute exactly what Cain desires and what is right according to his standard of values, and thus according to what will make him feel confirmed in his own position.

And in this too Cain is an example par excellence of all men. When God takes the liberty to do something which we do not understand and which goes against the grain, we are immediately ready with the question—and we have already met with it in many variations—"How can God permit such a thing?"

Job, for example, considered that it was right for the good to prosper and the wicked not to prosper. As long as God conformed to this favorite idea of his, to his conception of a moral world-order, he was all right. But the first time God did something that did *not* fit into this system of co-ordinates, when his children died, his house burned down, and his flocks were destroyed, he went on strike and withdrew into the sulking corner of the religiously disappointed.

When the pastor in Ernst Wiechert's novel, *The Jeromin Children*, comes to the point where he no longer understands the catastrophe of war and the excesses of inhumanity and is unable to reconcile all this with his conception of a just God, he shakes his fist at the crucifix. Instead of the hand of God, which supposedly holds the reins of the world, he sees only the hands of specters, and he says to a young person, "He *is* not, he *was* not, he never *will be*. Not the way it is written."

When God's thoughts are *actually* higher than our thoughts, we regard him as being refuted. For under all circumstances we want *our* thoughts to be the program according to which God operates. But the fact is that God is constantly *refuting* our human, all-too-human image of him. We, however, consider him refuted.

So Cain stands before the altar of God with a godless heart.

God isn't acting in accord with his program—any more than He acted according to Job's program. He reacts differently from what Cain expects and considers right.

According to Cain's expectations, the smoke of his offering must rise to heaven like a sublime mushroom cloud. This was, in fact, an ancient sign that God gratefully accepted a devout sacrifice. But in Abel's case, thinks Cain, considering his inferior station, there will be only a thin, fleeting bobtail of smoke which will go creeping and cowering along the ground. But it is just the opposite. The smoke of Abel's sacrifice rises up to heaven and Cain's offering is not accepted.

Thus God turns Cain's scale of values upside down. Consequently God is someone whom one must hate, for he permits himself to cancel out our calculation. Or consequently God is someone who doesn't exist at all. For, after all, what kind of an alibi does God have to offer? How can anybody exist who contradicts everything that I think makes sense? "He is not, he was not, he never will be. Not the way it is written," said the pastor in *The Jeromin Children* when he no longer could make sense of God.

"So Cain was very angry, and his countenance fell." Now we know who it was against whom he was protesting with distorted countenance. It is none other than God, for God cut straight across everything that Cain thought was right. God failed to give him the self-confirmation he desired.

Up to this point all this, if I may express it in pointed terms, is still confined to the "religious sphere." These are still only the first stages of a story of rebellion. But in the very next moment this hidden drama between Cain and God spills over into the realm of external realities and human relationships. Renunciation of God brings with it renunciation of the brother. He who hates God also hates his neighbor. The form this hatred takes is envy. Cain is cankered and corroded with jealousy.

We must consider for a moment what envy has to do with godlessness.

We moderns tend to psychologize everything and thus render it harmless. For us envy is something like a complex, like any other kind of inferiority feeling, which may possibly go back to a traumatic experience in our youth. In reality, however, much more than that happens when we are jealous. And since jealousy is an elemental process within us, since it can be a shattering, tormenting, destructive thing, we must take a good look at it.

What is jealousy?

When I am jealous I no longer see the other person as a "human being," as someone whom God has put in my way just as he is and furnished with particular gifts and accomplishments. I see only something *about* him, and most often something external. Perhaps I see in the other person only the owner of a car, while I go on pedaling a bicycle. Perhaps he may only have a bigger car than I, or his child has a doll that can open its eyes and say "Mama" whereas mine plays with a cheap thing from the five-and-dime—and is very happy with it! Or my neighbor has a better brand of vacuum cleaner, or my fellow worker has a workbench closer to the window. Or an assemblyman counts the number of lines reported in the press after every speech and is irked if his opponent is able to garner an average of a dozen words more than he does. Or a movie queen looks to see whether her pictures in the magazine are a quarter of a centimeter smaller than those of her rival. Or Cain watches to see whether Abel manages to make a higher annual profit with his flock than he—Cain—does with his cultivation of the soil.

It is incredible what trifles will kindle jealousy and how terribly I degrade the person of whom I am jealous, insofar as I look upon him only as the bearer of such trifles. I can literally grind myself to pieces with these petty, superficial differences in prestige. And all it does is rob me of my night's sleep. And meanwhile I no longer see the other person at all. All that he is to me—and how terrible this is!—is a representative of some petty, insignificant advantages.

I once realized the extent to which our neighbor actually disappears as a real person when someone who was jealous came to me and said, "Look, I always have bad luck, though I exert myself far more than Mr. Jones does and I have just as good a head as he does. But Jones always draws the winning ticket. His kids are always getting prizes in school while I have to spend good money to send my brats to an out-of-town school. And I'm always having bad luck with my personnel. But Jones has workers who are as good as gold. After all, anybody could get somewhere with people like that; that's no trick at all." And so the tale of woe went on.

Finally, with all this everlasting drawing of comparisons, "his countenance fell," just as Cain's did.

I then said to him, "So you would like to exchange for a lot of things that Jones has?"

"You can say that again," he replied.

"But look here, my dear fellow," I went on, "whenever such exchanges are made you have to take the whole thing. So I ask you, would you want to trade with Mr. Jones in every respect, really *everything?* His marriage, his health, his age—he has already had his first heart trouble!—his temperament, his convictions, his faith?"

He looked at me somewhat taken aback and then said, "Perhaps I wouldn't trade with him in *every* respect, because I don't know him well enough; I wouldn't know *what* all I'd be getting out of the deal that I'd be stuck with."

"Look here," I said in closing the interview, "you are devoured by jealousy, but you are only envious of something *about* Mr. Jones. And you have only been seeing something *about* him. As far as you are concerned, he himself is unknown; you don't know him at all. Who this Mr. Jones *really* is—with his secret cares and wounds, all the things he has to struggle with, the things that get him down and nobody else knows about—what he *really* is, what he is in *secret*, and what he is as only God knows him, this you don't know and ultimately you're not *interested* in it at all. Have you ever prayed for Mr. Jones? Only if you have brought yourself to do this in love, will you ever have any idea that in the eyes of God Mr. Jones is altogether different from what you choose to see in him when you enviously look at the outside of him."

And this is actually the way it is. Only he who has some conception of the fact that we are children who have a Father—a Father who alone really knows us—and that we are in need of forgiveness and help, that we are bleeding from secret wounds and have black stretches in our life that nobody knows about, but which Jesus knows, only he can accept another person from the hand of God and let him be what he is—even when it's hard for him and envy leaps up within him.

But because this is so, it will be quite futile for me to combat jealousy merely by will power and autosuggestion and by trying to doctor the accounts between the other person and myself and get more favorable results for myself by these everlasting comparisons. No, envy can be combatted only by letting God give me a new faith, a faith that accepts the other person just as he has been sent to me by a higher hand, as someone who has his place and function in God's plan exactly as I have, as someone who confronts me with the command of love and in whom God's higher thoughts come to meet me.

But how can I do all this and carry it out if I have fallen out with Him who sent him and made him what he is?

Now, I should feel that I had been thoroughly misunderstood if what I have said, namely, that I must accept the other person from God's hand, were taken merely as pious rhetoric or cheap pastoral consolation. I am utterly serious about this and I believe that here we are dealing with a fundamental reality of life. The corruption of our relationship to our neighbor and our own self-destruction—that self-tormenting feud that jealousy stirs up within us—can *actually* be overcome only by faith. We must learn to accept the other person from God's hand.

This is all there is to it, but it is really the whole cure.

But, after all, we can accept something from this hand only if we trust it, even when it does that which is different from what we wished or thought right. The point is that Cain did not accept Abel. This and nothing else was the root of the whole calamity. For the elder brother Abel was the great disruption of his concept of life. So Cain withdrew his trust from God when God, quite contrary to Cain's ideas, accepted his brother and let him, Cain, for a moment in the dark. And because he fell out with God, he also fell out with his brother.

All this, as we have said, is at first only an episode in a man's intimate relationship to God in his heart. But down in this inner domain, this so-called "religious sphere," is located the switchboard from which all the switches of our life are operated.

At first the story moves only in the realm of externals such as that his countenance fell and began to reflect hostility. Then follow the furtive glances at his brother and that clairvoyant jealousy that immediately notices whenever Abel has some bit of advantage. Then hatred condenses into complexes, and the image of the brother disappears behind caricatures and specters which poisoned imagination make of him. Then—and here is a new phase!—God intervenes with a warning, puts himself in his way, and tells him that sin is lying in wait at his door and desiring to get at him. But how can Cain ever hear this warning when he has long since shaken off the Warner? Then follows his invitation to Abel: "Come, let us go out to the field to have a talk with each other."

Only now does what began as a protest against God and what at first was only a thought beneath the surface in the interior of the self become an act. The deadly ax swished down upon Abel. But this is not the end of it. Cain's solo hatred soon becomes a whole chorus of hate and Cain's murder is followed by war and rumors of war and every brutal and subtle form of murder that history has developed. That *one* perilous spark that flared up in Cain's heart soon outshone the sacrificial fires on a thousand altars, became a prairie fire of blood vengeance and battlefields, and one day, as Robert Jungk says, will become brighter and more consuming than a "thousand suns" and lay the earth in ashes.

Why do we talk so much about atomic fires and why do we surrender to the self-destroying "lust for downfall"? Why do we indulge in visions of dread? Why have the novels about the future—we have referred to this before—long since ceased to wax enthusiastic over the progress of mankind toward undreamed-of heights of happiness? Why is it that today they present only delineations of terror?

The story of Cain and Abel calls us to order, because it says to us: "Don't keep looking spellbound into the atomic holocaust of the cosmos that threatens your earth, but look at the little sparks from which they come; look at the Cain within you. Return again to the altar and present your sacrifice in a way different from the way Cain did. All honor to your diplomatic endeavors and your peace organizations, but all this is only symptom therapy; it never gets beyond external patchwork if you refuse to go to the innermost seat of the disease, if you do not lay yourselves upon this sacrificial altar in order that God may be able to make something new of you.

"Why do you gaze so spellbound at rockets and future flights into space?" this story asks us. "Are you trying to divert attention from yourselves, you who are still bleeding from the wound of Cain? I am an ancient story from primitive times, but it's your story, and the question it puts to you reaches farther than the cosmic dimensions which you are now working to open up.

"You are always thinking about the remotest goals," says this ballad of Cain and Abel, "but you forget that everything depends upon the starting point. You stand at the altar and call yourselves Christians, you keep burning incense to "Christian civilization." Do you have any idea of what this means? Have you forgotten that all this is a matter of facing God, and nobody else but God —and not the scarecrow of a windy, shallow Christianity or an even more windy, conventional church?

"For God's sake," says this story, "it's a matter of God, of your being at peace with him. Everything else is charlatanry, religious or humanistic humbug, as long as this *one* thing is not in order. Your humanity becomes humanitarian drool and drivel, if you do not accept the existence of Abel, if you do not accept your neighbor from the high and holy hand of God, and if you no longer see his face gazing at you from the face of your competitors or even that of a functionary."

It is a constant source of amazement to me—you will permit me to add this in conclusion—that Jesus Christ never set forth a reform program for the abolition of slavery, for a new system of law and society, and a new and better world order—which, after all, is done by every revival movement that has any respect for itself at all. All that Jesus said was that we have a Father who is seeking us, a Father who grieves over the last thief and the last hangman beneath the cross, and plants a spark of true love in the corrupt heart of the woman who was a sinner. And then he lets us see our neighbor anew *beneath* the eyes and *with* the eyes of this our Father.

We must get this straight. He does not give us a new view of *society* or of so-called humanity—what is that anyway?—but rather makes us *see anew* the blind man there at the corner, the prostitute in her self-despising, the rich young ruler with his inner emptiness, the old woman in her loneliness.

He always shows us only the human being next to us. He makes us responsible only for a single milligram of the world's great burden. And even he himself, this Jesus Christ, whose arms embrace the globe and to whom has been committed all power in heaven and on earth, he too has time to be present for the *one* individual who needs him today, even though this one individual be only a poor wretch and certainly no key figure for the Christianization of the earth. For this one individual is a greeting and a charge from his Father.

When I hear this message of my neighbor and follow it in obedience, then at *one* small place I shall traverse the misery and discord of the world. Christians are not reformers, but they walk through life with their fellow men. The meek and the loving will inherit the earth, because they walk through it and suffer with it. But the conquerors are condemned to ruin. For, as Reinhold Schneider said, "the doers will never take heaven by force."

Jesus Christ would redeem the Cain within us and only so does he redeem the world. Love conquers all, because it traverses the world's misery at a single point, at the point where my neighbor stands—that neighbor whom I find so hard to love and who perhaps also makes things hard for me. But God himself put him right where he is. I can overlook him and I can hurry past him, but then I shall run straight into the arms of God. And if I do that, what will God be for me? What will I answer him when he says, "Where is Abel your brother?"

14

Where Is Abel Your Brother?

THE STORY OF CAIN AND ABEL: PART TWO

Cain said to Abel his brother, "Let us go out to the field." And when they were in the field, Cain rose up against his brother Abel, and killed him. Then the Lord said to Cain, "Where is Abel your brother?" He said, "I do not know; am I my brother's keeper?"
—*Genesis 4:8–9*

When Cain had slain his brother and the curtain rose upon the drama of world history, with one blow everything around him was changed. The bond between him and God and also the bond with his fellow man was broken. Now there is nobody left whom he can trust. Brotherliness has gone from the world. He himself has destroyed it.

Nor can he return to God, for, after all, he has renounced him. If he had still had God, he would have had at least one place of refuge in all his desolation. He could have said, "Father, I have sinned against heaven and before thee." Then he would have known that there was a hand from which he could accept all that now comes flooding down upon him: rejection, loneliness, fear—and also the judgment of expiation. For as long as that hand that gives and takes away is there, and as long as I can reach out for it and never let go of it, I am never *utterly* abandoned. Everyone who reads Dietrich Bonhoeffer's letters from prison senses something of the pressure of this kindly hand that turns even the darkest spot into a secure and homely place.

> Surrounded by heavenly powers, trusty and calm,
> Marvellously guarded and comforted,
> So with you I'll live this day with ne'er a qualm

—so wrote a man who was delivered over to the hangman's clutches but still escaped and conquered. For he was conscious of that higher hand that drew an enchanted circle of protection around him and, what is more, bound him to his neighbors even though he was separated from them by prison walls.

Cain has lost everything, and therefore he is the very prototype of the homeless one, the man displaced, "unhousel'd, disappointed, unanel'd."

Even the motherly earth broke faith with him, for she had drunk of the blood of his brother. Now the soil is mingled with a curse that is more harsh and hideous than that anathema of God in the story of the Fall which dealt only with relatively harmless thorns and thistles and other weeds. These hostile growths, these mischief-makers of the garden and the farm, were meant to indicate—we remember—that nature is no longer simply a friend and home for man, that it is no longer God's garden of paradise in which man can enjoy fellowship with all the creatures. Now nature becomes man's antagonist, an antagonist from whom we must *wring* our yield, who would keep it from us. Now the struggle for existence breaks forth into the primeval peace.

And Cain too had been compelled to wrest the fruit from the ground, for he too is a figure in the history between the Fall and the Last Judgment and stands this side of the cherub with the slashing, flaming sword. But now the soil itself had drunk his brother's blood. Now, not only the thorns and thistles, but this blood cries out in accusation. And so he is not only condemned to the struggle for existence, to painful wrestling with the soil. The curse has, so to speak, intensified itself. Cain's loss of God has also made him lose man. His brother is no more. And finally it made him lose his world. *For him the earth is no longer a home, a place of security.*

How great is the range of possibilities in which this can be said! Even the Christian can say, in an astonishingly similar way, that "this poor earth is not our home." But when we sing and say this as Christians, we do so, after all, only because our true home, our true security has appeared in Jesus Christ, and because, measured by *this* peace, our former refuges—money, prestige, job security, or vigorous health—appear to be ramshackle huts that really cannot assure us of a home. He who has found real peace sees through sham peace and sham security. He who has found the true home knows that all else is desert and wilderness.

So it is in *this* way, by finding the real standard for what is home, that we learn that this poor earth is not our home.

But Cain learned it in a different way. He experienced his homelessness in a negative way; he learned it from his unhappiness, from his being nowhere at home. When he looked upward, heaven was silent and only the grotesque face of unfeeling fate leered at him. When he looked about him, there was no longer a brother's heart beside him. He himself had seen to it that it ceased to beat. When he looked downward, the earth had lost its motherliness and appeared to him like one of the Furies, avenging spilt blood.

So Cain is hemmed in on every side. He is afraid because the noose grows tighter and there is no way out.

Do we remember how the destiny of curse began in the story of the Fall? There God challenged the man who had seized the forbidden fruit with: "Where are you?" Here again appears the word "where": "Where is Abel your brother?" God asks us not only what we have done with *him;* he also asks us what we have done with our *brother.*

The question of God is urgent not only in the vertical dimension, not only with respect to faith and prayer and the singing of hymns or with respect to despair and resignation. The question of God is equally cogent in the horizontal dimension, where we are dealing with society and community, with our associates and fellow riders on the subway, with friends and opponents.

Or are we to think that there really is such a thing as a religious "sphere," to which God must confine himself? These first pages of the Bible have a relentless way of repeatedly confronting us with precisely *this* question. Does God have to do only with heaven and the beyond, while we organize things on this side according to our own discretion? If he really were confined to the beyond, we would have a right to ask: "What has the way we run our business, our profession, our job to do with the hereafter? For the businessman, after all, it is quite simply a matter of the law of supply and demand, and of the further law that one must excel his competitors in gauging market conditions and beat them on price in order to survive. This is therefore a matter of very this-worldly things and any kind of intervention from the "beyond" is altogether out of place.

And what has politics to do with the religious sphere? Good heavens, you'll never get by with the Sermon on the Mount there! There it's less a matter of the Father of Jesus Christ than of the "God who made iron to grow."

And, finally, what about the rearing of children? Naturally, this does project a little into the so-called "religious sphere," because we must give the child something for his heart and, besides, these stories about the dear Savior are very acceptable for the training of the emotions. But otherwise here too what really matter are the naked, realistic questions: How can I feed and clothe them? How can I avoid the grossest educational blunders? What do I do when disturbances in development occur and how can I prevent children's diseases?

It's always the same old nonsense: we have to have religion, but it has no business except in the area between "heaven" and man's "inwardness." It belongs in a somewhat vague, difficult-to-localize area—somewhere on the margin of human existence. In normal everyday life, that is, in the here and now, it's a matter of realities which are quite different from praying and praising and giving thanks. Here it's a matter of being on the *qui vive* in order not to be taken in; what counts here is a head on your shoulders, elbows to shove with, and the speed with which you can shift gears.

But it is exceedingly remarkable that in both of the first two times God appears on the scene in the biblical account, it is emphatically not in the "religious sphere" at all that God breaks in. How impressive that would be, if he were to announce himself in a "religious" manner! What magnificent film material Hollywood could concoct from such accounts! Think of what could be done with trick shots and sensational dissolves in technicolor—we have already seen the possibilities in *The Ten Commandments*—in order to give people a little numinous shock as they sat in the movies! What a magnificent effect could be produced if God appeared in this "religious sphere" perhaps meeting Adam and Cain as a shimmering, ghostly, flood-lighted vision, something like a religious personification of a bad conscience, like a Shakespearean ghost! Perhaps this specter of God could appear in the night as a frightening dream, an avenging spirit, or in imperious majesty. In the morning Adam and Cain would wake up bathed in sweat and thank their lucky stars that they could get back from this religious sphere with its visionary horror-dramas into the light of waking consciousness, that Adam could go back to watching the animals and the flying birds, and that Cain could again attend to the respectable business of being a farmer, as was proper.

But God did not appear to either of them in the "religious sphere" or in any kind of subjective inwardness. He burst upon them in the midst of real, everyday life and therefore on that line of life which we have called the horizontal line.

Destiny with God caught Adam when he and his spouse were meddling with a tree that was none of his business, and Cain was accosted by God right after he had had a quarrel with another human being. It was then that he heard the voice saying: "Where is Abel your brother?"

A quarrel with another human being? Isn't that a pretty innocuous label for what happened? It was murder, wasn't it?

Of course it was. But it is conceivable that for his part Cain did not feel that he was a murderer. Perhaps he felt that Abel was a threat to his God-given position as the first-born and that therefore Abel was a disturbing element and hence must be eradicated. Perhaps Cain felt that he was facing the elemental alternative, which almost all of us face at some time in the struggle of life: either he or I! And isn't it a part of the law of self-preservation that one saves oneself at the cost of the other person and sometimes by main force? Why then must Cain have been what we call a dastardly murderer?

Perhaps it was hard for Cain to kill his brother. But he considered it unavoidable. Perhaps he even regarded his situation as tragic. Possibly he thought: This is a life and death contest; both of us cannot go on existing together. Therefore one of us has got to go. God has nothing to do with such ruthless, downright laws of the struggle for life. Elemental life is what rules here. "To be or not to be, that is the question." God belongs in the realm of altars, but not in the realm where real interests are in conflict.

May not Cain have indulged in the same arguments that we put forth today when we relegate God to the sphere of "religion" and "inwardness" and then go on to say: "We have to cope with this hostile life, its struggle for existence and its contests, alone and with means that are proper to the matter itself. Here we often have to employ questionable means; here we have no use for any divine interventions or nuisance raids from Sinai or the Sermon on the Mount"?

But the amazing thing is that God does *not* confront Cain in the precincts of the altar, in the religious sphere. He surprises him in his fields, in other words, in the midst of what we today call the world of work. Cain is not on his knees, he is not singing a hymn, he is not in church. His hands are gripping the plow and the soil is clinging to his boots, when suddenly God stops him in his tracks.

Nor does God announce himself with the words: "Behold, here I am, knowest thou me?"—and then perhaps supplement this reference to himself with an illustrative vision. No, God says not a word about himself. He speaks only of Cain's brother; he speaks only of Cain's fellow man, and he speaks only *indirectly* of himself. Naturally, Cain cannot miss the fact that it is God who is questioning him. But God emerged only in a cryptic, concealed way. Here he is hidden within the question about his brother.

I have often been asked by deeply serious people and particularly young seekers: "How does one really know that there is a God? How does one know that one believes at all?" "The great Christians, like Luther and Francis of Assisi," some may say, "obviously had something like an encounter with God. I have never had anything like that. In fact, if God called down from heaven through a loudspeaker: 'Here I am!' it would be a tremendous comfort. For then at least one would know where one stood. Then I'd bow my knees. But as it is, I don't know."

I am always touched when anybody speaks to me like that. For words like these bespeak the honesty of desperate searching. "I hear the bells all right," such a seeker may reflect, "and I have an idea that they are ringing peace. I want to heed them, I want this peace. But I do not know where the bells are hanging, and so I do not know which direction to go and find them. And yet I want to be honest, I don't want to be easy on myself. Dare I capitulate religiously and allow myself to be fascinated by the bells, simply because I yearn for the altars and their peace? Wouldn't it be cowardly flight simply to join the company of those who pray, just because some of these people impress me or because I envy their steadiness and I would like to have such steadfastness at any price?"

In connection with the Genesis story, one might express what such an honest seeker means like this: "God never yet said to me, 'Here I am.' And never yet have I heard a voice saying to me, 'Man, where are you?' I know nothing but a great silence. I don't have any luck in the religious sphere."

What can we say to such an earnest seeker?

Certainly the first thing the pastoral counselor thinks of is what a fortunate thing it is when a person is really grieved by the disparity between what he is and what he was meant to be. The sorrow of the seeker, who seeks with his whole heart and yet in vain, is a "godly grief" (cf. II Cor. 7:10) which is blessed with promise. Jesus himself calls blessed those who hunger and thirst for righteousness, despite the fact that they are menaced by the torment of uncertainty and assaulted by nothingness. For the very fact that they are seeking and that they are unhappy within themselves is in itself a sign that the Spirit of God is at work in them and that they are being shaken by the fever-crisis of an approaching cure. "We would not be able to seek thee, O God, if thou hadst not already found us"—once more we must think of this saying.

Perhaps they actually never did hear the voice of God seeking them and saying, "Man, where are you?" But they have heard a voice saying to them, "Where is Abel your brother?"

In other words, God certainly does not always announce himself in a "religious" way. He may approach us in the realm of very wordly-appearing topics, by confronting us with a social question or a human question, by inquiring, probably not about the person I have *killed*, but rather the person I have neglected and ignored.

What a staggering thing it is that in Jesus' great discourse on the Last Judgment (Matt. 25:31-46) there is no mention whatever of the great activities in vice—adulterers, murderers, and thieves—but rather that he speaks of those who neglected something and thus did nothing at all. "I was a stranger and you did not welcome me, naked and you did not clothe me, sick and in prison and you did not visit me."

Is not this perhaps the most subtle form of murder, that we overlook a person and his need, that we pass it off with a joke when he wants some question or difficulty of his to be taken seriously; that perhaps I was unable to deal with my own embarrassment and a certain awkward, uncomfortable feeling and therefore was unable to say the frank word by which I should have warned him, or stopped him from going the wrong way, or even have comforted him; that I have *not* written a letter to someone who is eagerly waiting to hear from me; that I did *not* raise my voice when the talk around a lunch table or at a tea party bore false witness against my neighbor and thus this neighbor fell among the robbers of reputations? *But I Never Spoke the Word.*[1] Many know this book by Alan Paton in which the guilt and destiny and terrible downfall of a man result from a single unspoken word.

And isn't there also another passage that compels us to prick up our ears? In the parable of the Good Samaritan there is only an incidental reference to the robbers, that is, the active villains, who beat up the man. Jesus' real indictment is concentrated upon the priest and the Levite, who passively disregarded him and let him lie there. It is precisely these laissez-faire people, these passive, thick-skinned, indifferent people, who will be asked at the Last Judgment: "Where is Abel your brother?" And the question will be *at least* as dreadful and emphatic and inescapable as the question that will be put to the active wrongdoers and the professional killers. For he who forgets his neighbor or disregards him has no love. He is too preoccupied with himself. So he has no eyes for others. Or he loves his royal Bavarian or Hanseatic comfort. Or he is too concentrated upon his own self to share the burden of another.[2]

At the Last Judgment he will try and vindicate himself, of course, by saying, "I never noticed a thing. What am I, a psychoanalyst, an X-ray eye, to be able to know the secret troubles of my colleague, my spouse, my cleaning woman? I'm up to my neck in work and in the evening I'm so dog-tired that I have to let down for the sake of my own self-preservation and it's impossible for me to bother myself with other people's petty

---

[1] This is a literal rendering of the German title of Alan Paton's novel, *Too Late the Phalarope*, in German translation. (Trans.)
[2] Thielicke, *The Waiting Father*, pp. 158–69.

troubles. I simply didn't see my neighbor. Show me *when* I was supposed to have seen him!" So, says Jesus, the accused will react at the Last Judgment.

But Jesus does not let this excuse pass. For it simply is not true that I must see the misery first, have it diagnosed for me, so to speak, before I can decide whether I want to help and to love. Anybody who is relentlessly honest with himself knows very well that this isn't so. My decisions with respect to my neighbor begin way back with the question whether I *want* to see him at all. Anybody who hears a drowning man who has broken through the ice cry out for help and then immediately begins to think: "You may get caught yourself under the ice if you leap in after him or you may catch your death of pneumonia"; anybody who in such a moment draws back from risking his own life, will very rarely do so by saying, "I heard the cry for help all right, but I won't help because it's too dangerous for me." If he admitted such a thing, he would have to admit that he was a coward. But, naturally, his moral instinct for self-preservation forbids him to do this. So he pretends to others and also to himself that he never even heard the cry for help. What I don't know won't hurt me. So he makes a big detour around his threatened neighbor who is crying for help and puts himself beyond the range of hearing—just as the priest and the Levite did. For he must not lose face.

There is a saying that "Love finds a way." This is certainly true, and we all know how love is capable of inventing all kinds of original methods to express itself. But before love becomes inventive it first becomes adept at seeing and finding. Goethe once said that one understands only what one loves. Yes, but there is even more to it than that. I actually *see* only what I love. So if we do not see or hear the other person, the reason for this does not lie in our deaf ears or blind eyes—it has nothing at all to do with optics or acoustics—but rather in our hard hearts which do not muster up any love and therefore overlook the other person altogether. Only he who loves has his eyes opened. But he who loves only himself stands in darkness and takes flight in an artificial way into an unconsciousness which will leave him thunderstruck at the Last Judgment.

But we have still to lay hold of the ultimate secret of why Cain's act of murder and our own Cainitic ignorance of our neighbor is so dreadful. Cain not only laid violent hands upon a human being who was a burden to him and whom he regarded as an intruder; he also violated the property of God himself. Abel the nobody, Abel the *declassé* belongs to the Lord God. Whoever touches him touches the Lord himself. And the Lord of the Last Judgment says the same thing: "It was I, Jesus Christ, who met you in rags and expected that you would give to me out of your abundance. It was I who languished behind bars in terrible imprisonments and waited for one small word of sympathy, one small look from your eyes or grip of your hand. In what you did or did not do to your neighbor you hurt me."

In our fellow man we are met by none other than Jesus Christ himself.

It is true, of course, that he is *hidden,* as Jesus Christ is always hidden and incognito. He was not seen by the Roman legionaries, the leaders of the synagogue, and the officers of the state. The ancient chronicles hardly mention him. One must love him greatly and be very near to him to discover his secret.

And so it is today also. *If* —yes, *if* the face of my colleague or my subordinate, which so often looks worn and depressed, were suddenly transformed by some mysterious dissolving view into the magic face of Jesus of Nazareth, wearing, perhaps, the crown of thorns, and I were to see the majesty of Jesus coming through him—yes, if that were ever to happen, then I surely would ask him: "What's the matter, what's wrong with you, what can I do to help you?" But this visual, religious miracle never happens. Something like this can happen, however: here is a weary, depressed-looking man going by, of the kind I see every day in the subway. What of it? Well, the fact remains that it is Jesus Christ who is suffering within him, and this Abel, the *declassé*, is stamped with the seal "God's property." Though nothing happens except what is always happening around me every day, the "drift of pinions" is passing by.

So against the dark background of this story of fratricide we meet two consolations.

The first is this: For us men the other person, the so-called neighbor, is as a rule the bearer of some function or other. He helps us or he hinders us in our work. He is the *useful* neighbor, whom we exploit and treat accordingly, as long as he is able to perform his obligations as a servant. Or he is the *irksome* neighbor, the trouble maker, the intruder, who is always showing up or making demands upon us at a time when we have no use for him. Or—and this is a third possibility—he has no function *whatsoever* in our life. If one day he doesn't show up we never miss him. Whatever night or anguish may have befallen him, we are not interested.

And this then is the comfort: For God no man is ever merely the bearer of a function, but always a *man*, a person—one to whom he gives a share in his eternity, whose sufferings he makes his own. The anguish of man is the anguish of God. That's what it means when it says: "God so loved the world that he gave his only Son. . . ."

And connected with this is the second consolation. For Cain his brother Abel is done for, once he is lying lifeless on the ground and has played out his function as an intruder and competitor. But for God no man is ever "finished," for this man, every one of us, are all a part of himself, we are all his property.

Men may never have been aware of the panic dread that broke out in a buried mine during an air raid. The earth covers up the explosion of misery with its peace. The grass grows green above the mass graves. The cries of the demented are swallowed up behind soundproof walls. The groans of the dying are forgotten while life goes on. The desperate dread, the strangling emptiness within us **we** keep hidden from the sight of others.

But it all comes to God; the mute blood cries out to him. For we live in his heart and *our* pain is *his* pain.

All the misery of the world, hidden and known, was concentrated in the cross of Golgotha, and there it became one great hurt in the heart of God. Only because we mean so much to him—while our fellow men pass us by afar off and do not even know that we exist—can he comfort us as a mother comforts her child.

That God espoused the cause of voiceless Abel and became the spokesman for him who is defenseless himself is shown in the fact that he called Cain to account. And when he asked the murderer, "Where is Abel your brother?" the answer he received (literally translated) was: "What is he to me? Am I to be the shepherd's keeper?"

What an outrageously insolent answer that is! Cain's cynicism can hardly be surpassed. For at a moment when life and death are at stake he cracks a rude joke and boldly utters a pun: "Am I to be the shepherd's keeper?"

Now it becomes apparent that Cain's secret godlessness, which was already devouring his heart as he made his burnt offering—we discussed this some time back—has now become an open, planned renunciation of God.

In these words the story of Cain and Abel provide us with nothing less than a brief sketch of the history of atheism.

Atheism began in the precincts of the altar. It was already developing in germ when Cain expected—and also would brook—nothing else from God but that He should bless him and exclude his competitor Abel. In the midst of the cultus and worship of God rebellion was already present, though it was hidden beneath a liturgical masquerade and a lot of Christian to-do. And yet this deceiving mask soon falls and naked, brazen-faced atheism comes to light.

Are we not still in the midst of this story of Cain today? We still have altars among us. We baptize and marry and confirm. The religious ceremonial still keeps on grinding away. At the high points of life we put on the ornaments and frills, just as laurel branches and red carpets are used. Do we still really hear the *message*, or does the ecclesiastical machinery simply have to be kept moving? We talk about the Christian West—though such talk has pretty well died down now!—and yet mean by it only the opposite of the slogans of Eastern tyranny. We talk about the liberty of faith and conscience and mean nothing by it except being left alone to do what we please.

The question is whether this whole business of Christianity promoting and identifying itself with so-called Western civilization is anything more than a gigantic camouflage structure, behind which one hears a great hammering and pounding because alterations are being made. The question is whether behind this board front the *transformed* Cain may not suddenly appear, the Cain who all this time has been coming to the altar, registering his children for baptism by the priest, and paying his church tax, and who now suddenly wears the hammer and sickle, talks about the opium of the people, advocates the idea that some lives are not worth preserving, and even stages a bit of atheistic propaganda.

I keep hearing this hammering and pounding behind the board front; day and night I hear it and my heart stops beating when I think of what I will see when one day this scaffolding, which is still covered with church flags and pious emblems, is torn down. We think—just as Cain did—that it is enough to provide altars with the bare necessities, to drop something in offering plates, and to pay the church tax. And yet even now the word goes forth: Weighed and found wanting!

We are still in favor of *man*. Oh, yes, we still lay great store by the word "humanity." But we have forgotten that man becomes a holy thing, a neighbor, only if we realize that he is the property of God and that Jesus Christ died for him. Otherwise he becomes a labor unit or a function. The community finally becomes a soul-less collective.

We also talk a lot about *freedom*. It is our pride, for, after all, we are the "free West." But is this freedom anything else for us but the freedom to achieve a certain standard of living? Is not freedom merely another item among the consumer's goods of Western comfort, along with freezers and television sets, which one uses and uses up? *We have become consumers of freedom. Do we really produce it in our lives?* But can we produce something when we no longer have any sources of supply?

We are only consuming the leftover impetus of a Christian tradition. The motor has been turned off, but the flywheel still keeps turning for a while longer. But more and more slowly. Already quite different motors are humming providing a new kind of dynamic.

Yes, it is a brief sketch of atheism that is contained in this account of Cain, and it is our story which is being told here. We shall never get by with the routine Christianity of the West. This kind of Christianity is merely an aggregate of misunderstandings which have formed about Jesus Christ. And underneath the fabric of this misunderstood Christianity there is a hammering and pounding going on; alterations are in progress.

Only he who drinks from the well of the eternal Word remains healthy. The polluted waters of conventional Christianity bring death.

Only he who believes abides. He who merely holds the Christian "point of view" will be swept away.

Only he who follows Jesus will conquer fear. He who tries to conquer it without Jesus is only repressing it.

Only he who knows Him who dearly purchased you and me and every one of us has compassion upon his brother and recognizes in his neighbor the naked, hungry Savior. He who does not recognize this Savior commits himself to a steep decline which makes of man mere "material" and turns the word "humanity" into a farce. It is a decline which, as Franz Grillparzer once said, leads from divinity to humanity to bestiality.

At this innermost point where we learn to spell and understand in all its immensity the Word of Jesus Christ—this is where we must start in order to regain our health and wholeness and "stay the sword that hangs above our heads" (Reinhold Schneider).

"Would that even today you knew the things that make for peace!" (Luke 19:42) These are the words that Jesus spoke when he drew near and saw the city and wept over it. The tears of the Lord: they are being shed over the Cain within us, over the unsuspecting, unheeding city, and over the hammering and pounding he hears beneath the façades.

15

Insecure Man

The Story of Cain and Abel: Part Three

Then the Lord said to Cain, "Where is Abel your brother?" He said, "I do not know; am I my brother's keeper?" And the Lord said, "What have you done? The voice of your brother's blood is crying to me from the ground. And now you are cursed from the ground, which has opened its mouth to receive your brother's blood from your hand. When you till the ground, it shall no longer yield to you its strength; you shall be a fugitive and a wanderer on the earth." Cain said to the Lord, "My punishment is greater than I can bear. Behold, thou hast driven me this day away from the ground; and from thy face I shall be hidden; and I shall be a fugitive and a wanderer on the earth, and whoever finds me will slay me." Then the Lord said to him, "Not so! If any one slays Cain, vengeance shall be taken on him sevenfold." And the Lord put a mark on Cain, lest any who came upon him should kill him. Then Cain went away from the presence of the Lord, and dwelt in the land of Nod, east of Eden.

—*Genesis 4:9–16*

What a remarkable conclusion to this story of fratricide! Cain is tormented with his guilt, encircled by visions of dread, smitten with the anathema of God, beset by the shrieking blood of his slain brother, hunted and hounded in a world that will never let him escape the omnipresence of this spilt blood. And yet—none of this cripples him or turns him into a pillar of salt or a block of ice. It rather drives him into activity and sends him off on aimless wanderings. It drives him into unceasing marching, traveling, and labor. Later (in vs. 17) it is said that he built a city, and his descendants were forgers of bronze and iron. And artists too—players on the lyre and pipe—were his descendants.

Cain and his family were obviously very productive. They cannot be regarded as antisocial riffraff. These people, who after all were descendants of a murderer, were by no means children of chaos but rather pioneers of progress. Fruitful fields and flourishing cities sprang up beneath their hands. The biblical texts are full of suggestions that Cain was something like the progenitor of human culture and civilization.

Isn't this a rather depressing prospect? When in the creation story God said to man, "Subdue the earth," we stated[1] that this might be interpreted as a command to pursue culture. For what else is culture but the creative process by which we make ourselves independent of the forces of nature, of cold and heat, storms and floods, day and night, the process by which we free our actions from the dictates of natural law and instead impose our will upon nature. We now subdue the oceans with our ships, cultivate the jungles and deserts and make them places of human habitation, and thus mold the world in our image. We "humanize" it.

Isn't that culture? And was not this what God intended when he said, "Subdue the earth?"

But here it would appear that the first realization of that command stemmed from Cain. Does not this imply the tremendous statement that in everything we men perform and construct there is at work, not only the original plan of the Creator, but at the same time a hidden curse, and that therefore everything fashioned by human hands is, well, perhaps not exactly "trumpery," but at least ambiguous and dubious?

We shall hold this question in abeyance for a moment and return to it later.

First we are told about Cain himself. He leads a life of wandering, working, and constructing. But whatever he may accom-

---

[1] Cf. Chapter 5, "Man—the Risk of God," pp. 67–68.

plish is under the curse that he was to be "a fugitive and a wanderer on the earth" and whatever he does is unstable and fugitive. The land of "Nod" means the land of wandering and restlessness. Perhaps today we would speak of the "endless road" or the "realm of nothingness."

We may feel impelled to resort to the metaphors of existentialism in order to illustrate this state of aimless, anxiety-ridden vagabondage. *What* is Cain really afraid of? After all, nobody knows him in the strange land to which he has been exiled; he can live there in anonymity and nobody will suspect that he has blood on his hands. So Cain has nothing *definite* to fear, no definite person who cherishes vengeance against him, no court, no police department. But it is this very indefiniteness that gives him anxiety.

As long as we men fear something definite—a business failure, an intrigue, a rainy vacation, or even a war—we can face it somehow by taking countermeasures against it, we are drawn into planned action and counteraction. Fear is not so fearfully bad when one knows *what* one has to fear and what can be done to combat it. But Cain has nothing definite to fear; he is anxious about a great X, an unknown.

What is it that produces this anxiety?

To understand this we need only to think of what Jesus says about being anxious.

How does the anxious question, "What shall we eat, what shall we drink, what shall we wear?" actually arise? Or the questions: "What calamity will come out of the East-West conflict and the Berlin crisis? What radioactive clouds will pass over us? From which stars will we soon be spied upon? Which bacteria are being cultured in which laboratories? What terror and what brainwashings are yet to come upon old Europe?"

Why do such anxious thoughts about tomorrow overtake us, unstable and fugitive as we are? Are we, like Cain, in the land of Nod? And why this anxious clutching at our throats when there is no immediate occasion for any such apprehensions?

Goethe once laid bare the secret of this anxiety in words that echo the Sermon on the Mount. After conversing with Wagner, Faust speaks of the care that "nestles deep within the heart."

> In new disguises she is always dressed;
> She may appear as house and land, as child and wife,
> As fire, as water, poison, knife.
> What never will happen makes you quail,
> And what you'll never lose, always must you bewail.

So in reality fire, water, poison, knife are not there at all! Actually it is quite possible to live fairly safely and comfortably in the land of Nod. And yet we go on trembling before this great "fire, water, poison, knife." Goethe visualizes this as being a definite basic stock or store of anxiety in the human heart. This heart, which, to express it in modern terms, is loaded with anxiety-producing substance, then operates as a projector which throws wide-screen, colorfully graphic pictures on the pure white walls that surround us, pictures of such vehement impact and convincingness that we see them as real specters leaping upon us, whereas they are merely expressions and products of our own hearts.

This sounds almost like a chapter on psychology, and some of you may ask what this has to do with this exposition of the Bible. And yet these products of anxiety are connected with the spiritual background of our life, which in turn cannot be understood apart from our relationship to God.

This immediately becomes clear when we remember the way Jesus fought against this spirit of care in us. This is to say, he by no means fought it in a "rationalistic" way. He did not say, "Now, children, be reasonable! You must see that what you are doing here is simply confusing reality with the products of your own anxiety. Where is a reason for the fear that you will get nothing more to eat or to wear? Where do you see any radioactive clouds anywhere on the horizon?"

Our Lord does not say anything like this at all; and it is very characteristic of him that he does not do so, for it would not help us anyhow. Strangely enough, no rational arguments are of any help in anxiety.

Instead he makes it clear to us that it is not what goes into a man, what comes to him from the *outside*, that defiles him and makes him afraid, but actually what rises up from his heart like air bubbles—*this* is the evil, the defiling thing, the thing that produces anxiety. If this heart of yours were still living in the security of the Father, if your hearts were sure, like the lilies of the field and the birds of the air, that you are sustained and cared for by this Father, you would have no more cares. Indeed, then you would walk bravely through the valley of the shadow; not because you could see a hundred yards ahead as with a radar—Christians live in the unforseeable just like everybody else!—but because you would feel the rod and the staff in your hand.

The man who carries with him the iron ration of the word of the Lord, "I am with you always, to the close of the age," will cross the threshold of each unknown tomorrow with cheerful composure, and for him this word is a "lamp to his feet." This lamp to our feet is not like an auto headlight that cuts a broad cone of light far ahead in the impenetrable darkness of the future. No, it illuminates only the next few steps, actually, only the very next step. But I know that the road for the next step but one has been prepared for me by a higher hand.

Hence there is something like a godly indifference to the step after the next one. A certain nonchalance can be a part of our worship of God—on condition, of course, that this unconcern is not the expression of phlegmatic indolence, but rather a small thankoffering to the Father, who, after all, knows what I need (cf. Matt. 6:32).

But Cain no longer has this security. Now he can say to God, "I must hide from thy face; I am an outcast. And therefore I must be a fugitive and a wanderer and go straying and stumbling on the endless road in the land of Nod.

"When the world becomes fatherless it becomes a weird and homeless place and I am driven into unending flight. Every tree, every milestone becomes a threat. So I try to charm away the weirdness with a talisman that dangles in my car. Or I consult the stars for some dodge by which to escape being caught in my run of bad luck. Or I procure lucky numbers to increase my chances and find out the dates and times when I must be careful because these are unlucky times. This is the law of life in the land of Nod where the security of home is gone. Here is where fear, superstition, and magic hold sway."

So Cain has no more happiness, no more enthusiasm. For, after all, we experience such uprushes of feeling only when there is something or other in our life that is worth living for, because it provides us with something more than the boredom of the daily treadmill. In John Osborne's play *Look Back in Anger*, Jimmy Porter says—and Cain might have said exactly the same thing!—"Oh heavens, how I long for a little ordinary human enthusiasm. Just enthusiasm—that's all. I want to hear a warm, thrilling voice cry out Hallelujah! . . . Oh, brother, it's such a long time since I was with anyone who got enthusiastic about anything."

But how can one possibly find anything in the land of Nod to get excited and enthusiastic about? Is there anything here but "looking back in anger"—anger over the bungled past that compels us to pay the consequences, anger over the meaningless mess that keeps driving us on to do things "as if it really meant something"?

True, I can fabricate a few illusions. I can work up some enthusiasm for certain ideals, and the fan clubs of our teen-agers are a pathetic and forlornly wistful attempt to break out of the land of Nod and find a star, precisely a star, that can serve as something like a guiding image. Thus they recognize themselves in a young star actor like James Dean with his melancholy and his oppression with the problems of life. We Christians ought not to smile about this and in a kind of pious snobbery dismiss these teen-age dreams with a wave of the hand. We ought to recognize the desperate homesickness that is trying to break through the iron curtain of the land of Nod. At any rate, when they reach the age of twenty-five at latest, this "star" worship will come to an end and then the odyssey begins afresh, except that now it will have become a bit more sober and hopeless.

In any case, there is one thing I must realize and that is that I shall find the great and sustaining thing in my life only if I see on every side in the desert the little signs and evidences of the loving God.

After all, what is a flower? A bit of vegetation that soon wilts and withers away, and when the wind passes over it it is no more. But for him who lives in the security of that peace which Jesus Christ bestows it is a lily, which, as Wilhelm Raabe said, simply discloses itself without making any fuss about it, a lily that neither works nor spins, but is simply "there," living without a care and more gloriously clothed by God than Solomon in all his splendid robes.

What is the love of my parents, who by the law of the generations will one day leave me orphaned, what is this transient love, if I do not see in it a parable, an analogy of him "Who, from our mother's arms, hath blessed us on our way with countless gifts of love" and will not leave us desolate.

All this Cain no longer knows nor possesses as he leads his fugitive and wandering life, even though he is tremendously active. For him the world holds neither parable nor message; it is dull and gray. For he who loses God has lost, not only heaven, but—as we have already made clear—also the *earth*. The Father of Jesus Christ is, after all, far more than merely a personage whose proper place is only in the "beyond." Ever since the manger and the cross stood upon our earth God has been the very utmost of "this-worldly" beings. Therefore our faith is by no means sustained merely by the hope that one day at our last hour he will be our stay and comfort and that finally he will help us "get to heaven." This is true, of course, but it is by no means the center of gravity in a Christian existence. We must even accept Nietzsche's charge that Christianity has often abused the hour of death and tried to make men tractable by threatening them with the terror of the hereafter.

Instead of thinking of the outskirts of life, of death and our last hour, we ought to impress it upon ourselves that God wants us to face and endure this frightening and fascinating world *now*, now when we are young and in the prime of life, when we are shaken by passions, when we are in the thick of things and we need to fight and resist.

Because the Word became flesh, God has come into the here and now. Right now he is in the midst of Pharisees and harlots, in the midst of people who are hungry and people who are ambitious, the snobs and the seekers, those who laugh and those who weep, the teen-agers and the executives. Jesus Christ is with us in the land of Nod, and he who has eyes to see observes to his utter amazement that this transforms this gloomy, frightening zone into the promised land and our home. For where God is there life is changed—*life*, and by no means only *death*. For now I have a purpose again, now I have something that is greater than myself, and therefore life is worth living.

The clouds and storms of life go on exactly as they did before. But in them shines the rainbow, a greeting from Him who never forgets me, who gives me goals and brings me to them. There are pitfalls and abysses to be sure, but there are bridges over them which now I cannot see. And the night is coming too, when no man can work; true, but even then the stars will shine and he who numbered them all will be there. There are our directions for life.

I think it is an encouraging thing that we should thus be able to recognize our own situation with its burdens and its promises in a biblical figure like Cain and in a biblical country like the land of Nod. Consequently, this Book does not contain strange and ancient stories that have no relevance to me—in any case, no relevance that is as great as the set-to with my boss that I must face tomorrow or the business deal I have to take up this afternoon. No, the Book contains my own biography. It does not talk about space flights; it is not even aware that our earth is a planet in the solar system; but it speaks about *me*.

What, then, do the Scriptures say about our homelessness and insecurity? It is remarkable how many connections there are in the Bible in which the idea of homelessness occurs.

Here is Abraham, the patriarch of faith. God says to him, "Go from your country and your kindred and your father's house to the land that I will show you." God often calls us, once we begin to take him seriously, to leave familiar ties. It may be that our faith will estrange and isolate us from old friends and companions, sometimes even from our own family, and we feel like strangers in an environment motivated by things and interests that are completely different from ours and whose passions and enthusiasms are located elsewhere.

But is Abraham, just because he is separated from all that is familiar, a man abandoned and fugitive?

No, he is not, for the very reason that he goes forth under the shadow of the outstretched hand of God. When God goes with us and we hold on to our faith no land is strange and the land of Nod does not exist. Abraham built altars to his God; but where his Word is present there is a bit of home. Many a prisoner of war in Russia who met two or three gathered together in "His" name, found that he was given a sense of security and meaning and purpose that took away all his feeling of being a lost and wandering fugitive and made him less lonely than perhaps he is today in the familiar rhythm of his everyday life at home.

And what about the homelessness of Jesus, who also left the security of his eternal home and went out into a strange land of hate and guilt and misunderstanding? "Foxes have holes, and birds of the air have nests; but the Son of man has nowhere to lay his head" (Matt. 8:20). Nowhere to lay his head, never to be able to relax, always surrounded and beset, and always exposed to the onslaught of the unknown: this is insecurity, this is the very prototype of the homeless one. And yet he goes on, mysteriously embodied in the plan of God, walking beneath the shadow of his higher thoughts.

We ought to read the Gospels sometime from this point of view, of how in this unique life homelessness and defenselessness are always connected with the guarding of the angels and the everlasting arms. "My hour has not yet come," he said one time —and the implication is that his Father put space and time at his disposal. And therefore he could calmly go to sleep in the little boat that threatened to capsize, while his companions' panic went beyond control. Even in that ultimate dereliction on the cross when the face of the Father vanished about the ninth hour and he could only cry out his rejection, "My God, my God, why hast thou forsaken me?" he framed his complaint in the words of a psalm of the Holy Scriptures, and thus prayed in the words his Father had given to him. So here again the circuit to the Eternal was closed and his Father was with him. And when at the last he said, "Father, into thy hands I commit my spirit," this was like a thanksgiving for the sheltering of a loving hand, like a prayer of gratitude that now he could let himself fall without a care, even though his body remained hanging helplessly from the nails of the cross.

Because all power in heaven and on earth has been given to this Lord, the world no longer reeks of alienness. When Eleanore von Reuss sings in her New Year's hymn:

> Why is our lot so full
> Of pain, and joy so brief? . . .
> That we may ne'er forget,
> What is so soon forgot:
> That this poor, stricken earth
> Is not our native home . . .

we must remember that this is being said precisely by someone for whom the terrors of the strange country have been shooed away by the lights of the Father's house. For they are a sign that we are expected and that we have a goal.

But even Cain is not altogether forsaken in the land of Nod. Even about him God throws a circle of protection and puts upon him a sign, the mark of Cain, which makes him taboo. Even the guilt-laden man remains God's property. He too is given room to repent. In case, there is no man in this world who is *only* guilty and of whom nothing more can be said except that he is a murderer and irrevocably condemned. Even the outcast is still included in a system of co-ordinates which is invisible to our human eyes. Even he still has a mysterious place in the grace of God and even the endless road that he walks as a fugitive and a wanderer is still the highway of God, and God alone knows and determines where it will end and arrive.

In centuries past the judge who had condemned a murderer to death would partake of the sacrament of the Lord's Supper with him before his execution. By doing this he was saying to him, "You poor, lost sinner, whom we are about to do to death, are nevertheless something totally different from what we human beings see in you. You are not *merely* a man who has been branded with the curse of society; you are still a part of another, invisible order, that can grant you a grace and pardon over which we human beings have no control. You bear the mysterious mark of Cain that makes you the property of Another—just as we judges are the property of that Other and therefore stand in an ultimate solidarity with you."

Cain may be restless and flee wherever he wills, but God's horizons will always surround him. Even if he takes the wings of the morning and dwells in the uttermost parts of the sea, even there his hand will lead him and his right hand will hold him (cf. Ps. 139:10).

The end of the story of Cain also leads us to that vista of culture which we spoke of at the beginning—of the children of Cain, the builders of cities, the masters of mines and ironworks, and the artists. In every culture—this is what the Bible is saying—there is a Cainite strain, in every culture the blood of the slain brother cries out and a cold breath blows out from the land of Nod.

I wonder whether in this intimation we see nothing more than a pessimistic view of culture, like that of Oswald Spengler, for example.

From now on—this is doubtless how the text is to be understood—the curse of fratricide is woven like a blood-red thread into the web of human life, even in its highest forms.

This web produces complicated and imposing patterns. In the great civilizations, as in the Egyptian or the Greek or the Gothic, it projects a great profusion of brilliant images—pyramids, temples, and soaring cathedrals. These great Gobelins on the walls of civilization are testimonies of our greatness. "Much that is mighty exists, but none more mighty than man."

But the strange thing is that the closer we come to these great tapestries the more clearly we see the red thread that runs like a pulsing, bloody artery through the myriad figures. This motherly earth, on which even the greatest of men walked, on which they erected cities and cathedrals and monuments, has drunk the blood of Abel, and this blood of the murdered and abused appears in stains and rivulets everywhere, including the greatest figures. Cain, the "great brother" and progenitor of all mankind, betrays his mysterious presence. Somewhere in every symphony the tone figure of death and anguish is traceable, somewhere on every Doric column this mark is to be found, and in every tragedy the lament over injustice and violence rings out.

Are not the slaves, the disfranchised, the misery of fellaheen and coolies a part of the greatness and the Apollinian brilliance of Greek art? Is not the greatest that men have ever produced founded upon an earth that has drunk the blood and sweat of these disfranchised waifs? Do we need Marxism to tell us this, or ought we not to know it ourselves, and know it far more deeply, because we know this story of Cain? Is it really true, as Treitschke once dared to say, that "one of Phidias' statues outweighs the misery of millions of ancient slaves"? Who is right—Treitschke or our Bible text?

Were not the stakes erected beside the Gothic cathedrals? Did not the lust for blood and the will to power burn, along with the flames of genius and mystical inwardness, masking pride and delusions of grandeur with crusaders' slogans and a humanitarian sense of mission? Is there not in every art the cry for redemption from the land of Nod and is not, as Gottfried Benn once said, every work of art like a laboriously fashioned oasis in a deadly desert?

And what about the builders of cities who are the descendants of Cain? Is it not our generation that has discovered the term, "the lonely crowd"? Is not the land of Nod in our very midst—in the midst of us who are literally surrounded by people, in the stations, in the trains and trolleys, and on the streets, and yet whom nobody sees and perhaps nobody wants to see?

Everywhere Cain is strangely present. Only those who have seen this can comprehend what a liberation Jesus Christ is in the midst of this Cainite world.

Cain says, "Whoever finds me will slay me." He fears the vengeance of blood. But this is only the primitive form of a law that has prevailed in this our world since the days of Cain. It is the law of the echo, the law of retaliation, an eye for an eye, a tooth for a tooth. At bottom this is the way we all react. We are like a forest that re-echoes what our fellow men—our colleagues, friends, and opponents—have shouted into it. And others again are just such a forest for us, that throws back the echo of our own friendly or malicious voice.

There is only *one* point in the world where this is not so, where the law of Cain is overruled. And that is the point where Jesus Christ stands, "who when he was reviled did not revile in return."

Is it merely weakness and passivity that this one Man should not retaliate?

No, it is something altogether different; he is taking the supreme initiative, it is a real new beginning in love. Here the deadly spiral of the world that keeps ascending ever higher and higher in its hostilities—in private antagonisms, commercial competition, and finally in the political opposition of whole hemispheres—here this deadly spiral is broken through at *one* point. And the breakthrough occurs wherever there is something like forgiveness and thus a new beginning.

How can it ever be possible that the world of Cain should collapse and from its ruins arise a new and redeemed world? When Jesus Christ forgave his enemies and conquered them in love, he did not do this because he no longer saw the evil, because he stretched a point and covered it up with the hypocritical mantle of so-called Christian love of one's neighbor. Jesus always called sins by their right names, he called lies lies, adultery adultery, and backbiting backbiting. But much as he hated sin, he nevertheless embraced the sinner in his compassion. He knew that his Father grieves over every sinner. He knew that the sinner—a man who had injured him, or perhaps me—was an erring child of this his Father. He knew that God holds precious an erring child and that he would let him, the Son of Man, die for that child. So deeply is God grieved when we go the wrong road. So deeply is God grieved also over him who persecutes me with his chicanery or intrigue or malice.

Shall I pitch my persecutor and trespasser even deeper into his Cainite madness by lashing out at him with my hatred? Or shall I let him know something utterly different? Shall I communicate to him this message: You have wronged me, you have even hurt me terribly; but I am grieved that you are taking such a wrong road? What is the matter with you, that you should be and act the way you do? I feel sorry for you out there in the far country, when all the time you are dearly purchased and the pinnacles of the Father's house are shining above the depths of your despair, and you are unaware of it.

Would not this little sign of compassion break through the law of retaliation at *one* point at least. and might not the fresh breath of air that brings release and liberation begin to blow through this *one* small breach which I have made in the name of my Savior?

"This I have done for thee," says the Crucified, "what dost thou do for me?" This is the question that breaks the world of Cain. And when it is broken, then there is no more "looking back in anger," then there is hope, a new future, a great breaking and thawing of the ice jam in our hearts.

THE STORY OF THE FLOOD

16

Floods and Fires

The Story of the Flood: Part One

These are the generations of Noah. Noah was a righteous man, blameless in his generation; Noah walked with God. And Noah had three sons, Shem, Ham, and Japheth.

Now the earth was corrupt in God's sight, and the earth was filled with violence. And God saw the earth, and behold, it was corrupt; for all flesh had corrupted their way upon the earth. And God said to Noah, "I have determined to make an end of all flesh; for the earth is filled with violence through them; behold, I will destroy them with the earth. Make yourself an ark of gopher wood; make rooms in the ark, and cover it inside and out with pitch. This is how you are to make it: the length of the ark three hundred cubits, its breadth fifty cubits, and its height thirty cubits. Make a room for the ark, and finish it to a cubit above; and set the door of the ark in its side; make it with lower, second, and third decks. For behold, I will bring a flood of waters upon the earth, to destroy all flesh in which is the breath of life from under heaven; everything that is on the earth shall die. But I will establish my covenant with you; and you shall come into the ark, you, your sons, your wife, and your son's wives with you. And of every living thing of all flesh, you shall bring two of every sort into the ark, to keep them alive with you; they shall be male and female. Of the birds according to their kinds, and of the animals according to their kinds, of every creeping thing of the ground according to its kind, two of every sort shall come in to you, to keep them alive. Also take with you every sort of food that is eaten, and store it up; and it shall serve as food for you and for them." Noah did this; he did all that God commanded him.

Then the Lord said to Noah, "Go into the ark, you and all your household, for I have seen that you are righteous before me in this generation. Take with you seven pairs of all clean animals, the male and his mate; and a pair of the animals that are not clean, the male and his mate; and seven pairs of the birds of the air also, male and female, to keep their kind alive upon the face of all the earth. For in seven days I will send rain upon the earth forty days and forty nights; and every living thing that I have made I will blot out from the face of the ground." And Noah did all that the Lord commanded him.

Noah was six hundred years old when the flood waters came upon the earth. And Noah and his sons and his wife and his sons' wives with him went into the ark, to escape the waters of the flood. Of clean animals, and of animals that are not clean, and of birds, and of everything that creeps on the ground, two and two, male and female, went into the ark with Noah, as God had commanded Noah. And after seven days the waters of the flood came upon the earth.

In the six hundredth year of Noah's life, in the second month, on the seventeenth day of the month, on that day all the fountains of the great deep burst forth, and the windows of the heavens were opened. And rain fell upon the earth forty days and forty nights. On the very same day Noah and his sons, Shem and Ham and Japheth, and Noah's wife and the three wives of his sons with them entered the ark, they and every beast according to its kind, and all the cattle according to their kinds, and every creeping thing that creeps on the earth according to its kind, and every bird according to its kind, every bird of every sort. They went into the ark with Noah, two and two of all flesh in which there was the breath of life. And they that entered, male and female of all flesh, went in as God had commanded him; and the Lord shut him in.

The flood continued forty days upon the earth, and the waters increased, and bore up the ark, and it rose high above the earth. The waters prevailed and increased greatly upon the earth; and the ark floated on the face of the waters. And the waters prevailed so mightily upon the earth that all the high mountains under the whole heaven were covered; the waters prevailed above the mountains, covering them fifteen cubits deep. And all flesh died that moved upon the earth, birds, cattle, beasts, all swarming creatures that swarm upon the earth, and every man; everything on the dry land in whose nostrils was the breath of life died. He blotted out every living thing that was upon the face of the ground, man and animals and creeping things and birds of the air; they were blotted out from the earth.

Only Noah was left, and those that were with him in the ark. And the waters prevailed upon the earth a hundred and fifty days.
—*Genesis 6:9–22, 7:17–24*

What is it really, that stirs us so in the story of the Flood? Is it the total destruction of a world, which is so weirdly parallel to our own conceptions of an atomic catastrophe, except that here the destruction is caused, not by fire and deadly radiation, not by deluges of fire, but by the element of water?

Or is it the seemingly problematical, crepuscular unsettledness of God, who, after all, found everything wonderfully good at the end of the creation, and now allows this his creation to be blotted out? What kind of a God is this who "repents" and then simply obliterates his bankrupt work and drowns it in a gigantic flood? A God who sets the scene for the kinship of the whole cosmos and allows innocent trees and flowers and animal creatures to perish because of human guilt? Do we not have here a prelude to the equally strange bankruptcy on Golgotha, where God seems to sink into suffering, impotence, and utter "ungodlikeness"?

What an extraordinary story this is! Here we have a whole bundle of themes and questions all bound up with one another. I shall try to cast some light upon the structure of this fugue.

The great catastrophe of the Flood tells us that here the second day of creation is being revoked in an awesome, dreadful way. We may recall what was said about the second day of creation: " 'Let there be a firmament in the midst of the waters' . . . and God made the firmament and separated the waters which were under the firmament from the waters which were above the firmament. . . . And God called the firmament Heaven."

Hence we have here the curious notion that the clouds, the seas, and the other vehicles of moisture on earth correspond to a kind of "heavenly ocean," a mysterious "beyond," a strange and elemental power, perhaps similar to what the Greeks meant by the menacing Oceanus beyond the edge of the world.

In view of these menacing powers, the first thing God the

Creator does is to create *order*. He separates the waters above the firmament from the waters beneath the firmament; he establishes boundaries and wards off chaos from the dwelling place of his children.

And yet the power of destruction, as represented by the "heavenly ocean," continues as before to lie in wait. The potential downfall of the world is, so to speak, always threatening and lying in wait. If ever the boundaries between the waters, if ever the firmament which God established should disappear and the conflux of the upper with the lower ocean produce something like a critical mass, the dammed-up chaos on the margin of the world would break loose and pour in upon us. And this is just what happened in the Flood when the floodgates of heaven opened and the dam between the upper and lower seas burst.

These are quite modern ideas, here expressed in terms of mythical conceptions. The igniting of the atom bomb has made us familiar with the idea of a "critical mass"—even though in this instance expressed in a different language, namely, in the terms of modern physics. The strange contiguity between the primeval age and our modern time is enough to make us shudder.

But, of course, if we are not to slip into the realm of fantasy and construct exaggerated similarities, we must get a precise bearing upon the determinative point in this similarity. This determinative point—this *tertium comparationis,* as it is called—I should like to describe as follows.

When God executes his great judgments, as he does in the Flood, he does so, not in the form of miraculous interventions and sudden bolts of heavenly thunder, but rather—as Paul expressed it—he punishes men by "*giving them up*" (Rom. 1:24) to the destructive consequences of their actions, by delivering them over to themselves. He gives the corruption of man the dreadful chance, as it were, to vent its fury and act out the experiment to the end—until five minutes after twelve, as Hitler used to express it—in order that he may see where his own initiative brings him.

This is, as it were, the "style" of divine judgment: man is

given up to his own fate and consequently he judges *himself* in that God judges him. "With man and horse and caisson the Lord of hosts did smite them," declares the song of Napoleon's mad campaign in Russia. But did not Napoleon judge himself in that the Lord judged and smote him and delivered him over to the inevitable fall of his own life-curve?

The powers of destruction are still present in the midst of creation. The atoms—did not God create them?—need only to be split, the bacteria let loose, hereditary factors monkeyed with, genes tampered with, and poisons need only to be distilled from the gifts of creation—oh yes, the powers of destruction are still with us and the heavenly ocean is still heaving and surging behind its dams. We live solely by the grace of God, who has fixed the bounds of destruction.

The dreadful secret of the world revealed in the first chapters of this old Book is that man is capable of *renouncing* and cutting himself off from this very grace which holds in check the power of destruction. At first, at the suggestion of the serpent, he desired to "be like God," and already he had overstepped the first and essential boundary. In order that Adam may not "become like one of us," this very Adam, this "man" is driven out of the peace of the Garden of Eden and compelled to suffer death, the boundary of his finitude. He must realize that he is "only" man, that he is dust and ashes. And as he learns this, the gates of mortality go clanking down before him.

Then comes Cain's murder of his brother, then comes the anguish of a bad conscience, then comes unrest and never-ending flight.

So the descent goes on and on. Corruption spreads like a prairie fire—and then the mighty force of the Flood breaks in upon it.

It's always the same old story: because man does what is unholy, he provokes the floods of dammed-up mischief. Because he no longer wants to live by grace, the dams which are held up by grace are broken.

And again we must not imagine that man always renounces God openly and purposefully in the style of Prometheus. Very seldom do people actually make the gesture of a clenched fist raised to heaven. We have spoken of this before. Nor does man need to be an overt atheist or antichristian. He can manage all this much more secretly. No sooner does he worship his own power—no sooner does he regard flesh or atomic power as his "arm"[1] and surrender to the illusion that he can hold the world in order and balance by military potential and political intelligence—than he has already renounced God's grace and breached the dam that holds the heavenly ocean. When he imagines that he can free men from need and fear by means of the welfare state he is already declaring himself independent of this sustaining grace and pressing the buttons which set off the secret signals of catastrophe. Above all, when we are people who calmly tolerate to be sure the routine business of the church's baptizing, marrying, and burying, but otherwise go on stubbornly worshiping our anxieties and succumbing to prosperity and its self-indulgence and superficiality; when therefore we are people who do not see their neighbor in his need and thus lose our souls, *then* and *precisely* then we too are playing fast and loose with that grace which guards the dikes of ruin.

And therefore this world, which we think we govern by our own power, may one day come crashing down upon us, because the thing we play with so presumptuously has gotten beyond our control, and because God is not to be mocked. He may suddenly cease to hold the ocean in check and the unleashed elements will sweep us into their vortex.

The Bible always has in view the possibility that this is the way our human history could proceed and finally be shipwrecked, and it is for this very reason that it has so much to say about the *end:* the end of corrupt mankind in the Flood, the end of the godless, whom "he sets in slippery places" (Ps. 73:18), the end of the world, when the stars will fall and the moon be-

---

[1] Jer. 17:5; cf. II Chron. 32:8; Ps. 44:3.

come like blood, the end of time in the Last Judgment and the return of the Lord.

And here again is a remarkable parallel to our own situation. Even those among us who are far removed from the message of this old Book are nevertheless aware of the possibility of the end. We know that the technical means exist for wiping out the human race and with it animals and plants, and thus life itself. Naturally, we have other terms and other concepts in which we think of this end.

Much as we like to turn up our noses at legends and myths, however, the story of the heavenly ocean and the possibility that evil lies in wait on the boundaries of creation fascinates us and our proud intellectualism has some inhibitions about indulging in sarcasm. We sense that here the theme of the end and the self-destruction of all things is being sounded.

And this is precisely *our* theme too.

Therefore we must be exceedingly careful not to allow ourselves to be influenced by the difference in the forms of conception and expression.

To begin with, how differently, even so far as *content* is concerned, the theme of the end is handled in the story of the Flood and in the atomic age! I am extremely hesitant about discussing here the apocalyptic conceptions of the end of the world in atomic ruin as they are dealt with in our illustrated magazines and paperback shockers. But I must at least bring out the central emphasis of these contemporary horror stories in order that we may see how grandly different is the biblical account.

As a rule we picture the atomic end of the world as leaving only a few people in some remote corners of the world, and, what is more, people whose genes have been injured and are nothing more than a dull, degenerate image of Homo sapiens. They are primitive again, as in primeval times, and begin anew with spears and bows. The elaborate machines of war have not only extinguished life on earth but themselves also. But the cathedrals are gone too, and the birds no longer sing. These new primitives who survive in remote mountain ranges and deserts no longer know who Hölderlin and Luther and Socrates were.

These are a few of the characteristic features of the atomic apocalypses which have appeared since the last world war, committed to paper in a thousand versions and run through the rotary presses by the millions.

Now one need only to read the text of the story of the Flood slowly and aloud in order to sense immediately that the themes and emphases of this story lie completely elsewhere and that here the atmosphere is totally different. Here there is no wallowing in fantasies of horror, as the medieval painters still loved to do. Here there are no farewell scenes before the great deluge, no weeping mothers, no descriptions of the terrors of drowning. The flood is merely suggested—as a modern stage set designer might do it—with a few lines and colors, nothing more.

For the catastrophic flood does not play the chief role in the drama that is enacted here, any more than the far country plays the main part in the parable of the Prodigal Son. The Flood and the far country are merely the dark wings that surround the real action on the stage.

This *real* action can be expressed in a very simple formula: God remembered Noah—just as the father remembered his son who was wandering in the far country. God remembered the one faithful one who held fast to the grace of God. For this *one* faithful one he held in readiness the ark, the place of refuge and safety.

The account of how one survived the catastrophe by resting upon the everlasting arms, how the dove with the olive leaf was sent to him as a sign of protection, and how he then was given a new world and once more saw the dawn of a new chance and a new beginning, in other words, how the words "Let there be" were spoken *once more—this* is the real theme of this story. For even though the subject is that of catastrophe and downfall, God can never be a God of the end of things. He always bestows beginnings. God is positive. His mercies are new every morning (cf. Lam. 3:23). One must only learn to see. And ultimately, faith is nothing else but seeing that this is so.

So everything in life depends upon getting this point of view, namely, that God has a purpose for Noah, for you, and for me, no matter what may be the envelope in which this plan of life is inclosed, whether floods and reverses or success and happiness.

What is the story of the Flood without this determining point of view, that God keeps faith with those who are faithful to him, that he knows how to preserve and guide and grant undreamed-of security?

Once you eliminate this central message, the account of the Flood is nothing more than a bit of meteorology and climatology. Then it is an account of a prehistoric flood which is in remarkable agreement with those preserved in the legends of many peoples.

But what the Bible tells us here is more than just one chronicle among others. The two biblical writers who composed this story are rather concerned to hear the hidden theme in this ancient story and they see in it the governance of an eternal Hand that makes heaven and earth serve the purposes of its judgment, and in the very midst of this judgment graciously establishes something new.

In other words, once you no longer see the judging and establishing Hand at work, then—immediately!—the story of the Flood becomes a confused and bewildering picture of a destructive catastrophe, an insoluble riddle of the meaningless death of thousands upon thousands of aged, women, and children—such as appears in the age-old flood stories of other peoples. Then this story strikes us the same way the report of the earthquake in Lisbon broke upon the enlightened world of the age of Rationalism and alienated men from God.

Let me illustrate what I mean by something that happens in our television sets.

When a person does not know how to operate a television set and turns the wrong knob, it may happen that, instead of a proper picture, he will get only quivering streaks and flashes on the screen. Now, in our scientific age we are far too rational-minded to conclude from these magic streaks and lines on our screen that the *transmitter* is sending out such crazy stuff. We know that it is our wrong adjustments that produce these optical confusions and that the transmitter is sending out sensible pictures. The confusion lies not in the sending, but in our receiving.

Now, the following observation strikes me as important. As soon as it is a matter of the ups and downs in our own lives we begin to think in a way completely opposite to the way we do when we look at our television screen. How often such chaotic mazes, such confused patterns of bad luck and meaningless accident appear on the screen of our life! We think of the death of a young mother, snatched away from her small children, while an aged man, weary of life and wanting death to come, cannot die. We grieve over the unsuccessfulness of work we have faithfully performed and can see no sense in it. I look on while my boss is transferred at the very time he was about to promote me. Such confused mazes on the screen of our life are simply proofs of the nonexistence of God. We feel like fatherless children who are caught in a dread circle of fateful forces and defenselessly exposed to the play of chance.

In terms of our illustration this means that the moment we are subjected to what is meaningless and even before we cry out "Why?"—because this question would be fruitless anyhow—we cease to look for the fault in our own wrong adjustments and say: The transmitter is not functioning or the director has probably left his celestial booth or there isn't any director at all. Does it ever occur to any of us that the confusion in our life which we can no longer make head or tail of lies in ourselves and our own wrong adjustments?

It would, of course, be unfair for me to conceal the fact that there is a limp in this illustration of the television. For we have not been promised that when we adjust the knobs properly, in other words, when we believe and keep in view the governing hand of God, we shall always get clear and easily understood pictures of how God guides our life and what he is trying to say to us in all these puzzling things. In many cases it will be true that "What I am doing you do *not* know now, but *afterward* you will understand" (John 13:7). Did Noah understand what was happening when he was ordered to build an ark while the sky was bright and cloudless? Did he grasp the meaning of this terrible catastrophe? After all, he saw people perishing in this flood who may have been dear to him and of whose guilt he was not convinced. He too may well have had an unsolved question on his lips.

But now I myself must raise an objection. May it not occur to us that this saying about understanding "afterward" is a rather dusty answer? Aren't we being put off with a rather cheap promise of heaven when for the moment we receive only the negative reply that we must be content with no answer to our question of Why? Why does God leave us so terribly alone with our riddles? Why does he make it so hard for us?

And here again the chorus of biblical witnesses reply that this is the way that God sets us a positive task. Perhaps nobody has uttered such profound thoughts about this question as Kierkegaard. He tells us that there are no absolute certainties except in mathematics. But they also leave us rather cold. Once we have grasped the Pythagorean proposition there can never again be any doubt about it. It never troubles our heart, for our intellect has settled the question of its correctness for us once and for all.

But then what about the other certainties in our life? What about the person, let us say, of whom we have thought so much and who suddenly does something we simply cannot understand, something which is certainly *not* as clear and intelligible as the Pythagorean proposition? What happens when we trust a person, where we utterly trust his honesty and the integrity of his character, and he suddenly does something that calls in question the purity of his nature? Nehru has said that when he was a young man he often **did not understand** the decisions of his teacher, Gandhi. But in the end, "afterward," they always turned out to be right. This experience, he said, had a remarkable effect upon his relationship with Gandhi. Whenever Gandhi did some something strange, indeed, something that appeared disastrously wrong and senseless, he, Nehru, was finally never able to bring himself to quit him brusquely and go his own way. These situations rather served only to put his trust in Gandhi to the ultimate tensile test. And the more uneasy this objective uncertainty concerning Gandhi's procedure made him, the more fervently did his heart, his trust, take flight to this superior man, the more did he bow to him intellectually. The more disquieted his heart became, the more troubled he was intellectually, the more he was thrown back upon his trust, upon venturing his faith in Gandhi, and the more this confidence grew and finally became unshakable.

In just this sense Kierkegaard says that precisely when I have no objective certainty, when I have no certainty that comes from touching, feeling, and seeing, the "infinite passion of inwardness" awakens.

This is only a very human example, even an example that comes from the non-Christian world. And it is also imperfect. Nevertheless this illustration can help us to see something of the mystery of divine guidance in our life and in the history of the world. The very time when we can no longer understand a catastrophe like the Flood or even the rushing streams and deluges in our personal life—when we are troubled and tempted by them—is the time when this very anxiety, this temptation, even dread, can become raw material for our faith. The more we learn to say in such times of disquiet, "Nevertheless I shall remain with thee," the closer will we come to the heart of God and the more confidently will we learn to say:

> Though the way I do not know
> Thou know'st it well;
> This fills my soul with peace
> And quietude.

As those who do not know, we trust him who does know. As those who do not know *why* he does what he does, we believe that he knows *to what end* he is doing it.

That's why the great believers of history, like Luther and von Bodelschwingh and Jung-Stilling, have always been sorely tried men, people who were often in deep waters rising to their throats, and often plunged into the abyss of darkest despair and perplexity. And this was precisely the reason they possessed a rich store of raw materials from which faith could be formed. All of them experienced, each in his own way, the miracle of transformation by which God is able to change the stones of dread into the bread of confident trust.

It is therefore very important to define the *theme* of our story rightly, and I must enlarge upon it in somewhat greater detail in order to do this as precisely as possible. This story is not concerned with a prehistoric epoch of climatic events which may be of interest to natural science or archeology. This story has only one theme: what happens to this man Noah at the hands of God. It is the story of a survival with God.

If Noah had looked only at the elements and let his eyes gaze upon the vast and watery wastes, he would have perished of mortal dread. For there his eyes would have found no resting place and even the time would have seemed endless and immeasurable. He would have been like the sinking Peter, who lost sight of his Lord as he attempted to walk upon the water and, left all alone with the elements, saw nothing but the waves, and therefore sank like a rock.

Noah, however, did not yield himself to the unnerving impression of flood and catastrophe, but simply held on to God's promise that He still had something in mind for him. He also knew that no ark could ever help him once he lost his hold on the hand that held him and his own above the flood. "I shall not die, but I shall live, and recount the deeds of the Lord"; it was by that kind of certainty that he *really* survived. The planks of the ark are nothing more than poor instrumentalities to effect that promise and without its blessing they would be worthless lumber. Unless the Lord builds and guides the ark, it is built in vain (cf. Ps. 127:1).

This presents us with one final question. Is not exactly the same thing true about the way we survive death, the deluge at the brink of our finitude? How did we ever get the presumptuous idea that death is *not* the end, that we are "immortal"? What exertions thinkers and religious men have made to prove this! Above everything else they have taught the immortality of the soul. They have asserted that the innermost self, the so-called soul constitutes a kind of ark that will bear us across the great flood of Styx, the river of death, to the shore of eternity. Only our bodies sink in that flood, but the soul is indestructible.

Surely it is astonishing that the Bible says nothing whatsoever about all this and that that kind of a doctrine of immortality did not grow out of Christian soil, though it has stealthily found its way into many of the church's sermons and funeral addresses.

Suppose that this doctrine of immortality, this principle of "the indestructibility of the soul" were true and I were to put my trust in it; would I not be like a Noah who trusted in the indestructibility and buoyancy of the ark of his soul and was indifferent to the *promise* of his Lord that He, and He alone, would bring him to the shore of a new beginning, and also indifferent to the *hand* of his Lord which would give him peace, security, and hope in the desolate watery waste? Does Noah's security really rest only upon the calculations of the art of ship-building and faith in the strength of its materials? Does belief in immortality, in our alleged superiority over death really consist only in the assumption that our soul-substance is indestructible, that nobody and nothing, not even death can harm this ark of the soul?

We need only to express it in this way to see that faith in the so-called immortality of the soul is no faith at all. It is rather a highly questionable assumption, which can be made even by a complete heathen and worldling. One can make it without caring two pins for God. One can still make it, even if one considers the resurrection of the Lord a highly superfluous spectacle of pious fantasy. Belief in immortality in this sense is nothing else but an insane trust in the ark—the ark of the soul—without any recourse to the hand that blesses our shelters and arks, without the light of that face the removal of which will cast us into dismay and dust and eternal death (cf. Ps. 104:29). This is *not* the way Noah sailed the watery waste.

Luther once stated in a very profound sentence the kind of immortality to which biblical thought points: "The man with whom God has begun to speak, be it in wrath or in grace, that man is truly immortal." That's it; that's the way it is! When God begins to deal with a man, when he speaks his Word to him, when his pentecostal Spirit touches him and the man responds, in other words, when he learns to trust God, receives forgiveness from him, and sets all his hope upon him, then *God never again ceases to deal with him.* Then he keeps faith with him; then not even death can come between them.

Our real immortality is nothing but another expression for the faithfulness of God, which is stronger than death and will never put our trust to shame. There *is* no such thing as immortality; God *gives* immortality. (God may also speak to us in wrath and, as Luther suggests, God deals with unbelief too. This "history" of God dealing with unbelief never ceases in all eternity either, and here, though it makes us shudder, we may speak of an immortality of terror. This, however, is not our concern in this connection.)

Then we understand why Jesus Christ is a necessary part of this immortality: "In order that"—I quote once more those comforting words of Matthias Claudius—"he may lift us up and hold us while we live, and lay his hand beneath our head when we come to die." For it is in him that God deals with us, has his "history" with us, that personal history through which he binds himself to us and gives a fellowship with him that survives death. For what can separate us from the love of God which is in this

Jesus? Can anything be mightier than his love? Can there be any sin that redemption is too weak to deal with, that therefore cannot be forgiven? Can death be mightier than the life that God would give us?

This would be the time for us to read together the Easter hymns of the church, in order that the scales might fall from our eyes and we would understand how we are being drawn by grace through floods and fires, through doubt and despair, through age and death, the grave and decay, because there is One who has broken through the dark encompassment of death and never gives us up.

This is the note—that we are Christ's companions, "where'er he goes, I too abide"—that runs through all these hymns. Sadness is compelled to retreat, for Jesus has entered the fray. And on the crumbling walls of this passing world the laughter of Christians breaks forth in triumph, because the hand that draws us up is reaching down into the bursting wreckage—including the wreckage of our perishing lives.

So we pass through the throes of death, just as Noah came through the floods. We are survivors, because we are in league with the Prince of life. This is the immortality of the patriarchs and prophets and disciples. And if we did not have it we would be of all men most miserable. We would be fanatics and charlatans if without it we dared to speak of the resurrection on the third day.

So Noah steers across the endless flood and his heart is at peace. He knows that his dove will find dry land and bring back the forgiving sign of the olive branch—if not today, then tomorrow or the day after.

Noah sees more than the waters. He knows the new life that will spring up deep beneath him. He knows that the day will come when God *once more* will utter his "Let there be!" across the wasteland, and that then *once more* his "history" will begin —"be it in wrath or in grace"—and that he will bring all things to their goal, the ark to Ararat, his own to eternal life, and the history of the world to the day of judgment. "For there is no escape," said Jung-Stilling, "from the providence of God." And that's because God is always stronger than the powers of destruction.

Not even man's corruption, which, after all, provoked the Flood, can ruin God's creation. Even though men today are trying to reconstruct it, even though they break marriages, destroy families, and turn things upside down as they are doing in China, they will never smash it, because God is stronger than everything that rises up against him and he circumvents even death, the last enemy, and it is no longer the ultimate at all.

But we dare not put our trust in arks, in political prescriptions and armament potentials by which we hope to survive the floods —and who knows what trials may be in store for us! No, we must hold fast to him who says in majesty: "Thus far shall you come, and no farther, and here shall your proud waves be stayed." Hold fast to him who dwells above the vastly deep and endless empty space and yet keeps his eye upon that tiny point where Noah floats upon his ark, never forgetting where you and I live our little lives.

As Noah sends out the dove and sends this message to his God: "I cannot see, but I wait for thee," God answers: "But I see thee, and I am coming."

Noah was a happy, blessed man, for he did not anxiously wait for what *might* come, but waited for him who most certainly will come, for him who will surely be there at the proper time.

17

Noah—The Adventure of Faith

The Story of the Flood: Part Two

Then God said to Noah, "Go forth from the ark, you and your wife, and your sons and your sons' wives with you. Bring forth with you every living thing that is with you of all flesh—birds and animals and every creeping thing that creeps on the earth—that they may breed abundantly on the earth, and be fruitful and multiply upon the earth." So Noah went forth, and his sons and his wife and his sons' wives with him. And every beast, every creeping thing, and every bird, everything that moves upon the earth, went forth by families out of the ark.

Then Noah built an altar to the Lord, and took of every clean animal and of every clean bird, and offered burnt offerings on the altar.

—*Genesis 8:15–20*

Surely the most shocking statement in the story of the Flood is this: "And the Lord was sorry that he had made man. . . ."

Did we really hear this aright? After all, isn't God omniscient, so that he could have foreseen this breakdown of creation? Isn't he powerful enough to prevent such a thing? Is a God who has to recant and revise and reverse himself a God at all? Doesn't this compromise his alleged divinity? Or better and quite bluntly: Do not such human-all-too-human features in this image of God make it painfully clear that it cannot be based upon "revelation," but that this is a purely human composition—a fabrication in which we men paint the picture of God according to our pattern and project upon heaven the portrait of changeable, uncertain, self-correcting man? Is God a man, that he should repent? (Cf. I Sam. 15:29.)

So right at the start I should like to state the contrary thesis with the same force with which I put the question: That which for a moment may look like a shortcoming, like something undivine in God is in reality the very secret of his heart. If we do not learn to understand this, the revolutionizing new thing in the gospel will remain closed to us and we shall not hear a single note of it.

Therefore we must first exert every effort to explain this statement that God was sorry and repented that he had made man. And to do this we must recall certain parts of the creation story.

We remember that there God gave to man something like "freedom." He set him apart from the whales, the birds, and the elephants. None of them can decide whether they wish to become fish, birds, or elephants. But to man the chance, and the burden too, has been given to decide for himself whether he wants to become human or inhuman, whether he wishes to realize or sabotage his destiny.

God does not want man to be a marionette that responds precisely and mechanically to the slightest movement of his finger. He wants living men, who have it in them to give their hearts to him, but who can also stand up to him as rebels and throw up the whole deal like Prometheus.

So this is the other side of the fact that God is great and good enough to grant the gift of freedom. Now he must accept the possibility that this man may also use this freedom *against* him and thus decide against him.

I wonder whether we see the implications of this at once.

If what we have said is true, then our human philosophies, all the superstitious pother our hearts cook up, even atheism and antichristianity and nihilism are nothing less than possibilities which God himself has put at our disposal. Then God has given me the freedom—just as the father did in the parable of the Prodigal Son—to renounce him and go off into the far country.

After all, this is the way it is in life: if I grant certain liberties to other persons—my children or my subordinates—if I give power of attorney or the right to make certain decisions to my fellow workers, then I have limited and partially surrendered my own freedom, for I make myself dependent upon what the other person may do with his freedom.

In reality this was the beginning of the suffering of God which reached its culmination on Calvary. God suffers the consequences of his goodness. He suffers from what men do with his gifts. This is the secret of the suffering God which is in the background of all Christian testimony.

I am always compelled to think of this whenever I hear people say: "How can God allow such a thing?" I can still hear this question being put to me during the bombing, sometimes in great sadness and sometimes in rude sarcasm. A sea of flames raged over the city. People ran through the streets like living torches. Children suffocated in the cellars. The refugee center crashed to the ground, killing thousands of fugitives. Dresden perished in horror and mortal terror. And sure as death, always there came this one question: "How can God permit such a thing?"

Have we ever stopped to think that all these witches' sabbaths were and are—and will be again in the atomic disasters that may come—nothing but consequences of man's playing hob with his gift of freedom; that they are all misuses of a God-given power of attorney, squanderings of the Father's capital, and basically violations of God's gifts? The question, "How can God permit this?" can also take on a very timely point and be put somewhat like this: "Why does God allow the tyrants and great tormentors of humanity to exist; why doesn't he smite them dead?" But, as Dorothy Sayers, the well-known detective-story writer, says, this would be "a question a little remote from us.

Why, madam, did he not strike you dumb and imbecile before you uttered that baseless and unkind slander the day before yesterday? Or me, before I behaved with such cruel lack of consideration to that well-meaning friend? And why, sir, did he not cause your hand to rot off at the wrist before you signed your name to that dirty little bit of financial trickery? You did not quite mean that? But why not? Your misdeeds and mine are none the less repellent because our opportunities for doing damage are less spectacular than those of some other people. Do you suggest that your doing and mine are too trivial for God to bother about? That cuts both ways; for, in that case, it would make precious little difference to his creation if he wiped us both out tomorrow."[1]

So when we ask: "How can God permit this?" and thus furtively imply that God is the chief culprit, that this merchandise called "creation" is no good, and that he ought to be dragged to a court where the mothers of the slain, the orphans and widows of those who perished so miserably could accuse him—I should say that when we whisper all this to ourselves this again betrays that disastrous talent of man for seeking a lightning rod to divert his own guilt: "God is at fault, God is guilty!" It's always the same old story.

Actually, why shouldn't the prodigal son have cried out among the swine: "Why did my father let me go? Why did he give me my inheritance? Why didn't he put me on a chain to protect me from myself? Now I am being strangled by my own freedom, the freedom I misused."

But just because the prodigal son did *not* attempt to do this and did *not* play the game of passing the buck, he did not get stuck fast in the far country. Precisely because he was able to say: "I am no longer worthy to be called your son," he was able to come home, and the father even came to meet him.

Do we understand now why God cares, why he should be

[1] Dorothy Sayers, *Creed or Chaos?* (New York: Harcourt, Brace, 1949), p. 9. The author quotes from the German edition, *Das grösste Drama aller Zeiten*, translated by Karl Barth (1959), p. 24.

sorry and repent? Can we really dare to go on asserting that this is the sign of a human-all-too-human God? Is not this rather the other side of the fact that God is a royal giver and that now he must discover in pain and sadness how everything we have is perverted and spoiled in our hands; how our power over creation leads to delusions of grandeur; how the joy of sex becomes brutish rut; how our reason becomes a meretricious whore; and how we use our knowledge of the elements and energies of creation to shatter this same creation?

Is there any greater pain than that which we suffer when we give and sacrifice our best to someone and he casts it disdainfully at our feet, after having first vilified and besmirched everything we love?

I think we understand now the pain that is expressed in this statement that God was sorry that he had been so kind as to grant us freedom. God has a heart that bleeds and winces beneath the blows of what we do, for we matter to him. His heart is a father's heart.

And therefore it is altogether understandable and deeply moving that the Bible also tells us something of the opposite way of "repenting," namely, that God is seized with compassion for our *lostness*, that he can also be sorry over the Flood, and that he wants to see an end to expiation. And *once more* he causes a new morning of creation to dawn, replete with "seedtime and harvest, cold and heat, summer and winter, day and night."

We would be ill-advised to conclude that this is just the "good, kindhearted" God at work, a God who could not bear the harshness of his own law of expiation, like the poor, feckless old man that Wolfgang Borchert pictures him to be. On the contrary, Luther once described what happens here in the metaphor of a struggle of God with himself: God, the Judge, wrestling with God, the Father. This is the great marvel, the absolutely unexpected message—that causes his angel choirs to sing forth peace on Christmas night, that he proclaims the turn of the aeons, and that now he wants to be wholly and nothing but the

Father, who meets us at the threshold of the father's house, even though we return from the far country laden with guilt and faithlessness.

If this were only the good-naturedness of "the good Lord," Jesus would never have had to die. Then there would have been no need for that sacrificial action and suffering by which he took upon his shoulders the weight of the whole world. No, what is at work here is the miracle through which God conquered the *ira dei* (wrath of God) by means of his love. Here pain and anguish struggle in God himself. And therefore, here again beats the heart that trembles and loves and pities and suffers with me. This is no mere principle of love, this is no God of the philosophers—as Pascal called him—here there is nothing except his loving heart.

The gospel simply means that by his wonderful act God has broken the law of retribution and that only his mercy prevails.

To appraise the surprise, the marvel of this second "repentance" of God we need only to look at the people of the New Testament who became witnesses to this marvel. From the shepherds in the field on Christmas Eve to Peter, who saw this marvel in the majesty of his Master, and many others who saw the healing and forgiving goodness of God in the fact of Jesus Christ, not one of them speaks of a "loving God" whom they had always known and therefore could be no surprise to them. On the contrary, their reaction is totally different: they were filled with fear, they fell to the ground, they took cover, they trembled and did not dare to believe what had happened to them. That God should deliver them from the primeval law of guilt and punishment, that he should accept them without demanding expiation, love them, and account them just, all this was so overwhelmingly unexpected that they could not bear it and had to stop and assess this new situation.

It is one of the dark sides of what is called Christian tradition that we are hardly able to re-enact the awe and the thrill of this wonder of God. We are a bit too accustomed to it. For many of us the gospel is no longer news, but an all-too-old and familiar tale. But it is important to know that the rise of a new world after the Flood and the beginning of a new aeon in Christ is founded solely upon this surprising marvel, a miracle, a new thing, which no man can demand or expect. This miracle is the "repentance of God." Now he is troubled by the troubles of his children and now he says, contrary to all expectation—and this time it is *God* himself who says it to his child who is lost in the far country—"Nevertheless I shall cling to thee."

In time of the Flood, the hour when the world lay in the balance, there was only one man in whom God was not frustrated: Noah. Who was this remarkable man?

"Noah was a righteous man, blameless in his generation; Noah walked with God." Was Noah, therefore, what we are accustomed to call a "morally upright" man? Was he the moral paragon of his time? If this were so, then it is certainly not the secret of his preservation.

The secret lies somewhere else. Noah was a man who listened and heeded, and also did the unusual when God required it of him; a man who, for example, built a ship, a real ship, when the sun was shining, built it on land, far from rivers or seas. For this is what God had told him to do. He obviously was not the kind of person who does something only because others are doing it, because it is "being done." There is not an hour of the day in which he is not inquiring about the will of God and then allowing himself to be led by it step by step.

Even as a child it made a deep impression upon me that Noah not only heard the general, blanket command, "Build an ark!" but also that he acted "according to directions" in every detail of materials, measurements, and caulking, that he was constantly open to guidance.

So Noah included in his fellowship with God even the little things of his life, the everyday details. Noah did not pray only for the great things in his life—that God would preserve him and his family in the coming catastrophe—but rather talked with God about the planks with which he built the ark, the partitions of the rooms, and the pitch with which he made this monster of a ship watertight. And surely, later on when he and his motley clan sailed upon the vast surface of the Flood, he talked with his God, not only about the whole store of provisions, but also the rations of fodder and food which he needed for all his hungry mouths each day. No topic is too small, too banal, to be brought to God.

And so it is with us too. It is only as we share with God the little things, not only when we talk with God about the great theme of world peace or the future of our children, but about the the toothaches that torment us, the letter we have to write, the anticipation of a sports festival, the flowers in a vase—only then do we have God constantly in our minds and hearts. For, after all, our life consists of a sum of little things.

This and this alone is the virtue of Noah—the fact that he was a trusting man, that he never made the great and the small decisions of his life at his own discretion, but always made himself merely an instrument.

In that which was decisive he took no part at all, but simply held his peace. For, concerning this decisive matter the Bible says in the spare greatness of its language: "The Lord shut him in." The Lord sealed him off and secured him against the elements. And a generation like our own may well prick up its ears at this. For we are ardently intent upon security and assurances. Even the majority of young people are after a dead certain career with a pension and have little stomach for adventure and risk.

Noah was by no means simply careless; he did not dally with the thrill of danger; but after he had done his part, he let God shut the door behind him. For we ourselves cannot dot the i's and put the period after our life-program. The moment comes when we must step back and allow ourselves to be pushed, because we know that Another has shut the door behind us.

So Noah sailed on—an adventurer in trust. He was cast entirely upon security in him who had locked the door on the outside. There were no latches or locks on the inside of the ark. Noah was confined in a narrow space. Sometimes he may have felt constricted, cramped, and oppressed, as if he were caught in a "bottleneck." Which of us is not familiar with this fear of being caught in a tight place, of being shut into a situation from which there is no way out? Who has not experienced that feeling of utter inability to break out of some situation where we are completely hemmed in and surrounded? Noah thinks of him who locked him in, who has the key, and will bring him out in his good time. And when he thinks of him, all is well.

For the adventurer of faith the next hour and the next day are always a great unknown. But the *ultimate* thing is always certain, and that is that the hand that locked us in will also open the lock, that our ark will land on Ararat, and that all the erring, zigzag ways of our life will end at the Father's house. That's why it is an adventure to sail with God. Nevertheless, it's not an aimless voyage.

So Noah knows that he is safe with God even in *external* things. He knows that God undoubtedly has control over this catastrophic Flood.

Is it true that faith in God provides only an *inner* support? Many people believe this. They say that religion is a very good and practical thing in life. Religion provides strength and creates spiritual reserves which enable us to bear more easily the hard things in life. Well, people who think in this way are not counting upon the living God at all, even though this may sound quite devout. For this God of ours is not merely the Lord of our spiritual stirrings and emotions; he is the Master of fate itself. He not only gives us the "inner" courage, the mental and spiritual attitude, so to speak, in which we endure a dreadful illness, but he can also heal us of the illness itself. He not only gives us something like calmness of spirit when the little ship of our life is pitched to and fro in the storms; he needs only to speak *one* word and the waves are stilled—the actual, *external* waves, not merely the waves in our soul and the fevered beating of our heart.

In this very same way he not only gives "peace of soul" to Noah in his ark, but also sees to it that the flood cannot harm him. He also took in hand his *outward* fate.

I find it wonderfully good and comforting that here God is at work in a really "outward" way, completely outside any religious, spiritual, "inward" sphere whatsoever, that he is also with dogs and cats and elephants and wrens, who cannot have such a thing as a mental attitude or courage, and that he rejoices when the evening praise of Noah's family rings out across the desolate wastes mingled with barking, mewing, trumpeting, and warbling.

Nor should we drive our animals from the room when we have our family worship. After all, God is by no means so "spiritual" that he will associate only with men and, if possible, only with pious, spiritual-minded and highly moral men. After all, "the eyes of *all* look to him" and "out of the mouth of babes," out of the song of the lark and the croaking of frogs has he brought perfect praise.

So the ark went floating along, both men and beasts singing the praise of the Creator. For God loves every living thing.

When the angels sang on Christmas night the sheep were there, and ox and ass stood by the manger. God is not confined to the realm of the human spirit. It's only the so-called religious people who think this way. The living God is also the Lord of sick and healthy bodies, of floods and fires, and the cosmic orbits of the planets. The hand of him who says, "All authority in heaven and on earth has been given to me" can touch in blessing a small child's tousled hair, even though his nose may be a bit runny; at the same time His arms embrace the light years of the universe.

The fact that Noah is the great believer and that God therefore remembers him also comes out at the *end* of his voyage.

When he stepped out of the crowded ark with all the pairs

of animals and the fowls set up a joyful cackling and the people stretched their rusty bones, his first act was to erect an altar and present his sacrifice of thanksgiving.

A teacher who had told the story of the Flood to his pupils as colorfully, vividly, and graphically as possible once told me that at the close he challenged the children not to hesitate to ask any question they might have. One little girl raised her hand and said that the part about Noah kneeling down to give thanks as soon as he stepped off the ark surely couldn't be right, because then he and his children must have had to kneel down in the mud, and that would be "nasty."

One does not always get the impression when children ask questions that they have gotten the essential point. And that is just the reason they are so amusing (except for people who have no sense of humor and have not yet found out that God can laugh too).

Nevertheless I suggest that this little girl caught something that is perfectly valid, namely, that it really should give us pause when we hear that for Noah the first thing, the *very* first thing is the prayer of thanks.

For, after all, when he left the ark he was in a crisis situation: there he was suddenly thrown out bag and baggage and facing a desolate chaos of mud and mire. Normally in such a situation of elementary need one does the elementary thing: one looks for tents and emergency shelter, for spring water and food.

But before Noah raised all such questions, he erected an altar. Long before he thought about a roof over his head, he built the place for the worship of God. Consequently, *this* is the elementary thing for him, namely, not to break off contact and communication with God. Consequently, this foundation is the first thing to be marked out, for all future building and all future life is to be founded upon it.

I believe that we people of today are such fanatics for security, such blind, mad, sham-realists, because we no longer understand that this is the basic, important thing—to get into the clear with God and put the altar at the beginning. Because we have forgotten this, we live in the delusion that we must do everything ourselves. We think: first I must set my job in order, put my business on a solid basis, pass this particular examination or get over that hurdle in my path. First I must settle the so-called elementary areas of life—and only then, when I have all this behind me, can I permit myself to think about the inner comfort of life; then I'll have time to cultivate my soul and the inner man a bit.

But when I think in this way I have already gambled away the decisive thing in life. For it is axiomatic that God does not come when it fits my schedule. There we have him down for the time after our second heart attack. But, alas, the God who is thus put down in our date book never shows up. God doesn't allow himself to be dealt with dilatorily, for he insists upon being the elementary thing in my life and not just the symbol of a bit of additional spiritual comfort or of certain pious symptoms of advancing age.

Noah and his family knelt in the mud, and, measured by *this* standard, the securing of dry ground, the procuring of the vital needs of life are completely secondary. I suggest that this account contains an unmistakable question addressed to us. Don't we often nervously start up our ship's motor in the morning before we have hardly wakened and let it run full speed even before we have set our course? In the realm of faith there are not only "wicked servants," but also wicked captains, who are addicted to the error that the elementary and important thing in our voyage into the new day is to get the motor of our mind and also of our body moving as quickly as possible and turn it up to high speed. They forget all about navigation and the goal. And that's why our day's work is often less like the singleness of purpose in a ship's course and more like the furious spinning of a top that keeps revolving around itself, turning about in the void and never getting anywhere.

This means quite simply that the person who does not *build the altar*, like Noah, before the landscape of the new day gains clear contours, before he enters the new world of such and such a date with its programs and tasks and appointments, the person who does not set the theme and the course of the new day by that altar but steals into it without the Lord's Prayer and a word from the Holy Scriptures, that person is beginning the day as a "wicked" businessman, a "wicked" father or a "wicked" mother. And he need not be surprised when at evening the voice of God overtakes him: "The things you have prepared, whose will they be?" (Luke 12:20).

We may be doing piece work and our tempo may be so fast that we get a heart attack. But in our labor we neglect to ask the question: In whose barn are we really gathering which harvest? Aren't we constantly, day after day, heaping thing after thing, coin after coin into a bag full of holes? And the result is "a long day's journey into night." (Eugene O'Neill).

Noah sacrificed the best of his cattle on the altar he had erected. He who does not offer the most vital and wide-awake hour of the day does not create a "pleasing odor" (vs. 21). For God is either the headline of our life or we are writing the chronicle of our life without him. He does not run with the "also rans" and he refuses to appear anywhere except in the "banner heading."

As Noah erected an altar at the beginning of the *new world*, so he had already set up the sign of his faith at the end of the perishing antediluvian world. His life was all of a piece and "his purity was to will one thing" (Kierkegaard).

When he received the command to build the ark the weather was still peaceful. His neighbors and friends may well have wondered why he would begin to build a ship on land while the sun was shining brightly and all the weather prophets and political prophets were predicting dry and untroubled times. In the evening couples came out for a stroll to see the spectral ship in the moonlight; people ate and drank, married and were given in marriage, and shook their heads in derision over this queer old saint.

When Noah set about this highly fantastic undertaking, which no reasoning could ever make plausible, he was living a faith that sees nothing, that has no reason to point to, and is constantly under the necessity of fighting down the objections of his own reason.

Undoubtedly there must have been many times when he asked himself uneasily whether he had not been a fool and a fantast to bind himself so blindly to this odd command of an odd God and simply trust that it was right and that God would not let him down. The head-shaking of these amused people around him—these rational, commonsensical people—may actually have gotten on his nerves. The sun shone and shone and all around him nothing but dry land—and here he was building a ship! Noah, the admiral of the land marines—it was a bitter thing to hear what was being said and what in moments of weakness he felt like saying himself.

Is not what God here requires of Noah the same as what we may say to a young person? We say: See to it betimes, that is, in season and out of season, that you get a foundation under your feet, that you build an ark for yourself, for the storms and cloudbursts will come. The young person may then react the same way the people of yore did when Noah said to them: "These bright skies will be darkened, the floodgates of heaven will be opened, and I am building an ark for myself and my family." Involuntarily these people would then have asked themselves, despite the oddness of this Noah: "It won't do any harm to be on the safe side; oughtn't we too get hold of some kind of floating foundation in case a flood should come?"

But the thought scarcely emerges before it dies. In the next moment they are reassuring themselves: "Today is today! Instead of working our heads off for such an eventuality, we'll have a palaver at the village pump this evening," or, "At the moment we're about to play hockey or go sailing or on a camping trip.

Let the old folks worry about a stay in life and a boat for the river Styx when rheumatism comes or calcification and coronaries send out their harbingers."

I once read of an old actor who was on his deathbed and in his distress called for an old friend and associate to come to see him. After groaning a bit and indicating that he was exceedingly troubled, he finally asked his friend to say the Lord's Prayer. In rather painful self-deprecation, however, the friend replied, "I regret it, my dear fellow, but I have no prompter." Perhaps in that hour he would have given much to be able to recall from memory such comforting and sustaining words as "Nevertheless, I shall abide with thee" or "My thoughts are not your thoughts" or "I have called you by name, you are mine."

So the people in Noah's time would probably have given everything if they had had an ark in that decisive moment when X-Day broke upon them and the great trial came.

If only the warning signs had appeared *beforehand*, if only it had thundered a bit and a few stormclouds had appeared on the horizon! But the skies were blue and it was vacation time. Nor did one from the dead come to warn the rich man's five brothers (cf. Luke 16:27 ff.). As Jesus expressed it, they had only "Moses and the prophets" and had to decide whether they would listen or close their ears.

The great fateful questions of faith are addressed to us very privately and almost inaudibly. They are unaccompanied by the rumbling of thunder and propaganda. Any advertisement for brand name stockings or beauty soap is far more noisy.

True, when the fountains of the great deep burst forth and the windows of the heavens were opened, the people cried out to God in prayer. Who hasn't done this and does not still do it? Don't we remember the hours in the cellar during the nights of bombing or the time when that *one* dreadful telegram arrived? But the strange thing is that the curtain hardly rises upon a prayer that has its premiere only at the moment when peril has already broken in; such a prayer has not been "learned and rehearsed." It seems never to get beyond the ceiling of the room, and contact with God to whom I am crying just doesn't take place any more.

Such a prayer—we have already touched upon this in another connection—is all too likely to be sucked into the panic of the moment instead of breaking through the panic and letting in the breath of peace. For faith is like a seed that must grow in order to provide fruit in the time of harvest. This is a slow process and takes time. Every pastor is familiar with the difficulty experienced at many a deathbed where he is expected to say a word of Godspeed and comfort—right now, when the time has grown short. Here he should be able to take hold of such words as he would fruit that has grown in the soil of this person's life. But how can one sow and reap in the same hour?

Besides it is a disastrous superstition, which has also spread among many teachers, that the things of faith are something that must be spared the immature child and that they become important only after they have reached the stage of maturity and ability to make decisions. This means that as far as faith is concerned, it can wait until the floods of life actually arrive; it has no place in the alleged peace of the paradise of childhood. What shall we say to this?

Most certainly Jesus Christ is the friend of little children, and his Word is so simple that the praise of babes and sucklings can put to shame many who are wise and certainly many who think of themselves as intellectuals. Nevertheless, it is *also* a Word which is always above and beyond us, which we grow into step by step. We adults are bound up with children in a mysterious solidarity. We too continue to grow and ultimately we are never fully grown up; we too continue to know only in part and wait for the hour when we shall know and see face to face what we have believed.

Therefore we should not smile when a little boy or girl recites the Catechism or be amused when the little fellow walks about in oversized armor, in which is concentrated the spiritual experience of centuries and the burden of mature knowledge. The armor is there for us to grow into.

The eternal words are always greater than ourselves. And therefore they will never become too small for us, as children's verses grow too small for us. They will not be too small for us even if we reach the peak of human knowledge and become doctors of the wisdom of the world. We can never grow beyond these everlasting words; we can only grow into them more deeply.

Why are we touched and moved when the clear voices of St. Michael's boys proclaim in song the ultimate mysteries of all judgment and all grace? Who smiles because these boys still do not know *what* they are singing? They are still as it were in Advent and as "babes" they are singing praise to that which for them is still to come. But later on, if God grants his grace, they will repeat and perfect this praise in all its registers, the register of the heart and life's experience and also the register of the praiseful intellect. So who dares to smile when the little ones proclaim the Infinite with childish voices, when they sing of the depths, though they themselves still pass over them like unknowing dreamers, when twelve-year-olds sing of the heavenly Jerusalem, which even the aged apostle did not see until he reached the Nebo of his life?

So Noah's faith is exactly like our own—a growing faith. As the Flood destroyed and buried every living thing Noah's faith grew and bore him high above the abodes of catastrophe. And this is the very miracle and wonder of faith—that the very thing that kills and buries and overwhelms is now compelled to bear him up. Anybody who has made this venture of faith and knows it from his own experience knows that this is just simple truth. Everything that comes to us like an assault of fate—dread of the future, human disappointments, embroilments in our life, trials and afflictions—all this becomes for him who has faith an element which can no longer swamp and bury him, but mysteriously bears him up, as Noah was borne up by the Flood.

Many a person who has experienced this has also testified that faith actually needs the perilous elements to prove its lifting and sustaining power.

And that's why Jesus Christ does not say, in the face of troubles to come: When these things come upon you, then take cover, dig yourself in, lie flat on the ground! No, he says: When things grow really hard for you, "look up and raise your heads, because your redemption is drawing near."

Why does faith rise up and take heart like this? Why does it go striding through the storms with head held high? Because it hears the footsteps of Another, striding toward us in these very storms, because the tempests never come unaccompanied, because there is a voice that calls to us in every gale and a hand that holds us in every dark and dismal place.

THE BUILDING OF THE TOWER OF BABEL

18

The Fear of Our Fellows

THE TOWER OF BABEL

Now the whole earth had one language and few words. And as men migrated in the east, they found a plain in the land of Shinar and settled there. And they said to one another, "Come, let us make bricks, and burn them thoroughly." And they had brick for stone, and bitumen for mortar. Then they said, "Come, let us build ourselves a city, and a tower with its top in the heavens, and let us make a name for ourselves, lest we be scattered abroad upon the face of the whole earth." And the Lord came down to see the city and the tower, which the sons of men had built. And the Lord said, "Behold, they are one people, and they have all one language; and this is only the beginning of what they will do; and nothing that they propose to do will now be impossible for them. Come, let us go down, and there confuse their language, that they may not understand one another's speech." So the Lord scattered them abroad from there over the face of all the earth, and they left off building the city. Therefore its name was called Babel, because there the Lord confused the language of all the earth; and from there the Lord scattered them abroad over the face of all the earth.

—*Genesis 11:1–9*

This story is quite different from everything we have discussed to this point, with the possible exception of the story of the Flood. Elsewhere in these first chapters of Genesis we have met with individual men and their personal struggle with fate, with guilt, and—in both—with God: Eve and Adam, Abel and Cain, and finally Noah. And again and again it was amazing to discover that each one of these figures was a part of ourselves. The more closely we examined them the more they helped us to find a clue to the mystery of our own life.

The story of the building of the tower of Babel, however, has a definitely universal theme. Here the subject is not the individual man but rather a destiny beyond the personal. Here we are concerned with mankind in the large and with the rules by which the history of the world is enacted. Even the determinative questions of the age of technology and space travel are sketched out in the lines of this story. In other words, the Bible speaks not only about God and the individual soul; it also makes the whole realm of history its theme.

This ancient chronicle actually contains a compendium of the course of this world and the history of the cosmos. We shall attempt to understand its suggestive lines and hieroglyphs.

Originally, it is said, the world "had one language." What bound people together was once stronger than what separated them. And this is what God intended the world to be when he created it. When we hear those words "one language," it is as if for a few seconds the harmony of the original creation salutes our sundered world and tries to tell it how it was when men and beasts and clouds and stars still possessed a binding center and were still turned in common praise, in the music of the spheres, to *Him* who called them into being.

But now, suddenly, a new and alien note is struck in God's creation. Now man proposes to be his own master. Did not God himself summon him to dominion? Did he not say, "Subdue the earth"? And man's reaction was: "All right, then we'll be masters too!"

It was not that man simply renounced the supremacy of God. Eve—we remember—desired to remain a devout lady and even engaged in a religious discussion of God with the serpent. Even the serpent is at first glance quite mannerly and is careful not to appear as a representative of atheism. At first the declension from God takes place quite secretly and, so to speak, by degrees measured in millimeters. Eve and the serpent are simply exchanging views on the question whether God actually said this and that, whether what he said is properly documented. And this is an altogether serious and proper subject for discussion. Even conferences of ministers and laymen discuss it.

Actually, this is always the way it is when men begin to separate themselves from God. Even the prodigal son, when he departed from his father, did not create a public scandal and utter a rabid renunciation of his parental home. He rather went on living on his father's capital and was glad to have it. So he availed himself of what the father had given him—except that he mismanaged it and used it in a way altogether different from what the father intended. There is never a moment of open and rude rebellion. But every time the prodigal son took a dollar from his purse he slipped another imperceptible millimeter away from the will of his father. The father had altogether different plans for him.

And when God said to man, "Subdue the earth," he too had something totally different in mind. What God was saying to him was: "Cultivate and fashion this created world in my name and as my representative. Pursue the art of reading and writing, practice the arts and sciences as a service of God, and as you do so remain sound and orderly and close to the source of all things."

But all this turns out quite otherwise. "I am the master," says man, "and therefore I am not going to go on stumbling over the prohibitions of this allegedly higher being. I am free, and therefore I can do what I will, and therefore I can experiment and see how far I can go. I have reason and intellect and therefore I'm not going to be tied to standards and stipulations which I can't verify for myself and accept in freedom. With my intellectual equipment it is utterly impossible to expect me to believe in something that is invisible and commit myself to these alleged commands of God. Am I not autonomous, am I not Homo sapiens?"

So man—what was his name? Adam, Cain, or . . . was it your name or my name?—so man exults in the rapture of his power and keeps probing to see how far he can go, to what extent he can use his Father's power of attorney according to his own taste and discretion. He feels confirmed in his dream of freedom when God does not immediately rap him on the fingers.

Finally he becomes so obsessed by his ability and his technological omnipotence that he concludes that he can make anything and everything. He makes dogs with two heads, he interferes with genes, and he attempts to reconstruct human beings for his own purposes as one would reconstruct a machine. No wonder that every year he is somewhat baffled by the idea of thanksgiving for the harvest. It is really this so-called creation, is it really the hand which is behind it that is to be praised and thanked? Should we not rather praise human production; do we not owe our prosperity to the market which can be manipulated by influencing supply and demand? Harvest thanksgiving? Really we have only ourselves to thank, and especially the tractor factories and the producers of artificial fertilizers.

Now I ask you, am I really getting away from the subject into general secular considerations which have no place in an exposition of the Bible? *Or* am I actually describing our inner history, the history of people who were dowered by the Father with a multitude of gifts and kindnesses and then made off with this dowry somewhere else altogether?

What have we done with our gift of sexuality? What have we done with the gift of will power or our intellectual and artistic endowment? Have we served others with these same gifts? Have we used them to help even *one* person? Or have we done nothing but make hay for ourselves? Have we served our own vanity, our megalomania, with our gifts and merely consumed them? Now *is* this my inner history and yours or am I talking about something else?

So whenever we cease to be men who serve, men who praise God in everything they do, the same things always happens: we make gods of ourselves. In Nietzsche's book, *Joyful Wisdom*, there is a section entitled "The Madman." This appalling creature lights a lantern on a bright morning and goes out to search for God. And finally he declares that God is dead. "We have killed him," he cries. "The holiest and the mightiest that the world has hitherto possessed, has bled to death under our knife,—who will wipe the blood from us? With what water could we cleanse ourselves? . . . Is not the magnitude of this deed too great for us? Shall we not ourselves have to become gods, merely to be worthy of it?"

So there it is: the upper limit has vanished and men have evacuated heaven. Now they themselves propose to fill the vacuum, to advance as supermen, and declare in howling triumph that they have outgrown the old ingenuous God, indeed, that they themselves will bring heaven—read: "technological and social perfection"—on this earth, instead of expecting it from some unreal world in the beyond. Has not Sputnik surpassed "dear old God"? Has not man seized God's prerogative of reigning over the heavens?

I often wonder why it is that we are not altogether happy about traveling in space—even though the accomplishments as such must give us a certain thrill!—and that somehow we have a vague, uncomfortable feeling about it that lingers in the background of our mind and troubles us. I do not believe that this uneasiness is caused by the fact that it was the representatives of the "other" hemisphere who first succeeded in penetrating into space and that this prestige may possibly have incalculable consequences.

Does not this uneasiness originate on an altogether different level? That is to say, may there not be another sound reverberating from space along with the ticking of Sputnik, something like sardonic laughter that implies: "Look here, how illimitable we are; we can make everything possible; nobody is there to stop our excursion into the celestial fields? Are we not proving ourselves month by month to be more than true gods? Isn't the old God of our pious imagination about at the end of his tether?"

But because down underneath man does not quite trust himself in the role of superman—in hours of fear and loneliness there creeps under his skin and into his vitals that saying, "The wind passes over it, and it is gone, and its place knows it no more"—I say, because man does not quite believe in his own greatness and the golden epaulets of his godlikeness, he tries all the more to convince himself of his greatness. So he builds a mighty tower "with its top in the heavens"—that is to say, it reached exactly to that heaven where God then appeared to be enthroned.

If he should succeed, so he speculates, in gaining possession of this heaven and this universe unscathed, if no one rushes at him from infinity and pulverizes him to dust and ashes, this would prove that man and nobody else is the master of the universe and that there are no limits to his greatness.

So man creates an architectural symbol of his greatness, the colossal tower of Babel "with its top in the heavens." He develops the disease of giantism. And now he must constantly be doing something that will convince him of his greatness, because in reality he *cannot* believe in it. And now, as he looks at the pinnacle of his gigantic tower, and as, several milleniums later, he points somewhat familiarly and jovially to the stars where he will soon establish his vegetable garden, he says to himself: "All this thou hast accomplished, O holy, glowing heart."

At this moment then, when the tower of Babel is complete and man seems to have proved that he is worthy of the rank of a god, something like a touch of humor breaks out for the first time in this old Bible, and it is only with a certain Christian amusement that I call attention to it here. What it says is that God finally "caught on" to the fact that men were planning to attack him and occupy his throne, so "the Lord came down to see the city and the tower, which the sons of men had built." Do we catch the laughter of God between the lines?

After all, isn't God "omniscient"? Certainly he must know what is going on on earth. He knows every hair on our head and every sparrow that falls. But here, despite all this omniscience, he doesn't "get wise" to what men are up to in this giant building project, their idea of storming heaven. No, God really doesn't catch on, for this tower is too far away. From the real heaven it looks too small and God can't see it with the naked eye. And certainly it must be terribly tiny, this tower, if even the all-knowing God cannot see it without glasses and a telescope.

So he takes counsel with his heavenly court and resolves to take the extra trouble to come down and make a local inspection on earth.

If this is not irony, I don't know what irony is. Here these men thought they had built a structure so colossal that it would take God's breath away. They thought: Here we, mad Promethian fellows that we are, have broken into God's celestial domain with our tower.

But from the *real* heaven all this looks like something built by brownies, goblins, or Lilliputians, so tiny and microscopically small that it cannot be seen with the naked eye. "He who sits in the heavens laughs; and the Lord has them in derision." Seen from where God sits, everything looks different. This is the abiding consolation which this old story communicates to us with its half-concealed laughter.

But still these people have no suspicion that the God they thought was dead had long since set out to come to them. They think: If God says nothing and we see nothing of him—if he cannot be found in a microscope—this proves his nonexistence.

But God's judgments come on dove's feet.

And immediately we ask, do they, really? Does not God finally intervene like a thunderbolt and confuse their tongues, disperse and scatter them to the four quarters of the earth? At least, isn't that what it says in this old Book? But where do we see any such spectacular judgments taking place today? This, after all, seems to be our trouble; we are always being expected to believe contrary to all appearances and contrary to our own experience.

T

Nevertheless, it would be wrong to think of God's judgment upon Babel as something like a miraculous thunderbolt from the Beyond. As the story of the Flood has already shown us,[1] the judgments of God are very often quite different in style: He just lets men go on as they are in order that they may see where it brings them. He let the experiment of the Third Reich run its course to the bitter end and not one of the seven or eleven attempts on Hitler's life was able to interrupt the experiment; nobody was permitted to prevent or anticipate his coming judgments. And so it is here.

How then are we to envisage this dispersion, this explosion of rebellious mankind?

Perhaps some of you have already noted a passage that crops up, somewhat hiddenly and enigmatically, at the very beginning of our story: "Let us build ourselves a city, and a tower with its top in the heavens . . . *lest we be scattered abroad upon the face of the whole earth.*" Hence, long before the judgment of dispersion fell upon them, men already had a premonition, a dim fear that they might break apart and that even their languages might be confused. They sensed the hidden presence of centrifugal, dispersive force.

This arises from the fact that they have suffered something that might be called the "loss of a center" and that now that they have banished God from their midst they no longer have anything that binds them to *each other*. Always the trend is the same: wherever God has been deposed, some substitute point has to be created to bind men together in some fashion or other. You start a war, perhaps, in order to divert attention from internal political dissensions and thus create a new solidarity by making people feel that they are facing a common threat. Or you build a tower of Babel in order to concentrate people's attention upon a new center by rallying them to united and enthusiastic effort and this way pull together the dispersive elements. Or you whip together by terror those who will not stay together voluntarily.

[1] "Floods and Fires," The Story of the Flood: Part One, pp. 238–239.

Or you utilize the powers of suggestion, "propaganda," and "ideology," in order to generate the feeling of community by means of psychological tricks and thus make people want precisely what you want them to want.

All of these are substitute ties, conclusive attempts to replace the lost center with a synthetic center. But this attempt—this *experimentum medietatis*—is doomed to failure. The centrifugal forces go on pulling and rending and a hidden time-fuse is ticking in the piers of all the bridges.

Now, what has gone wrong here? And to answer this, we need to make clear the following. Suppose I have a colleague or a business partner who believes in nothing, for whom there is no authority whatsoever, to say nothing of commandments of God, a man in whom I cannot find anything that looks like an inner sanction. I would be on guard against such a man. I would distrust him. Perhaps I would even be afraid of him.

Why? Simply because he is completely unpredictable and probably capable of doing almost anything. On the other hand, when I know that someone is bound to God and that his conscience has a secure orientation, then I can "predict," as it were, how he will act in such and such a situation: that he will feel bound, for example, to keep contracts and promises, that he will not perpetrate crooked acts or that at least he will have a bad conscience if he does.

Of someone else, who does not have these ties, I do not know this. In other words, if he is no longer subject to God, then he is under the domination of his instincts, his opportunism, his ambition, his will to power. The day may come when he will stick at nothing if it seems opportune to him. For every one of us has some kind of a lord, we are all driven by something—if not God, then an idol, if not from above, then from below. That's why I am afraid of a man who has no ties and am on my guard against him.

I believe that Hitler was just such an unbound, authority-less person and that we can apply to him what Jacob Burckhardt once said of Napoleon, that he was the personification of absence of guaranty. For him there were no binding ties, humanitarian, legal, or religious. The very moment he signed a treaty he was prepared to break it, if this served his interest. For he thought only of interest and not of any tie of loyalty, of any obligation to any authoritative court of appeal.

I even believe that it can be historically proved that the ultimate cause of the Second World War and thus of the greatest Babylonian confusion in our century did not lie in the Czech or the Polish crisis or in any other external provocation. The real cause of this our disaster, of our divided country and the East-West conflict, lay rather in the fact that Hitler could no longer be trusted, that he could no longer be considered a "reliable firm," capable of keeping an agreement, but only as being absolutely unpredictable. When something like this is found to exist in the realm of government the sole aim of the responsible leaders of the nations is usually to destroy this vicious and unpredictable thing.

The story of Joseph illustrates these forces in the background of historical events from a similar point of view. Joseph, as we know, was sold into Egypt by his jealous brethren. But then there ensued a chain of circumstances which his intriguing brothers could not have foreseen even remotely. It turned out that Joseph did not perish in that foreign land, as they hoped he would, but rather made a career for himself. He became what might be called the Egyptian minister of food and agriculture. Pharaoh put him at the head of a "seven-year-plan," and it was his task to administer a planned storage economy for the coming dry periods and the resulting lack of harvests. And when the famine did in fact come, the word about the gigantic grain reserves stored up in Egypt got around.

Thereupon, among many others, Joseph's brethren also set out for Egypt to make large purchases of grain. On this occasion they were received in audience by Joseph, the food-controller, without their knowing that he was their brother whom they thought was long since dead.

When Joseph finally made himself known to them their knees began to shake. And quite understandably! For they were compelled to say: Now he is on the long end of the lever, now he has become a person to be held in respect, a person of high rank; one flick of his little finger will be enough to make us all disappear in his dungeons. Now he can enjoy a cool revenge.

But then something remarkable happened. Joseph found the one word with which he was able to reassure these brethren of his in their trembling fear. He said to them, "Fear not, for am I in the place of God?" What he was saying was: "My dear people, I too am only a man of flesh and blood. I admit that the old Adam in me may actually be itching to take advantage of this piquant situation and let you all swing for what you did to me. But I am not under the dictatorship of my instincts; I am under God. And because you too are under the same God, you know the course that I am obliged to take. This God, in whom you believe and in whom I believe, is not a God of vengeance, but a God of forgiveness. He has freed me from my unpredictable blood, which may be crying out for vengeance; he has appointed me to love, and therefore you shall be my brethren again."

Suddenly the fear is gone and trust enters the situation.

And that's the way it is. When a man stands in humbleness before God and his conscience is firmly bound to the promises and commandments of the Lord, he radiates confidence, he becomes a neighbor to his brother, and then his brother knows what his intentions toward him are. Then bridges are built from person to person and the security of community comes into being.

But the opposite is equally true. When I know that a person has lost the center of his life I must reckon with the fact that he will be aimlessly and arbitrarily carried away by his instinct and his egoism. For a time I may get along fine with him, that is, as long as common economic interests or political expediencies bind us together. But the moment this specific interest ceases to bind us together he loses his interest in me. Then he doesn't give a hang for me; it is as if he never knew me. Or it may be even worse: he regards me as his mortal enemy because I am his competitor or because he wants my job.

In a society which has lost its center and consists of not much more than interest groups, employers' associations and labor unions, tenants' and home-owners' associations—we call it a "pluralistic society," without realizing the fateful Babylonian curse that lies behind this pluralism!—in such a society fear and distrust prevail, precisely the centrifugal forces which exploded with a vengeance at the tower of Babel.

Do we understand now that this story is something like a compendium of what we experience every day in ourselves and all around us? For a moment God opens the armored strongbox and lets us see the secret survey map of the course of this world.

At all events it no longer requires a thunderbolt from heaven to drive men apart. Since they have become godless the ferments of decay and disintegration are at work everywhere even without a blast from heaven.

So what the biblical narrator saw is this: The tower of Babel was a masterpiece of ancient technology and architecture. But even though all the grandeur of human culture and all technology —even that which grapples with the light-years of the universe— shines with glory, may it not nevertheless be the demonic splendor of man's deranged, unhinged, unobligated reason? May it not be the gaining of the world by a man who has forfeited his soul and who now not only gathers together the beams for his mighty world-structure and a new order of society, but also brings with him the worms that gnaw unceasingly in these beams, eating away the very foundation of the world?

When the first words which come to a man are no longer those which he speaks to his God, when there is no more prayer, language itself ultimately breaks down. How, for example, can one have any common understanding of what freedom means without God, without him who makes us free?

In the East people say: "Freedom is the ability by which I gain insight into the inevitability of historical processes, so that I can influence the course of history." In the West we say: "Freedom means that I can do what I will."

Both use the same word and mean something completely different. So the iron curtain runs right through our language. Our terms are in Babylonian confusion. Our words are not much more than specters and empty masks. A language in which one can no longer pray—and this appears to be so not only in the East, but also threatens to be very generally true in the West—collapses upon itself. The praise of God is a rejuvenating fountain of language as well. Was not our own mother tongue mined from the pits of the Bible? But when the center, when God the Lord disappears from our circle, language too sinks into the grave; we begin to talk at cross purposes with one another and the result is a real Babylonian confusion of tongues. Indeed, the result is that perverse state of affairs in which language becomes an instrument of cloaking and veiling, rather than of communication and confession.

On my trip to Asia the word "Coca-Cola" was the one word I understood in every language; it sprang out familiarly from signs written in the most alien characters. What's wrong with a world in which this is the only word that has survived the Babylonian confusion of tongues? We can still talk to one another about Coca-Cola, but not about freedom, not about God, not about what a neighbor is.

Well, what can we do about it?

It would be putting the cart before the horse if we were to attempt to restore something like this lost community by means of organizations, systems of confederation, disarmament treaties, and other schemes for thawing out the cold war.

Not that we have anything against these attempts and endeavors! It would be unrealistic and falsely spiritual to cast any discredit upon them. And yet this story makes it clear that all this is nothing more than physicking the external symptoms of the disease and suffering of the world. Anybody who wants to get at the real seat of the illness must know that this focus is localized precisely at the point where we—exactly like the people in Babel—have ceased to be "under God," where we have lost the center and where this fear of our fellows, where these centrifugal forces, then gained power over us.

Even we "Westerners" are all too prone to say that religion is a private affair, a personal concern that each must settle for himself. Anybody who reads this age-old story will find that such trivial assurances will get stuck in his throat before he utters them. For this account of the building of the tower of Babel is not concerned with our pious inwardness, our private spirituality. On the contrary, it presents a program for everything that happens among mankind as a whole. It embraces global concerns. Not only he who wants to know his own soul, but also he who wants to understand the history of the world, must listen to this voice that comes through to us across the milleniums.

But here too we find what we always find when the word of the Bible is heard: the history of the world as a whole is only the reflection of the history of my own heart, and Francis Thompson rightly says:

> ... all man's Babylons strive but to impart
> The grandeurs of his Babylonian Heart.

It is strange and wonderful, but true, that anybody who wants to release the forces of healing in our maimed world must begin with himself and his own Babylonian heart. This new departure occurs when a man finds his way back from madness to peace, when he suddenly realizes that the God whom men in their madness would drive from the heavens in order to occupy them themselves, that this same God loves him, is interested in him, sought him in pain and torment, and took the burden of his life upon his own shoulders in the cross of Jesus Christ, when a man begins to stammer in all humility, "I believe, help my unbelief." When that happens a bit of healing from the hill of Golgotha comes into this world. For then a whole series of chain reactions break loose in my life. Then for me God will no longer be anything so pale and diluted as a "higher Power" or the content of an anxiety complex, but instead I shall then be free to love and I shall also have to pass on the love I have received. Then I shall discover in my life the neighbor God wants to entrust to me. Then fear will be gone and with it the anxiety and the weight of our haunting homelessness. Then I shall be able to breathe again, and because I can breathe, there is at least *one* point in this world at which the freshness of eternity and the breath of life has broken in.

The counterpart of the story of the tower of Babel is the event of Pentecost which is recounted in the New Testament. Here the common language is suddenly present again, and Parthians, Medes, and Elamites understand one another. Here the spell is broken and all the confusion banished. When Jesus Christ becomes the Lord of our life, then there is healing of hearts, of bodies, and even of language.

Therefore we shall not set our hopes upon the marvel of some great turn in the history of the world, nor in the "miracle men of history," as Luther called them. We shall not think that power or chance are determinative. The expanses of the world are *not* governed or healed by the hands of the mighty. God's peacemakers do not come marching through the triumphal arches which the great of this world build. They come through the needle's eye of an individual's heart, very quietly and very secretly.

God's kingdom begins with tiny seeds and little particles of leaven. When *my* heart and *your* heart find their way home to the peace of the Father's house a little light is kindled in the great world's night and there is a tiny oasis in the desert.

He who allows this to be bestowed upon him finds that the evil virus has no power over him. And not only the bad, but also the good is infectious! Because this salt is present, the earth cannot go utterly bad. Only ten righteous men in Sodom and Gomorrha stay the judgment. For their sake all the promises remain in force. The question is whether you and I are among these ten. All our destiny lies in this question.

19

Outlines of a New World Order

And when the Lord smelled the pleasing odor, the Lord said in his heart, "I will never again curse the ground because of man, for the imagination of man's heart is evil from his youth; neither will I ever again destroy every living creature as I have done. While the earth remains, seedtime and harvest, cold and heat, summer and winter, day and night, shall not cease."

And God blessed Noah and his sons, and said to them, "Be fruitful and multiply, and fill the earth. The fear of you and the dread of you shall be upon every beast of the earth, and upon every bird of the air, upon everything that creeps on the ground and all the fish of the sea; into your hand they are delivered. Every moving thing that lives shall be food for you; and as I gave you the green plants, I give you everything. Only you shall not eat flesh with its life, that is, its blood. For your lifeblood I will surely require a reckoning; of every beast I will require it and of man; of every man's brother I will require the life of man. Whoever sheds the blood of man, by man shall his blood be shed; for God made man in his own image. . . .

I set my bow in the cloud, and it shall be a sign of the covenant between me and the earth. When I bring clouds over the earth and the bow is seen in the clouds, I will remember my covenant which is between me and you and every living creature of all flesh; and the waters shall never again become a flood to destroy all flesh."

—*Genesis 8:21—9:6, 13–15*

There still rings in our ears that thrilling mandate addressed to the first human beings, which we have encountered again and again in the most diverse places: "Be fruitful and multiply, and fill the earth and subdue it."

After the Flood this mandate and general authorization is renewed. It is as if after the tragic interlude of guilt and destruction the world were once more permitted to rise out of the catastrophe of the Flood, as if the touch of creation caressed it once more as on the first day.

And yet as the first passage of the creation symphony, "Be fruitful and fill the earth," is now played once more, it is nevertheless not merely a repetition. On the morning of creation this passage rang out in a brilliant A major, like the proclamation of peace in the *Missa solemnis* (*"pacem, pacem!"*). But now it is repeated in that strange, dark D minor with which the somber military march begins in Beethoven's Mass.

One has the feeling that deep shadows are emerging from these new and altered tones, for now the Lord says—and this was *not* what he said before!—"The fear of you and the dread of you shall be upon every beast of the earth. . . ."

Thus, wherever man exercises his dominion, all creation will live in fear. Now a sinister pall will hang above the world and change its climate. God knows that from now on there is a gaping rift in the composition of his creation, that it is no longer a harmonious hymn that he can listen to with delight and then break out in the words: "Behold, it is very good." He knows that henceforth the dissonances of violence, injustice, and megalomania will reverberate and shrill throughout the earth; that Cain will have his successors and man will lay violent hands upon his fellow man, despite the fact that he is the image of God. So here the text says menacingly: "Whoever sheds the blood of man, by man shall his blood be shed." And this too is a new note, which was not there before.

Whereas before it might have been said that the harmony of creation was something like "eternal rest in God the Lord," now the face of God appears in altered lineaments. Now God is a profoundly alarming power; he is the Avenger and Judge. Now he himself puts down with power what rebels against him in violence.

We can state the question this text puts to us as follows: How does God operate in the enigmas of history?

A NEW WORLD ORDER

For history is constantly presenting us with dark and puzzling riddles. We have already met with some of these questions in the story of the Flood. And now that we are coming to the end of our exposition, let us take them up again and thrust our drill still deeper into the rock.

What we asked was this: Where is there anywhere, any clue whatsoever that God is holding the reins of history in his hand and thinking his thoughts about us? Isn't it a fact that the heaviest artillery and the most inflammatory propaganda are what really rule the world? Do not the representatives of God—men like Luther and Bodelschwingh—appear in the ranking lists of the great movers of men merely as "also rans," without their ever being able to get hold of one of the main switches in the switch tower of history? Do not the reporters record with camera and notebook every wrinkling of the brow, every smile, even the most trivial comment of the so-called great men of the world—even when they are only paltry ephemerids—whereas the flash bulbs go dark, the notebooks snap shut, and the loudspeakers grow silent when it comes to the men of God who know the tremendous mystery of the world and want to make it known? Where is there any sound of the voice of God and his people, where can even the slightest whisper of it be heard?

The concluding part of the story of the Flood, which we must hark back to, shows us how the hand of God is at work, with incredibly quiet but sure and purposeful power, in, with, and under the errings and confusions of history.

How does this hidden hand rule the world?

In his exposition of the first chapters of the Bible, Luther expressed some very profound but also exceedingly curious ideas concerning the nature and the purpose of the *state*.

If we were together in a small discussion group, I would be tempted to throw out a question: Just guess at what point in these chapters Luther broached the subject of the state. I would bet in the framework of the creation story. And certainly one could mention several reasons that would suggest such a guess. The following, for example. The Creator did not create men as isolated individual beings, but rather for each other. He ordained Adam and Eve for each other. He established the continuity of the generations in the relationship of parents and children. It is therefore quite logical that the *state* should belong in this line of creation. Is not the state too an expression of the fact that God designed men for "togetherness"? Is not the state a form of community—except that it is in large form? God's creative hand fashions not only the small family cells in which he repeatedly performs the miracle of generation and birth; he also takes these cells and forms the great organisms of human societies; he creates states and nations.

It must be admitted that such an answer sounds very plausible.

But Luther broached the question of the state *not* in the context of the creation, but, of all places, in connection with the story of the Fall.

What he says is this. Originally God was able to rule the world with a mere flip of his little finger, for then men kept their eyes upon his finger and heeded the twinkling of his eye. But after they had declared their disobedience to God, and thus turned their eyes away from him, this possibility of naturally accepted direction and easy, harmonious mutual understanding ceased to exist. Then, said Luther, God was obliged to rule the world with his *fist*—and thus no longer with his finger!—with the restraint of force—and therefore no longer with a wink of his eye! *Therefore* he called the state into being. For then there would be criminal law and police and magistrates to keep men in check. Then the wicked would be punished and the good rewarded. And a superior force, that is, the power of the state, would compel the rebellious to observe order.

This, then, according to Luther, is the distinguishing mark of the new, hard world order, the order in "minor key": the state is a perpetual reminder of a fateful decree pronounced upon man in his past.

Nevertheless, it is a great mercy that men were not permitted to rend and devour one another—in a war of all against all—

and that God instead preserves them until his "good last day" by means of the compulsion exerted by the order of the state, and even in these forms of compulsion exerts his preserving goodness.

This is Luther's understanding of history and its ordinances.

So, until the sunset of the world glows upon the horizon and the last day dawns, we go on living in a Babylonian world: here one is against the other, interest group against interest group; here each man is his own neighbor; here power goes before justice; here there is competition and suppression and the rule of the stronger.

This is the utterly realistic ground upon which the biblical picture of history is painted. Here there is no room for pale utopias and dreams of progress. Here there is only the sober account of a world in which we are afraid, in which the shouts of war and rumors of war are heard and the mighty and the rich fight to hold on to their privileges and the rest strain at their chains, for "darkness covers the earth, and thick darkness the peoples" (Isa. 60:2).

It is an unspeakable consolation that the men of the Bible are conscious of all this and that they never slipped into any kind of religious daydreams, which we oft-burnt children could never honestly "buy" from them. Only because they cling to this cold and incorruptible realism can we listen to them and then take seriously the fact that this same book speaks of wonderful Christmas light that breaks in upon the darkness that covers the peoples and the despairing hearts of men.

The truth is that ever since man cut himself off from God and declared that God is no longer the measure of what we do in our marriages, the rearing of our children, our offices, and our laboratories, the world has been an alien, haunted place. The atheisms and atrocities are only some of the many symptoms of what lies in wait, ready to pounce upon us, in our Western world as well as in the East. The fatherliness and the security have vanished.

This is certainly true. In one way or another every one of

us has experienced it in his own life. And yet the dark minor strain of this message contains the comforting news that God will not abandon us and that—incredibly and yet rejoicingly—he therefore keeps faith with this rebellious world.

How he does this and how he means it to be understood is shown by the words: "Whoever sheds the blood of man, by man shall his blood be shed." We must not think that this refers only to the death penalty. What the text means lies several feet deeper.

This is what it means: Wherever man brutally asserts himself with his egotism and his slogan, "Might makes right," there God mobilizes his ordinances against this kind of rebellion, there he sets the penal power of law against the revolt and directs the power of the state against the divisive egotisms of individuals and groups.

This text provides us, as it were, with training for the eye: We are to acquire an eye for the place where the miracle of grace occurs; for the miracle occurs not only at the place where the words, "Your sins are forgiven" or "Rise, take up your bed and go home," are addressed to you. The miracle has long since been operative and we were already its beneficiaries before these transforming and comforting words are spoken to us. The miracle of grace has already occurred in the fact that we are surrounded by the ordinances of God and graciously preserved despite all the threats and blows of life. The mere fact that we are alive, that we are *physically* alive, gives us the chance to participate in that which is *more* than mere physical life: we can become pardoned, reconciled men.

This text is something like the foundation stone of all Christian teaching concerning the state. "Wherever there is a state, there a miracle occurs," says Luther; there is a sign that God is still at work even in a fallen, faithless world, keeping faith with his faithless children.

In other words, he not only preserves our souls. He not only grants us faith and peace of heart and the joy of security. He is not only our rod and staff in the valley of the shadow and our Comforter when our conscience torments us. *God is also the Lord of the world;* he causes his eternal ordinances to prevail over all our mutual destructiveness and all the powers of overthrow. He directs this feverish, threatened world straight to the goal, which it itself knows not: his throne.

We men may do what we will, Nebuchadnezzar may come and Genghis Khan and Mao Tse-tung; none of them can break God's plans, but rather must fulfil them—against their will! Even though what we hear now is the dark minor tone, *what is being played is still God's symphony,* and it will be played out to the end. The individual tones may think they are who knows what; they may want to assert themselves and swing out on their own. And yet they have all been composed into a score of which God alone is in command and in which everything, when it is heard from heaven's vantage point, has its place in God's succession of tones that end in his final chord. "The rich of this world are in process of going, but the kingdom of God is in process of coming," Blumhardt once said.

Therefore, even in the pressure zone of mass means of destruction and growing tyranny, we must have the long view and the confident calmness of those who know they have a secure place in the score of God's eternal symphony. For above the battle of the powers—the outcome of which we do not know—above all the crises and threats in our personal life there sounds, like a peaceful, comforting bell, the promise of God: "While the earth remains, seedtime and harvest, cold and heat, summer and winter, day and night, shall not cease." Every time the world goes to its autumn rest and every day as the peace of evening descends anew upon the earth we are to receive this message, like a blinking signal from the Eternal: "I calmly pursue my course through all the convulsions and derangements of your life. And just as I direct the rhythm of days and seasons, so I encompass the islands and the continents, the men of faith and the atheists, the constitutional states and the tyrannies. Don't ever think that anybody will ever be able to break away from serving me, though he renounce me ten times over! Even in the extreme perversion of authority, as in the tyranny of a totalitarian state, men are compelled despite themselves to preserve a remnant of my order and they can never succeed in consistently devilizing and ruining my world. And I, who have power of the whole world of space, should I not be able to encompass your little life, hear your questions and your groans, and unravel the tangled skein of your need?"

But now I hear a question, the expression of an honest doubt. All this, you say, sounds very comforting, so fine that it might almost carry us away. But isn't it nothing but words? Where is there any clear evidence—*again* the question must be asked— where is there a single trace of Him who allegedly rules in the midst of all this world's confusion and bends it to his purposes? And there sure enough, is that monumental statement: "While the earth remains, seedtime and harvest, cold and heat, summer and winter, day and night, shall not cease." And what this means after all is that the quiet, stable rhythm of the divine activity endures through all the unrest and chaos that men bring into the world. When my parental home burned down during the air raids, a blackbird sang the next morning in a fire-blackened tree as if nothing had happened. And sometimes in a sleepless night when we rack our brains and wonder how things can ever go on this way, the sun rises in the morning—glorious and unmoved by all the misery; and in the everlasting harmony of things, in the change from day to night, in the courses of the stars God sends to us his comforting sign: "Look, I am at work, I cause life to go on. I do not forsake you. I am watching out for you and also for your daily bread and the space you need to live in today, and for the birds who sing their songs for you."

Nevertheless, I must ask, because we want to be honest and stick to the truth: Isn't all this just romanticism? Are these really signals from God? Can't the courses of the stars and the change from day to night just as well be interpreted altogether differently, and much less comfortingly? Can't we say that it means nothing more than the eternal, unfeeling turning of the wheel of the world?

> It is as good as had it ne'er existed,
> And yet in cycle moves as if it were.
> Eternal Emptiness would I prefer.

At any rate, this is the way many skeptics may feel. (And this time this saying from *Faust* does not apply—as it did earlier—to the empty revolving of human existence; it goes further and now seems to point to the meaninglessness and futility of the whole cycle of cosmic processes.) In the Hindu doctrine of salvation this despair emerges in the concept of *samsara*, the great cosmic wheel and the unending, soulless recurrence of all things.

The likelihood is that we have all had very direct experience of this in our own lives: I had a bad day; perhaps I fell out with the person I loved most; perhaps I have returned from a visit to the hospital where the person closest to me in all the world is waiting for the end in torment; perhaps it was the collapse of my hopes for my job and my material existence. That night I looked up to the skies and there were the stars, marching across the firmament in everlasting harmony.

Now, was this for me—remember that we want to be completely honest!—a comforting message from the Eternal? Or did I curse perhaps: "What do you know, you who move, unknowing, cold, untouched, across the sky in your geometrical arcs; what do you know about what is breaking my heart this moment? 'Up above the starry skies dwells a loving Father'? Don't make me laugh. It's nothing but heartless mathematics, and all the rest is sentimental slush."

That *could* be the answer too, couldn't it?

Ah, but this very shock that the starry heavens can deal us is nevertheless, despite all appearances to the contrary, a sign from our Father. For everything we are told by the men of the Bible, who had their own experiences with God, is this—and we have now learned it in any number of ways from these texts: "God's way is through the sea, his path is through the great waters; and yet you do not see his footprints" (cf. Ps. 77:19). In order to know where God is going and whither he wants to take us, we do not need to know his footprints; we need rather to know his heart. Whoever sees in what Luther called the mirror of the divine heart, whoever sees in Jesus Christ the very presence and reflection of the Father, for him all the vicissitudes of his life, his griefs and successes, his fortuitous and meaningless experiences, become exercises in trust.

And then at the end of the story of the Flood, as a sign that we are thus lovingly and protectingly surrounded on every side by God's higher thoughts, we are told: "I set my bow in the cloud, and it shall be a sign of the covenant between me and the earth."

So, as the monumental pictures of the Bible testify, the history of the whole world is set down and enclosed between this bow that shines above the catastrophe of the Flood and the end of the primeval world *and* that other rainbow which John the Seer saw around the throne of God, where one day the history of the world must end (cf. Rev. 4:3). True, this road of history between the two rainbows is dark. It leads through abysses and the lightning flashes along its way. But the point is that this road *begins* in the name of a great love that is faithful to our disjointed world and *ends* in a great fulfilment, that is to say, precisely at the point to which God wants to bring us all: the Russians, the Chinese, the Americans, the prisoners in the jails, the little old lady in the home for the aged, the children who are born to us, and the dead in the distant seas.

No matter what happens, no matter how meaningless and stupid the things that oppress us, and despite every human view, our way leads from the rainbow of grace at the *beginning* to the rainbow of triumph at the *end*. We can rest upon the Father's heart and be safe in his mighty power.

So God would always have us see his bow of grace and triumph whenever life grows hard for us. Have you ever observed what happens when a rainbow appears in the sky? Suddenly the sun breaks through the clouds with a marvelous brilliancy while the downpour is still falling upon us and tumult has not yet abated. And then comes the marvel; never does light celebrate such a festival of color as when it is broken into its spectrum. And this feast of light occurs precisely when the radiance of the sun, the divine sun of grace, encounters the tempestuous elements of our earth.

We understand, do we not, what is being conveyed to us here under the guise of metaphor? It is precisely in pain and suffering, in the abysses and storms of life that God wills to declare his glory and show forth the fulness of his grace.

Do we understand this? Do we not understand it best when we look back upon our own life? Have we ever known God's nearness so clearly as in the moments when we were exposed to the most frightful peril, when there was no protecting cellar vault to shield us from the shells, when there was no doctor to help us and no friend to say a comforting word?

The rainbow always shines most comfortingly in the dark places. God loves most of all to reach down into the deep, dark places of life. But we must see this and be willing to trust God's promise.

And as we go on into the future it will continue to be so. At exactly the right moment a helpful message will be there as his messenger. At the very moment I need it, it is there. His love will greet us in a person whom he sends to us unexpectedly, or in the smile of a little child, or in some wonderful preservation from harm, or in a liberating prayer that he answers by taking away our fears and cares.

Because we have a Father, we are not mere gamblers in a game of chance; we are people who live by the surprises and miracles of their God. We are people who know where we have come from and where we are going and therefore have the courage to live. Above the dark valleys through which we must walk are the hills from whence comes our help, and already their peaks are red with the light of the glory to come. No lightning bolt can strike us. All that is there is lightning flashes and dark rumblings. The ways are prepared "where your foot may walk," and they are prepared by *Him* who also points the clouds and storms their course. And everywhere along the way the surprises of God are waiting.

Blessed are the eyes that see what is prepared for us.

> All around us lightning flashes,
> Give us hearts set free from fright.
> Down upon the world's confusion
> Cast thine everlasting light.

POSTSCRIPT FOR THEOLOGICAL READERS

20

Postscript for Theological Readers

Considering the discussion which is now in flux concerning the relation between the Old Testament and the New Testament, law and gospel, prophecy and fulfilment, the history of salvation (*Heilsgeschichte*) and the interpretation of the history of salvation, history and demythologizing, etc.—in short, considering the many unsolved hermeneutical problems in the area of the Bible,[1] it is a venturesome thing to preach and to publish a series of sermons on Old Testament texts. As a theologian the preacher must indeed have worked through these problems and

---

[1] An excellent introduction to the history of these problems down to the present is provided by H. J. Kraus, *Geschichte der historischen Erforschung des Alten Testaments von der Reformation bis zur Gegenwart* (1956), esp. pp. 382 ff. The significance of these historical and critical problems is well explained by Fr. Hesse, "Die Erforschung der Geschichte Israels als theologische Aufgabe" in *Kerygma und Dogma*, 1958, pp. 1 ff. Fr. Baumgärtel's book, *Verheissung, Zur Frage des evangelischen Verständnisses des Alten Testaments* (1952), has elicited numerous fruitful controversies (cf. esp. the essay by Gerhard von Rad in *Evangelische Theologie*, 1953, pp. 406 ff. and Baumgärtel's reply, *ibid.*, 1954, pp. 298 ff.). An important compilation of the theological problems of the Old Testament—the possibility of contemporizing it, the typological interpretation of it, the relationship of prophecy and fulfilment and the interpretation given to it by modern Judaism—may be found in *Evangelische Theologie*, 1952, Nos. 1/2. For these problems further reference may be made to L. Goppelt, *Typos, Die typologische Deutung des Alten Testaments im Neuen* (1939). The Dutch systematician, Arnold A. van Ruler, *Die christliche Kirche und das Alte Testament* (1955), entered the debate with some very revolutionary theses and posed some questions which have not yet been solved (cf. my discussion of van Ruler's position in *Theologische Ethik*, Vol. II, 2, §4274 ff. Among the commentaries on the first chapters of Genesis which may be recommended to those who are not familiar with Hebrew the following are mentioned especially: Gerhard von Rad, *Das erste Buch Mose in Das AT Deutsch, Nr. 2*, 1st ed. (1949); W. Zimmerli, *Die Urgeschichte 1 Mose I-XI* in *Prophezei*, 2nd ed. (Zurich, 1957).

taken a position with regard to them, but he has no opportunity —unless it be in other publications—to justify *in extenso* and in the light of this discussion the statements he may make, and therefore he must speak from an unguarded position. He can only cherish the hope that the specialist will note between the lines the reflections the author has turned over in his mind—and often been compelled to leave unsettled!—before he permitted himself to make this or that preached statement in the style in which he did.

The author has been aware of the venturesomeness of this series of sermons in still another respect. This is connected with the necessity of giving sharp kerygmatic focus to a text, a necessity incumbent upon the sermon; and this means that certain relevant emphases must be enucleated from the total corpus of the texts and that consequently an appropriate selection must be made. Thus certain parts of the text remain unexposed.

The selection of specific points of emphasis—and thus the choice of the text—is, of course, a subjective thing, even though the margin of discretion never permits a purely arbitrary choice; there must be good reason for it. The criteria by which this choice is made are provided partly by the question of how the individual sermon and ultimately also the series as a whole can be kept within certain time limits and partly by the question of what must appear to be especially important to the person who is seeking to find the origin, meaning, and reality of life. But even these criteria leave room for difference of opinion with regard to what is to be treated and what is to be omitted. Thus I debated with myself for a long time whether—to mention only *one* example—I ought not to make the verses concerning the "heavenly ocean" (the idea of an original chaos) the text of a separate sermon, particularly since Karl Barth has devoted a section of his dogmatics to a definitely kerygmatic exposition of this portion of the text.[2] If in this and similar cases I have nevertheless decided in favor of incidental treatment, I have done

---

[2] So, it is quite possible to do this! Cf., on Gen. 1:6 ff., Karl Barth, *Kirchliche Dogmatik*, III, i, pp. 153 ff.

so, not because I was of the opinion that these texts were lacking in kerygmatic content, but rather because I shrank from the long marches that must be negotiated before this preaching content can be laid bare. Here the preaching situation seemed to me to necessitate some definite external limitations. I believe I can say, however, that I have not evaded the homiletical treatment of such texts because of any desire to shirk the difficulties in the *content*.

Likewise in the presentation—not in the meditation of the texts—the contour of the various individual sources has not been mentioned, at least not explicitly, even in the case of such diverse theological intentions as those pursued by the Priestly and the Yahwist accounts of the creation of man (cf. Genesis 1 and 2). Even though here too the specialist may be able—I hope!—to ascertain or at least sense that in each case the specific intention of the particular source has been noted and worked into the content of the preaching, I nevertheless felt that in the presentation itself I had to forgo any differentiating elaboration of the profile of the sources and that I might be allowed to speak in the name of the redactor who composed the section in question.

My position with regard to the problem of *apologetics*, a problem particularly apparent in just such texts, I have already indicated in the introductory chapter. In any case I have endeavored to lead my hearers from the wrong front to the right front, and thus from the wrong offenses to the right *skandala*. So I would be grateful if theological readers too were able to muster up a certain receptiveness to my opinion that the attempt to speak a language which is modern, secular, and, let us hope, not "slovenly," is by no means merely an attempt to make the message of the texts of the primeval story more "popular and palatable" and enclose the kerygmatic medicine in sweet-tasting capsules.

It is rather my belief that when a person hears these messages spoken in his own language they not only strike home to him, but, what is more, they strike *menacingly* home to him. It is precisely when they are addressed to him in familiar language that their very strangeness can shake him, indeed, he may even feel that they are hostile. On the other hand the well-worn terms of traditional ecclesiastical speech frequently allow him to remain indifferent, no matter how aggressive may be the substance of the statements hidden within those accustomed phrases.

Consequently, we must distinguish between accommodation in speech and accommodation in substance. The former is aggressive because judgment and grace are thus held up to the hearer at the level where he can see them. The latter is apologetic because it confirms the hearer in the position he has already taken.

Thus accommodation in speech is not intended to be tactical in purpose. The pedagogical clarification which it produces is at most a secondary effect. The real reasons for this form of accommodation is rather twofold:

First, the road of the gospel must be pursued to the place where it meets man, wherever he may be in the hedges and the market places. The incarnation of the Word is in principle nothing else but the meeting with man. At the same time it is the barrier against any kind of *cooperatio*, by which man must first put himself in a particular place and fulfil certain conditions in order to share in the message. It is therefore the barrier against any false doctrine of justification.

The second reason for accommodation in speech is related to the following. The hearer must be able to say after he has listened to the sermon: "I was in it"; perhaps also, "I was in it in a way that doesn't suit me at all, because I want to think of myself in a different way, and so I feel challenged to oppose. Nevertheless, I was in it."

Dare I say something else that is very harsh?

Corrie ten Boom once said, "I have traveled through half the world and I have found that nowhere is there such correct preaching as in Germany, but nowhere else is it so lacking in power and authority."

The mirror that is held up to us in this statement is inexorable. For its thesis describes a listener's reaction which may be expressed somewhat as follows: "It was all perfectly right; but I wasn't in it." The preacher who encounters this reaction will be disquieted. He will not look for the fault in some error of technique—in the fact, let us say, that he slipped too much into the style of merely lecturing, that he was too abstract, or never got beyond the theological. He will rather seek the fault in a spiritual infirmity, in the fact that he may have "heard" the text wrongly. And he has heard the text wrongly in every case, if he *himself* has not been in it. For then he will on no account succeed in making it plausible that the *other* person, the listener, is in it. Nor will a pious statement like, "This applies to you too," tacked on at the end, be of any help. By that time nobody will believe it anyhow.

It was out of disquietude over this situation of preaching that the preceding sermons arose and were delivered. Whether they have brought us a little farther on remains a question. But in any case the disquietude accompanied them all along. The author was never secure and confident about them. Among the many illusions that threaten a preacher there was one at any rate that he did not have, and that was the false comfort of routine. Thus form and language were never meant to be an end in itself—at least in intention!—but rather were honestly tested at every step in the light of the message and were meant to be a part of the message. I would be thankful if my brethren of the pulpit were to perceive in this book the same disquietude and the same searching, by which they are as surely troubled as am I. What we have to preach is greater than we, and we fall far short of it. And there is the cause of the disquietude; there too is the source of that "godly grief" (II Cor. 7:10) which has the promise of every blessing.

In closing I should like to pass on a bit of very practical experience. When in the second part of the series we were obliged to arrange another parallel service on the preceding afternoon, I observed what a relief it was for harried and fatigued city people to have an opportunity to attend a service late Saturday afternoon and thus be able to sleep later on Sunday morning. I am not entertaining the idea of dropping the service on Sunday morning—how could I?—but simply asking whether it might not make sense to schedule one of the additional Sunday services for late Saturday afternoon in order at least to provide this opportunity. Perhaps the church has given too little consideration to the inclusion of this largely free day in its plans.